THE KNOWER
AND
THE KNOWN

Current Continental Research
The Center for Advanced Research in Phenomenology
and
University Press of America, Inc.

CURRENT CONTINENTAL RESEARCH 803

Marjorie Grene

THE KNOWER
AND
THE KNOWN

1984

Center for Advanced Research in Phenomenology
& University Press of America, Washington, D.C.

To Michael Polanyi

Preface to the Paper-bound Edition

This book was written during the years 1961–1963 at Queen's University, Belfast, when I was lecturing in Greek philosophy and gaining, I hope, some little insight about the subjects of my first two chapters—for in philosophy, it seems to me, teaching and learning are inseparable. But at the same time I was reading Merleau-Ponty, alas, for the first time, and indulging, perhaps over-rhetorically, in an enthusiasm too unfashionable to be shared in that environment. At Queen's also (unlike Leeds, where I had done a most fruitful year's teaching in J. R. Ravetz' history of science course) I was debarred from teaching in the field of history and philosophy of science, so that my speculations around evolution and allied subjects had, probably, some of the perversity that voices crying in wildernesses are wont to have. Were I to write this book now, I would perhaps tone down the rhetoric and would certainly (in chapters 7 and 9) separate more prudently than I did then the strictly empirical scope of evolutionary theory from its metaphysical associations or implications. And also, as several younger writers in the field, as well as my scientific colleagues, and of course my students, have been helping me to do, I would try to separate more sharply functional, teleological and hierarchical (or systems-theoretical) explanations. Some of these improvements, as I hope they are, are exemplified in my *Understanding of Nature* (*Boston Studies in the Philosophy of Science*, vol. 23; in press). I would still stand by the criticisms made in Chapter 7 of ambiguous and overambitious evolutionary thinking, and of course by the main theme of Chapter 8; but I confess to having been unfair to the stricter evolutionists who have always seen clearly what they were *not* explaining, and to having overestimated the relevance of teleological thought for evolutionary theory—which I would now place at zero. But the wheat and chaff in Part Three are too closely interspersed for an easy separation; and I hope the wheat, even there, is sufficient to merit this reprinting.

University of California, Davis
January, 1974

Acknowledgments

The following have kindly allowed me to reprint, with omissions and revisions, material from articles of mine already published: *Encounter*: 'David Hume' (1955), 'The Faith of Darwinism' (1959); Routledge and Kegan Paul: 'The Logic of Biology' in *The Logic of Personal Knowledge* (1961); *The British Journal for the Philosophy of Science*: 'Statistics and Selection' (1961); *The Cambridge Review*: 'Biology and Teleology' (1964). Part of Chapter 6 is based on a contribution to a symposium, 'Die Theorie der deskriptiven Aussage und der Begriff der Existenz', held in 1963 under the auspices of the Institut für Wissenschaftstheorie of the Internationales Forschungszentrum für Grundfragen der Wissenschaft at Salzburg. (See *Deskription, Analytizität und Existenz*, ed. P. Weingartner, Salzburg: Pustet, 1965).

I also wish to thank the following publishers for permission to quote from copyrighted material (full bibliographical details are given in the footnotes): for permission to quote from Hugh Tredennick's translation of Aristotle's *Prior* and *Posterior Analytics* and from W. R. M. Lamb's translation of Plato's *Meno*, Loeb Classical Library, Harvard University Press; from the Hicks *De Anima* and the Haldane and Ross translation of Descartes's *Rules* and *Meditations,* Cambridge University Press; from Merleau-Ponty's *Phenomenology of Perception,* Routledge and Kegan Paul and Humanities Press; from Bertrand Russell, *Human Knowledge: its Scope and Limits*, George Allen and Unwin and Simon and Schuster; from A. N. Whitehead, *Modes of Thought,* Cambridge University Press and Macmillan (Copyright 1938 by the Macmillan Publishing Company, renewed 1966 by T. North Whitehead); from F. J. J. Buytendijk, *Mensch und Tier*, Rowohlt Taschenbuch Verlag, Reinbek bei Hamburg (Copyright 1958); from Wilfred Owen's 'Greater Love', *Collected Poems of Wilfred Owen*, Chatto and Windus, Ltd. Copyright 1963 (reprinted by permission of New Directions Publishing Corporation.)

Davis, California, 1966
Ithaca, N.Y., 1983

Contents

Introduction

The seventeenth-century revolution in philosophy stood – and we still stand – under the authority of the 'new science', and this was primarily the science of inorganic nature. 'Bits of matter, qualified by mass, spatial relations, and the change of such relations': such were the bare realities out of which experimental ingenuity and mathematical exactitude built their new universe. Once the new simplicity and clarity were extended to all subject matters, we should, as Descartes put it, have solved all the problems that would ever confront the human mind. Today, although such optimism has, fortunately, left us, the hope of a universal mathematics, of an exact science of life, of man, and of society, founded on the automatic manipulation of unambiguous, 'objective' variables, remains a predominant ideal of scientists and philosophers. Both the ideal of reason as analysis, in each of its guises and disguises, and the revolt against reason by more subjectivist philosophers, have remained, whether as acceptance or rebellion, within this single conceptual frame.

We have come, or are coming, at last to the end of this epoch, the epoch presided over by the concepts of Newtonian cosmology and Newtonian method. We are in the midst of a new philosophical revolution, a revolution in which, indeed, the new physics too has had due influence, but a revolution founded squarely on the disciplines concerned with life: on biology, psychology, sociology, history, even theology and art criticism. Seventeenth-century thinkers had to free themselves from the bonds of scholastic discipline, and we have had to free ourselves from the bonds of Newtonian abstraction, to dare, not only to manipulate abstractions, to calculate and predict and falsify, but to *understand*. The revolution before us is a revolution of life against dead nature, and of understanding as against the calculi of logical machines. The Newtonian ideal, said Whitehead (in a context to which I shall later return in more detail), has turned scientific procedure into 'a mystic chant over an unintelligible universe'. The conceptual reform in which we are now engaged must restore our speech about the world to intelligible discourse and the world it aims at describing to significant and coherent form. Nature must be understood once more as the multifarious scene, not only of an invisible billiards game played by chance against necessity, but of a vast variety of forms, energies and events, living and non-living, sentient and insentient, of processes alive, active and striving, as well as of conditions, dead, passive and inert. For the Cartesian-Newtonian world was, in the last analysis, a world without life. That simple fact had, and still has, disastrous consequences for the conception both of the object of knowledge and of the subject who knows it. These consequences lie so deep in our habits of thought that the recovery from them is slow and difficult. Many thinkers have already tried to assist us on the road: philosophers like Dilthey, James, Dewey, Whitehead, Bergson, Collingwood, and many biologists and psychologists as well. I should not venture to better their instruction. But I think that looking back over the history of western thought we may find some clues to help us in understanding the need for and direction of such conceptual recovery.

My own starting point is in the theory of knowledge developed by Michael Polanyi in *Personal Knowledge* and other writings, or better, in my interpretation of that theory; for whatever I have *mis*interpreted, I alone bear the responsibility. As I see the matter, then, Polanyi restores knower and known to their healthy functioning by stressing the personal commitment of the knower and the tacit, unspecifiable element in knowledge. His approach has much in common with some forms of existentialist and phenomenological thought as well as with the *Lebensphilosophie* of Dilthey and the organismic philosophy of Whitehead. Particularly striking, however, is the convergence between the arguments of Polanyi in *Personal Knowledge* and of Maurice Merleau-Ponty in the *Phenomenology of Perception*. As is evident from what follows, my debt to both books is pervasive. My own view of the history of thought, especially of the influence of Descartes, is, again, strikingly paralleled by the argument of Erwin Straus in his *Vom Sinn der Sinne*, a book to which, unfortunately, I had access only when this manuscript was nearing completion. I also regret that I did not have the opportunity of reading Edward Pols' *The Recognition of Reason* and Maurice Natanson's *Literature, Philosophy and the Social Sciences* until after my MS. had been completed.

Belfast

MARJORIE GRENE

Part One
Knowledge as Conjecture

1 The Legacy of the *Meno*

THE PATTERN SO POWERFULLY IMPRESSED UPON WESTERN MINDS through the rise of modern science was the conception of knowledge as completely impersonal, explicit and permanent: the ideal of total objectivity. In terms of this ideal, as Polanyi has put it, we suppose that if we had an infinite blackboard we could write down one after another in final and precise form all the knowledge there is to be known.[1] The optimism of the seventeenth century and the Enlightenment have contributed centrally to the form of this ideal, which has dominated philosophical thought in the last few generations. But the dream of 'manifest truth' has a much longer history than that: it began, in our tradition at least, in the first great syntheses of Western thought, in Greek philosophy. There are three chief versions of this ideal of impersonal and explicit knowledge with which we must reckon: in the philosophies of Plato, Aristotle and Descartes. For all three knowledge is final, impersonal and certain. But what makes Platonic certainty possible is the eternity, the superior, intrinsic reality, of its transcendent object, itself by itself, apart from relativity, contradiction, or decay. This is certainty beyond, even against, the world. What makes Aristotelian certainty possible is the secure natures of kinds of things within the real world itself, and ultimately the eternity of the world itself; it is certainty within the world. Cartesian certainty, finally, relies neither on a really real beyond the world, nor on rootedness in the structure of the world itself. It is the pure, intrinsic certainty of the knowing intellect itself, needing no support beyond the luminous self-evidence of its own act of understanding.

In this and the two succeeding chapters I shall present some aspects of these three types of objectivism. I shall try to show what can be learned from them, and through criticism of them, with the ultimate aim of establishing a revised, and more adequate epistemology.

I have taken the *Meno* as the text for my study of Plato. True, the dialogue deals ostensibly with an 'ethical' subject, but there is, for one thing, no strict delimitation of subject-matters in Platonic philosophizing, and for another, this after all is one of the chief sources for the theory of recollection, itself a cornerstone of Platonic certainty. But my chief reason for choosing the *Meno* was a chance confrontation of two recent uses of this dialogue by contemporary philosophers. Karl R. Popper, commenting in his British Academy lecture on Plato's argument, and Michael Polanyi in his 1964 Duke lectures read the *Meno* in sharply contrary senses; yet both find it important as a starting point for their own appraisals of the history of thought.[2] These two very opposite uses of the same Platonic text suggest that we re-examine the dialogue itself to see what it can teach us, both about Plato's problems and purposes and about the nature of knowledge as we see it, or should see it, ourselves. Our leading question is this: does the *Meno* record Plato's confidence that men by their very nature possess the power of grasping ultimate and absolute truths, or his despair of their ability to acquire, whether by reasoning or experience, any knowledge not already implanted in their minds before birth? Does it teach the actuality of knowledge or the impossibility of discovery?

According to Popper, the *Meno* marks the beginning of Cartesianism, of that dangerous doctrine that 'truth is manifest' which lies at the root of so much mistaken philosophy and even of pseudo-science. The theory of recollection, he believes, exhibits Plato's most optimistic mood: man *is* in possession of absolute knowledge. Let but Socratic questioning awaken him, his latent opinions will come to view, and not as opinions, but as the secure knowledge of the really real which was his in an earlier life. Yet few philosophers have accepted this unlikely story, and even Socrates is made to remark that he is himself unsure of the details of the soul's destiny. What matters most in Plato's formulation, according to Polanyi's interpretation of its significance, is not the optimistic cast of the doctrine of recollection itself, but the urgency of the problem in response to which Plato has developed the theory: the problem of discovery. If you really know nothing of the nature of virtue, Meno asks Socrates, how do you propose to find out? How can we ask for something if we do not so much as know what that something is? We shall be like a detective looking for a murderer without a single clue: not even so much as that he is a dark man with prominent cheek bones and a recent cut on his left hand. Not knowing it, we could not even recognize 'virtue' if we found it. So the theory of recollection is proposed as an answer to the contradictoriness of learning, the impossibility of formulating, even as a question, what we do not yet know. What is most significant for us, on this view, is not the quaint and implausible story Plato devised in answer to Meno's challenge, but the challenge itself: how can knowledge come of ignorance? How can we know the unknown, describe as our goal what is, as yet, undescribable? What is this whole business of searching for definitions, with which Socrates was so constantly concerned? Looked at this way, the *Meno*, far from exhibiting Plato's optimism, presents us with a contradiction at the very root of our intellectual situation: a contradiction which Plato never resolves, or 'resolves' only by denying that it exists, since he believes that, in a way nobody could credit, we already 'know'.

II

What, then, has the *Meno* to tell us if we ask about Plato's view of knowledge and learning? Most of what I want to say about the *Meno* could be elicited as commentary from two or three brief passages; but let me put these in context by recalling the general course of the argument, pointing out along the way some themes with a special bearing on our problem. (It should be remembered, of course, that I am by no means attempting to comment on the dialogue as such, but only on aspects of it bearing on the question with which I started. Even for this purpose one has to take one's start from the whole conversation, since there is in Plato no formal separation of one 'field' from another – there are only the dialogues.)

The *Meno* falls into three main parts. In the first, Socrates tries to elicit from Meno a definition of virtue; the second puts forward the theory of recollection; and the third returns to Meno's original question: is virtue teachable?

(1) *Towards a definition of virtue*

At the start,[3] Meno has asked whether virtue comes by practice, teaching, nature or 'some other way'. This reference, at the very beginning of the conversation, to 'some other way' has a certain importance, for it points towards the eventual conclusion of the dialogue, where Socrates will indeed invoke 'another way', divine dispensation (theia moira) as the source of human excellence. Virtue is knowledge-*like*, Socrates will argue, but since good men fail to teach goodness to their sons, it cannot *be* knowledge (for if it were, it *would* be teachable): it must therefore be right opinion given to men irrationally (without understanding) by some divine destiny. Divinity or holiness – something more than ordinary human efficiency, rationally definable – as the source of virtue *or* of knowledge: this is a theme only lightly touched on in the dialogue, but essential, it seems to me, to Plato's problem and his solution of it. Imperialism abroad and demagoguery at home had exhibited to Athenians of Plato's generation the collapse of a merely human ethic, of convenience, expediency, or a merely customary 'decency' as the ground of political behaviour. Something more than 'convention' *must* be the source of our standards if they are to withstand the lure of greed and power or the extraordinary pressures of civil war. But they do sometimes withstand these lures and pressures: notably, for Plato, in the case of Socrates himself. There is, therefore, something transcending mere human contrivance at the source of the principles by which experience is ordered: something set apart as 'holy' or 'divine'. I am not here ascribing to Plato a quasi-Augustinian anticipation of a Christian theodicy, but only recalling a recurrent Platonic emphasis. The defence of the just life, in the *Gorgias* or the *Republic*, for example, demands myth, something beyond rational explanation, for its completion. In the *Republic* too, the philosopher-king himself, who fulfils the suspended conclusion of the *Meno* and shows how political excellence *can* after all be knowledge, is described in what Socrates is made to call 'the greatest wave of paradox'. Together with the Good, the knowledge of which makes him what he is, his nature and his training are expounded as a parenthesis to the main theme of the discourse, too difficult, too strange to be woven in craftsmanlike fashion into the fabric of a straightforward argument. All this, indeed, the *Meno* does not yet try to present, even as paradox or parenthesis. Yet even this dialogue, anticipating, as most of the early dialogues do, one motif or another of the complex harmonies of the *Republic*, points the way toward Plato's leading political principle. Although, he will tell us, virtue is after all knowledge, it is a knowledge inaccessible in its full nature to most men, and accessible even to a few only through hard and sustained discipline–above all, through a *turning* of the mind from the sensible to the intellectual plane, from the pseudo-world of fleeting perceptions to the real world of Forms. Such a conversion is strange, difficult, from the everyday point of view even perverted. It needs the guidance of holy men, a dispensation of the gods, an initiation into mysteries–something beyond bread-and-butter efficiency–to achieve it. There are, again, only brief hints of this theme in the *Meno*, but in connection with our opening question we should not forget it. If for Plato truth *can* be manifest, this can happen only by a hard, perilous reversal of our ordinary attention, from the seeming world around us to the really real. Cartesian certainty, as we shall see later, is attainable by any mind 'however mediocre'; not so Platonic truth. Granted, all men in some sense 'recollect'. As Plato puts it in the myth of the *Phaedrus*, no soul that has not seen the Forms can ever enter into the body of a man.[4] But only the rare soul, by its purer vision holier, nearer to the Gods, achieves the perfect recollection that is not opinion, but knowledge. And such knowledge will be, in the *Republic*, virtue too. The *Meno*, like the *Protagoras*, is still puzzling over this Socratic equation. The hints of divine dispensation, of prophetic lore, suggest the difficulty, the more than workaday direction, of the eventual solution.

All this, however, is to anticipate. The first part of the *Meno* displays no such difficulties, nor even suggests them. It is a straightforward piece of Socratic argument. Professing ignorance, as usual, Socrates pleads that he cannot tell of what *sort* virtue is, that is, whether teachable or no, when he does not yet know what virtue *is*. This part of the dialogue illustrates Socrates' habit of seeking 'universal definitions'; it is not our primary concern here, but it does in conclusion[5] lay the groundwork for our problem. Meno has tried to define virtue as action done justly. Justice, however, is *a* virtue, that is, a part of virtue, so he is trying to define virtue in terms of a part of itself. That is what happens, Socrates concludes, when you try to define an entity in terms 'not yet agreed', or of which you are 'still in search'. We cannot give a satisfactory *formula* for virtue because we do not yet know *what* it is. This is just the difficulty which Meno will soon transform into the question, 'How can you seek what you do not know?': the question to which, in the second main part of the dialogue, Plato presents the theory of recollection as his answer. In the present context, it is a typically Socratic rebuke to Meno for his unseemly haste in trying to predicate characters of an unknown subject; but it also reflects Plato's conviction that knowledge always involves an aspect of acquaintance. Definition is not just putting words together, but depends, when it yields knowledge, on the mind's confrontation with the object to be known. Moreover, this confrontation at the same time transforms the person himself who attains knowledge. Remember Socrates' warning to the young man who has waked him before dawn, eager to hurry off and enrol for the lectures of the sophist Protagoras:

> When you buy victuals and liquors you can carry them off from the dealer or merchant in separate vessels, and before you take them into your body by drinking or eating you can lay them by in your house and take the advice of an expert whom you call in, as to what is fit to eat or drink and what is not, and how much you should take and when; so that in this purchase the risk is not serious. But you cannot carry away doctrines in a separate vessel: you are compelled, when you have handed over the price, to take the doctrine in your very soul by learning it, and so to depart either an injured or a benefited man.[6]

Moreover, these two aspects of knowledge, the ontological and the existential, are identified, for example in the *Symposium*, where the philosophical lover, he who has seen the beautiful itself, is at the same time the only person who can 'breed true virtue, since he is in contact not with illusion but with truth'.[7] But here, Meno, lacking both the confrontation with being and the transformation of himself through that experience, is floundering. Not knowing, not being moulded by, 'virtue itself', he is trying to define it by its many appearances or by its parts. Where our terms are not understood, as Socrates will put it later, the chain is missing to tie down opinion, even right opinion, and make it knowledge. The chain, of course, as the *Phaedo* or the *Symposium* makes plain, is knowledge of the Forms, or, in the *Republic*, of the Form of Forms, the Good. Plato cannot and does not go into this ontological foundation of definition in the present dialogue. On the face of it, this is Socrates exposing ignorance and fraud and seeking for definition, an ethical and a logical task rather than an ontological one. But Plato is also foreshadowing, I believe, his own solution, if solution it be, both of the Socratic task of definition and of the task of Socrates as gadfly to Athens. As to the first, he is showing the impossibility of achieving definition without knowledge, in this case knowledge of 'virtue itself', knowledge of the being itself that we are seeking to investigate, not some part or aspect of it, but the one behind the many, and this is at the same time also the ethical task of Socrates: for only through such knowledge can a man discover the standards which can justly and properly shape his life. In the present context, however, the emphasis is on the cognitive side. As in the *Theaetetus* Plato will demonstrate that perception alone cannot be or produce knowledge, so here he demonstrates that verbal manoeuvring cannot evoke a statement of essence unless we already *know what* we are talking about. We cannot even characterize, let alone define an entity if we do not know the being of what we seek.

(2) *Learning as recollection*

But, then, Meno can go on to ask, how *can* we seek what we do not yet know?[8] To seek it, we must know it; but if we know it, there is no search. This is the question to which the theory of recollection is the answer; question and answer, preceded by Meno's famous likening of Socrates to a sting-ray, it constitutes the second main part of the dialogue.

Has Meno's analogy any bearing on our question; that is, on Plato's theory of knowledge? Again, our main concern here is not with the vocation of Socrates; yet we should notice in passing the characteristic effect of Socratic questioning, which is stressed later also in the interrogation of the slave boy on geometry. Socrates professes ignorance; and by contact with him others also achieve ignorance. That is, they come to question what they formerly thought they knew. Socratic seeking, which Plato is here interpreting as an aid to recollection, is not by any means simply a pointing to 'manifest truth'. It is an insistence on criticism, on the re-examination of beliefs so far unreflectively held.

But now let us look at Meno's question itself. Socrates, in reply to the sting-ray likeness, has concluded:

So now, for my part, I have no idea what virtue is, whilst you, though perhaps you may have known before you came in touch with me, are now as good as ignorant of it also. But none the less I am willing to join you in examining it and inquiring into its nature.[9]

To this Meno replies:

Why, on what lines will you look, Socrates, for a thing of whose nature you know nothing at all? Pray, what sort of thing, amongst those that you know not, will you treat us to as the object of your search? Or even supposing, at the best, that you hit upon it, how will you know it is the thing you did not know?[10]

This is the question which, in Polanyi's view, forms the root problem of epistemology. It is the question of *heuristics*, of the *raison d'être* of discovery. Philosophers, recognizing that there is no *method* of discovery, are inclined to neglect this aspect of knowledge and to content themselves with analysing the logic of theories and of their verification, or falsification, as the case may be. But the paradigm case of knowledge in our culture is science, and the paradigm of science is its advance, the discovery of new, and the reinterpretation of old, truths. Unless we can make sense of this process, the very heart of science, we can do no more in the theory of knowledge than to run round in continually dwindling circles of argument, doubtfully relevant to the substantive question.

That question is, as Meno put it, how can we seek what we do not already know, or, in more modern terms, how can we recognize a problem, how can we advance to discover the unknown? Polanyi's *Personal Knowledge* and his writings since then provide philosophical instruments to answer this question. My argument here, as I have already said, starts from Polanyi's theory, and it is also intended to guide the reader towards an understanding of that theory. But let me give at this point a brief indication of the theory, as applied to the case of problem-solving.

First, a negative point. If we insist that all cognitive acts are wholly *explicit*, that we can know only what is plainly, or even verbally, at the centre of our attention, then, indeed, we can *not* escape the puzzlement of Meno's question. The same point, central to Polanyi's argument, is also made by Lachièze-Rey in a passage quoted by Merleau-Ponty in the *Phenomenology of Perception*:

Whoever tries to limit the spiritual light to what is at present before the mind always runs up against the Socratic problem. 'How will you set about looking for that thing, the nature of which is totally unknown to you? . . .'[11]

But, Merleau-Ponty continues,

> we must define thought in terms of that strange power which it possesses of being ahead of itself, of launching itself and being at home everywhere.'[12]

In other words, as Polanyi and Merleau-Ponty seem to agree, this single question asked by Plato at the very start of inquiry into the nature of knowledge already puts paid to the centuries of effort in which men have sought to formulate canons of wholly *explicit* truth. Instead, we must admit as essential to the very nature of mind the kind of groping that constitutes the recognition of a problem.

How, positively, can we do this? Polanyi's solution rests on the distinction, which he introduces in Chapter Four of *Personal Knowledge*, between two kinds of awareness: *focal* and *subsidiary*. The kinds of knowledge grounded in these two kinds of awareness he has later called 'knowledge by attending to' and 'knowledge by relying on'. His central thesis is that no knowledge is, or can be, *wholly* focal. And in the case of a problem the subsidiary aspect looms large. We do not know, in the focal sense, what we are looking for, and yet we *can* look for it, because we *rely* in looking for it on clues to its nature, clues through which we somehow anticipate what we have not yet plainly understood. Such clues we hold in subsidiary rather than focal awareness.

The class of examples through which Polanyi has introduced this distinction is that of tool-using. When I use a hammer to hammer in a nail, I feel through my arm and hand the nail and the wood into which I am hammering it. I rely on my own bodily awareness to attend to the performance with which I am concerned. Reading is another paradigm case: I follow the marks on a page, relying on them in order to attend to the meaning, to attend, in fact, indirectly, to the person who wrote them.[13] The same structure holds for a problem. Focally, at the centre of attention, we are aware, so far, of the problem only as a puzzle, a discomfort, a conflict. If, however, it is a good problem, and if we are on the track of a solution, the clues on which we are relying do have a bearing on the solution: they are in fact aspects of the entity we are seeking to comprehend.

At the same time, such clues are also aspects of ourselves: they are points in our own attitude, skills, memories, or crypto-memories, hunches. To put it in existentialist language, they are aspects of our transcendence. So we live in the tension between what we are and what we seek: between the world whose facticity we share and ourselves whose shaping makes the world a world. Our explicit awareness, the focal core of consciousness, is always founded in and carried by the tacit acceptance of something not explicit, which binds, heavily and concretely, ourselves to and within our world. This means, thirdly, that knowledge is always personal. The impersonal aspect of knowledge arises from and returns to personal participation in the search for and acceptance of the object to be known. For only the explicit, formulable core of knowledge can be transferred, neutrally, from person to person. Its implicit base (since it is not verbalized and cannot be formulated and so impersonalized) must be the groping, the orientation and reorientation *of someone*.

Now all this, it may be said, is twentieth-century embroidery, far from Plato's theme. If we find Meno's question fundamental to philosophical reflection about knowledge, Plato, it may be objected, does not consider it a really important question. For it is, he says, a disputatious, or eristic, argument and we ought not to pay attention to it. Meno's question is in fact similar to the sophistic arguments Socrates is made to play with in the *Euthydemus*. Are we then justified in putting so much weight on it here? I think we are. For it *is* this argument which the doctrine of recollection is invoked to refute—and we may understand better what Plato's 'manifest truth' is and what we may learn from his description of it if we take seriously the question from which his exposition starts.[14]

Let us then see how Plato makes Socrates deal with this 'eristic argument'. It is not, he counters Meno, a good argument, and to explain why not, he reports what he has heard 'from men and women wise in divine things'. 'What was it they said?' asks Meno.

Socrates: Something true, as I thought, and fair:
Meno: What was it, and who were the speakers?
Socrates: They were certain priests and priestesses who have studied so as to be able to give a reasoned account of their ministry; and Pindar also and many another poet of heavenly gifts.[15]

If at the close of the dialogue, it is virtue as right opinion that comes 'by divine dispensation', here it is recollection itself, the source of knowledge, not opinion, that is known through 'men and women wise in divine things', or 'poets of divine greatness'. This may be a reference to the Pythagorean origin of the doctrine of recollection. But it seems to me there is more to it than that. Taken at the explicit verbal level, as the sophistic disputant would take it, Meno's question *has no answer*. Socrates does not answer it, as in the *Euthydemus*, by counter-argument, but by moving to another plane: by invoking the authority of priests and seers, of divinely inspired men. Now it is true that the poets and prophets are for Plato divinely inspired because they do *not* know. Like Ion, they are irrationally moved to speech. So right opinion at the close of the dialogue is said to be divinely inspired, not because it is superior to knowledge, but because it is inferior to it. Virtue as right opinion comes by divine dispensation *without understanding*. But there is nevertheless an ambiguity here which is essential to Plato's thought. He may, as in the *Ion* and the *Gorgias*, wholly condemn irrational pursuits as mere persuasion, without principle and without knowledge of what they are about, but he may also distinguish, as in the *Phaedrus*, between a false and a true or between a lower and a higher madness. The flash of fire that brings knowledge of the real[16] is more than, not less than, rational. By a sudden step, a turning of the mind, it brings men (the few men capable of it) face to face with the really real, the eternal, itself by itself. They step across the gap that separates becoming from being, seeming from real, many from one, from the world of word-juggling give-and-take to that other world where only those can guide us who are steeped in 'divine things'. As in the *Theaetetus* again, so here, Plato is not explicitly dealing with the Forms; so he can only suggest the step across the gap, not build it up laboriously as in the *Republic*, and he suggests it by invoking the authority of those expert in more than mundane things. The reference is admittedly a slight one, but it should be kept in mind as giving the frame of reference within which the doctrine of recollection is introduced.

Indeed, it is, in general, the suggestions surrounding the theory of recollection as Socrates propounds it that I want to stress here, particularly in the passage immediately following the lines just quoted. After his initial statement about immortality and the poetic lines with which he has emphasized it, Socrates continues:

> Seeing then that the soul is immortal and has been born many times, and has beheld all things both in this world and in the nether realms, she has acquired knowledge of all and everything; so that it is no wonder that she should be able to recollect all that she knew before about virtue and other things. For as all nature is akin, and the soul has learned all things, there is no reason why we should not, by remembering one single thing–an act which men call learning–discover everything else, if we have courage and faint not in the search; since, it would seem, research and learning are wholly recollection. So we must not hearken to that captious argument: it would make us idle, and is pleasing only to the indolent ear, whereas the other makes us energetic and inquiring. Putting my trust in its truth, I am ready to inquire with you into the nature of virtue.[17]

It is this passage, together with the hint of extraordinary authority on which it is made to rest, which, it seems to me, gives us such significant clues toward understanding Plato's answer to Meno–and may give us in some respects some guidance to our own answer. We may take the reference to those skilled in divine things as our first point. What other themes does this passage suggest? For one thing, there is the statement that there is nothing that the soul has not learned, and, related to this, the argument that, since all nature is akin, the soul, having remembered one thing, can discover everything else. This is, to me, the most puzzling aspect of the situation as Plato describes it. It is the converse in a sense of the thesis of the *Seventh Letter*, that to try to understand one thing we may have to search through the whole universe.[18] Socrates has been insistent that we must not inquire about the characteristics of virtue until we know its nature, and the Socratic technique seems to be in large part directed to pinning down the peculiar nature of the thing inquired into, virtue, holiness, rhetoric or whatever it may be. But why would this matter if all nature were akin in such a manner that when we knew one thing we knew all? The Forms themselves, surely, are many, and must not be confused with one another; discrimination is surely as important as synthesis for Platonic knowledge. Hazarding a guess at the kind of thing Plato might have meant by this statement, the best I can do is to suppose that the turn from becoming to being, from perception and opinion to dialectical reasoning and understanding, the shift of attention that constitutes recollection, brings the mind to the intelligible world where it can move unimpeded by irrelevancies and, knowing being, dwell in a vision of 'all things'. But it is still a puzzling statement.

Third, there is recollection itself: the contention that 'what men call learning' is in fact remembering. We need not consider here the problem of the sense in which Plato held this theory.[19] What is important for us is the philosophical import of the theory as the reply to Meno's eristic argument. If we are to be able to search for knowledge, knowledge wherein we become, as it were, at one with the object of knowledge, and if such knowledge must be wholly explicit, wholly luminous, wholly at the forefront of attention, then we are bound to conclude: the everyday world of sense-experience and word-bound judgment is unable to produce such knowledge. It must have some literally super-natural source. The alternative would be: either that there is no knowledge, or that it is not of this explicit and self-sufficient kind. In other words, that instead of learning being really recollection of what we already know, the only kind of knowledge we have is in truth only learning; and that for Plato would not be knowledge.

Fourth: look at Plato's *reason* for accepting the evidence of his 'priests and priestesses' rather than listening to Meno's argument. The latter would 'make us idle', the other 'makes us energetic and inquiring', so we should 'have courage and faint not in our search'. This moral reason for the theory Plato stresses again in another crucial passage, which summarizes this second portion of the dialogue.

At the close of the interlude with the slave boy, when Socrates has reiterated and expanded his statement of the recollection theory, Meno comments:

> What you say, Socrates, commends itself to me, I know not how.[20]

and Socrates answers:

> And so it does to me, Meno. Most of the points I have made in support of my argument are not such as I can confidently assert (*lit.* would fight for); but that the belief in the duty of inquiring after what we do not know will make us better and braver and less helpless than the notion that there is not even a possibility of discovering what we do not know, nor any duty of inquiring after it—this is a point for which I am determined to do battle, so far as I am able, both in word and deed.[21]

It is not, then, the details of immortality and recollection that Socrates 'will fight for'. What matters, as against these details, is the fundamental antithesis: between the belief that we have a duty of inquiring after what we do not know and the belief that there is no possibility of finding out and so no duty to try. And between these two mutually exclusive possibilities, further, it is the former he will defend *because* it will make us *better and braver and less helpless*. Let us reflect a little on the implications of this repeated and emphatic statement. The kind of knowledge that is virtue, the knowledge of the Good, which Socrates will approach circuitously and under protest in the central books of the *Republic*, Plato cannot touch on in the context of this dialogue. He can only leave us with a paradox less blatant than that with which the *Protagoras* concludes, but still a paradox. Virtue seems to be wisdom, or knowledge, yet no one teaches it, so it cannot be knowledge, for he who has knowledge can transmit it. Therefore it must be, so far as one can see from here, some lesser knowledge-like condition, god-given without understanding. But the point of reference he stresses is that, at least, confidence in the existence of knowledge and the possibility of attaining it will make us better than the want of such confidence. The linking of 'goodness and courage' to the true knowledge of the soul's true destiny is surely no mere literary accident, but a pointer to the richer context of the inquiry which only the *Republic* is to complete. There we shall find the true statesman who (other things being equal) can transmit his virtue, which *is* knowledge, to his successor. This forward reference, in fact, Plato explicitly makes at the close of the *Meno*:

> ... unless there be somebody among the statesmen capable of making a statesman of another. And if there should be such, he might fairly be said to be among the living what Homer says Teiresias was among the dead: He alone has comprehension, the rest are flitting shades.[22]

Finally, let us look once more at the fundamental contrast as first stated in our initial passage and again at the summary of 86C. What, Socrates is sure, will make us more energetic (81D) and better, braver and less idle (86C) is the belief that we can know, rather than the belief that inquiry is impossible. Now the same emphatic contrast, in turn echoing 86C, between what Socrates puts forward as conjecture and what he asserts with complete confidence, is presented once more toward the close of the dialogue, this time, however, in a different form. Socrates has been trying to distinguish between knowledge and right opinion. In general, he says, he, like Meno, 'speaks as one who conjectures':

> yet that there is a difference between right opinion and knowledge is not at all a conjecture with me but something I would particularly assert that I knew; there are not many things of which I would say that, but this one, at any rate, I will include among things that I know.[23]

So it is now the fact that knowledge exists and differs from opinion that Socrates is confident he not only guesses at but knows. How is this contrast related to the earlier one? Very closely. To know we can learn is to know there is knowledge to be had; to stick to opinion only is never to know, or to know that we know, and so to have no energy or courage to seek the knowable. Working back from this concluding distinction we can say that in Plato's view: (1) there is a firm distinction between knowledge and conjecture; (2) only if there is knowledge can we strive for knowledge, that is, only then is learning possible, not impossible. But (3) learning, aimed at knowledge of a non-conjectural kind, is possible only if, as holy men tell us, learning is recollection of what we have already learned in a former life. (4) This insight, the knowledge that learning is recollection and that therefore there is knowledge, is in fact the knowledge that is virtue, since it makes men braver and better than the contrary attitude exemplified in Meno's argument.

This seems to me, in bare outline, the conceptual framework within which the argument of the *Meno* moves, the context within which Meno's question and Socrates' answer should be interpreted. It hinges on the difference in kind between knowledge and conjecture, a difference without which in Plato's view there could be neither learning nor goodness, since—though it is beyond the scope of this conversation to show it—the life of inquiry in the light of true knowledge is also the good life.

The details of the slave-boy's geometrizing need not occupy us here; we have already stressed the conclusion of this part of the dialogue. Suffice it to mention in addition what was already emphasized in the first part: that is, the critical function of Socratic conversation.

The slave-boy began with a false opinion. Now he has had 'stirred up in him like a dream' true opinions of things he does not know. From here he could proceed to knowledge which was somehow in him all the time but which needed criticism and reflection, the Socratic sting, to bring it from forgetfulness.

(3) *Is virtue teachable?*

Meno persuades Socrates to return to his original question. For our present problem – knowledge and the possibility of learning – this part of the dialogue is the least apposite. Against the background of recollection, it bears somewhat the same relation to the philosophical climax of the whole that Alcibiades' praise in the *Symposium* does to the speech of Diotima. Interwoven with the argument is the contrast of Socrates and Anytus, who are the human counterparts of the contrast between confidence in knowledge and reliance on conjecture, between true virtue and the illusion of virtue. The particular points which do bear directly on our problem, the distinction between knowledge and opinion, and the reference to divine dispensation, I have already mentioned as reinforcements and revisions of earlier themes.

Such, then, in so far as it concerns us in our inquiry about knowledge, is the gist of the *Meno*. Looking back, we may say that there are three stages in Plato's argument about knowledge. First: *Socratic criticism*: Socrates is saying, we are both ignorant, let us seek together for what we do not know. This means that we look critically at our accepted, unreflective opinions and try to come, like the slave-boy, from wrong opinion to a dream-like right opinion, and perhaps, with luck, from there to knowledge. Secondly, *Meno's challenge to the possibility of this reflective movement*. Thirdly, *Plato's answer to him*: invoking a divine source of the knowledge of what knowledge is, stressing the unity of the knowable, the distinction between knowledge and conjecture, and the knowledge of this distinction, or of the soul's destiny, in which this distinction has its foundation, as the source of goodness and courage.

III

Let us now return to our original question: the use of this dialogue by Popper and Polanyi. It is of course stage three of Plato's argument on knowledge that Popper is objecting to. This is where he believes Plato betrays his shameless arrogance and over-optimism. And, on the premises which he and Plato have in common, so he does. For both Plato and Popper, knowledge, to be knowledge, must be explicit and wholly impersonal. It is *theoria*, something the mind confronts and to which it must submit as more than itself, but which is at the same time separable from it. There is for Plato one nature in which, having found a toe-hold, we can move anywhere. For Popper, indeed, there is no such One Being in which we dwell as knowers; but there is the one impersonal, objective and sacrosanct 'method' of science which moves serenely apart from and unperturbed by the hopes and disappointments of interested individuals, and from this issues, no explicit knowledge indeed, but its negation: explicit error.

Now there is indeed some truth in both these views. There *is* one reality to which all our conjectures are directed, but Plato was wrong in thinking we could ever attain the knowledge of it as such. All our successful gropings after knowledge succeed by making contact with some fragmentary aspect of reality and only in awareness of their fragmentariness can they succeed. To deny this would be, not the courage Plato advises, but *hybris*. And Popper is also right in stressing the standard of disinterestedness in science; but it is a standard nevertheless which must inform individual minds. They must learn it and dwell in it through long apprenticeship and it has no existence apart from their individual striving, or rather the convergent strivings of numbers of individual minds shaped in the same traditions. My point here however is simply this: on either view, Plato's or Popper's, there is really no such thing as learning. We must agree with Popper that there is no manifest truth, no radical cut between knowledge and conjecture. But the knowledge Popper is after, if he could get it, would still be Platonic knowledge: wholly explicit, finished and final. And in terms of such a conception of knowledge, as Lachièze-Rey rightly argues, Meno's paradox holds: there can be no learning. For Plato there is the knowledge of truth through recollection; for Popper there is the knowledge of error through falsification. In the one case knowledge in a former life, in the other case conjecture (hypothesis) is the point we start from. In the one case we make explicit once more knowledge we formerly possessed; in the other, we achieve through deduction and controlled observation the knowledge of the falsity of conjectures we somehow happen to have. But neither in the one case nor the other is there any reasoned account of learning or discovery. There is either, for Plato, nothing new, or, for Popper, novelties thrown up so far as one knows at random.

Let us look a little further into this situation. If all knowledge were explicit, if it consisted of pieces of information immediately present to the mind and impersonally transferable from one mind to another, then there would be no learning and *a fortiori* no discovery, which is the learning of what no one ever knew before. No one could 'see' a problem or, in any accountable way, find a road to its solution. Knowledge on this basis would be a miracle. It is this solution or something like it which, it seems to me, both Plato and Popper are driven to adopt. If we seek along the road of ordinary everyday experience for explicit truth, we find none, and no road to it either. To support his confidence that there is, nevertheless knowledge, Plato turns sharply away from the everyday world around us to immortality and the fantasy of recollection for support. This Popper obviously cannot do. But so deep is the need for the explicit, the formulable, that he grasps at the converse of truth, at explicit error, as the straw that will save the traditional ideal. At least, he claims, we can know publicly, explicitly, impersonally, when we are mistaken. That is the mark, Popper believes, of genuine knowledge, the dividing line of science and speculation. If knowledge were indeed only explicit, this would be a reasonable answer.

But Popper has paid no serious heed to Meno's question. He has not only cut off the level of Platonic recollection, fastened to the reality of the Forms, but the recognition of problems as well. It is in fact the critical stage of Socratic questioning at which Popper stops. Criticism is for him the be-all and end-all, because there is no explicit knowledge, no manifest truth, and so we rest with the manifestness of error, in which criticism for its own sake becomes the primary tool of knowledge. Yet this is to ignore the whole context of discovery which Meno's question has raised: of the way we grope our way forward to make sense, and more sense, and different sense, of our experience, so that we discover not only the error of our past prejudices but the possible truth of our conjectures. One does not, Popper insists, just counsel young scientists 'Observe'. There is always some hypothesis in relation to which they are conducting their observations. But neither does one counsel them simply 'Falsify!' Both observation and criticism are in context, not only in relation to an explicit 'hypothesis', but in relation to the tacit field out of which and in which alone explicit questioning and explicit answering can grow.

In other words, both Plato and Popper take as their starting point the demand that knowledge must be explicit. Plato insists further that knowledge is different in kind from opinion. For opinion always has something beyond that escapes it. It may or may not be chained by right 'causal' reasoning to its object—there is an inescapable ambiguity, a want of explicitness in its relation to what it claims to know. For Popper, on the other hand, there is, in a positive sense, nothing but conjecture: we never know we know. But the conjectures we make are still interpreted as all on one level of explicit formulation, and to keep them from disintegrating into meaningless and unmotivated guesses, he retains one point of attachment still for unambiguous, explicit knowledge, and that is: we can know error. We have only conjectures but we can find out they are false. So the body of accepted, and for the moment acceptable, conjectures is stabilized by an increased mass of rejected hypotheses, which we know, Platonically, unalterably, forever, to be wrong.

Now it is indeed the case that falsification of hypotheses is logically sound, whereas verification is not. But to reduce the process of knowing to its skeleton in logic is to produce a travesty of so-called 'scientific method' and scientific advance, or, more generally, of the process of achieving knowledge. What other alternative is there?

The Platonic miracle of the knowledge of truth and the Popperian miracle of the knowledge of error are, we have argued, equally consequences of the demand for wholly explicit knowledge. And the conclusion which they jointly lead us to draw is that already quoted from Merleau-Ponty: if knowledge is wholly what is present to the mind, at the centre of attention, we are driven back to Meno's question, and there is no learning. But there is learning, there are discoveries. Suppose, as Polanyi does, we start from that as our given. We must then abandon our search for wholly explicit, wholly impersonal knowledge. In agreement with Popper, we reject the difference in kind between knowledge and conjecture, but we admit that if truth is not manifest, if we do not explicitly know we know, neither do we always and necessarily know when we do not know. We are always, as human beings, beings in a world, in advance of our data in the aspiration to knowledge, yet caught in the ambiguity of our finitude between the explicit surface of our knowledge, the formulable, impersonal aspect of it, and the tacit, often even unknown clues to it in reliance on which we attend to that explicit core. There is no absolute, once for all, knowing by human beings, neither in supernatural confrontation with Really Reals nor in a logical checking off of falsified not-knowns. There are only ourselves, using all the means at our disposal: bodily orientation, sensory images, verbal formulations with all their over- and undertones, social taboos and imperatives—including all the lore of practice and procedure of any given discipline we have been trained to—and, finally, our deepest, widest vision of the world we dwell in: using all these as clues to the nature we are in a given instance trying to understand. In this sense understanding, knowing, *is* learning to understand: always susceptible to error, but also, though never wholly and though never *known* to be so, capable of success.

IV

Our conclusion, then, is: that we must reject the claim of a wholly explicit knowledge, if we seek to escape Meno's question by denying the reality of the kind of knowledge of which Plato was in search and which indeed he did believe he had achieved. But let us look back once more at the dialogue and ask, finally, what we can say that we have learned from Plato's argument. Is it only the false ideal of manifest truth—and further of totally explicit knowledge (of truth *or* error) that the *Meno* by implication warns us to reject? Plato insists that unless there is knowledge as distinct from mere conjecture we shall not try to discover what we do not yet know, but even though we reject his dichotomy, I think we can go between the horns of his dilemma and still assent to a number of the theses which directly or indirectly the *Meno* states or suggests.

First, there is the paradox itself of Meno's question and with it the hint of something dark and difficult in Socrates' reply. No pat formula will tell us what learning is. Destined somehow to seek we know not what, we need, not words only, not eristic skill, but the stranger vision of 'priests and priestesses', of those 'learned in divine things', to put us on the track. There is a hint here, I believe, of the theme that Plato develops much more explicitly elsewhere: that is, of the existential aspect of knowledge: the fact that, as the *Protagoras* passage tells us playfully and the 'knowledge line' of the *Republic* will tell us in all earnest, people are changed in their very inmost nature by the 'acquisition' of knowledge. All that Plato says here is that the secret of what learning is has some kind of priestly lore as its source: that at least marks it off from the external, verbal plane of eristic argument.

Secondly, whatever we seek, it is not some definite thing which will reveal itself self-sufficient and complete, but a point of entry to a reality that is in some sense more than any one object we aspire to know. What Plato meant by the One behind the many I suppose no one can clearly and unequivocally state. And as for us, we must surely deny that we can know we know even one thing, let alone all. There is no 'all' of knowledge. But in the sense that we grant one ground, one being, of which in all our gropings, our efforts to make sense of things, we are trying in a segmented and abstract way to understand some aspect: i.e. that all knowledge ultimately is metaphysical knowledge, this much of Plato's vision we may still grant.

Finally, and most important for us, I believe, is Plato's emphasis in the *Meno* on the unity of theory and practice. We cannot accept recollection, a turning about to another world, as the prop for our zeal in inquiry. Nevertheless learning as the process of discovering significant form is the source of right practice as well as right opinion. In fact, there is only one process: that is ourselves trying to make sense of things, trying to find significance in what would else be chaos. This is learning, the only kind of knowledge we have or can have, and it is the same process whether it happens in a given context to be more or less closely related to the ends of 'practical' life. Learning is a transformation of the whole person, as any action is; in fact as the ground of action it is the continuing, manifold transformation which makes us what we are.

2 Aristotelian Certainty

I

KNOWLEDGE, PLATO HAS MADE SOCRATES SAY, DIFFERS DEEPLY
from opinion; only this confidence makes possible the courageous
and persistent pursuit of truth and right. To justify this dichotomy,
however, Plato had to turn his back on the changing world of sensible things and affirm a pre-natal confrontation with truth. His
certainties lay in a vision beyond and opposed to the everyday,
visible world. But must we in fact set out, as Plato did, from the *un-*
certainty of things as they seem? Is not the structure of the world
itself, *our* world, stable enough to let us rest with the certainties *it*
provides? For Plato's greatest pupil, for Aristotle, the Platonic
starting point, the thesis that 'sensible things are always in flux and
there is no knowledge of them', was itself a mistake, and so the
intellectual conversion away from the perceptible world to the really
real of the Forms, was illusory and unneeded. The source of certainty,
Aristotle believed, is with us and around us in the nature of things
and in the natural concordance between our own intelligence and the
world. For Aristotelian certainty rests on two related conditions: the
power of our minds to apprehend the essential nature and to formulate the definition of each kind of thing, and the natures of things
which are exhibited *in* them in such a way that we can so apprehend
them and state their definitions. He accepts, indeed, Plato's cut
between knowledge and opinion. Knowledge is the assured, indubitable union of the mind with what is, the possession of manifest
truth. Opinion, on the other hand, is the mere assertion *that it is*,
where our statement may have hit the target or have missed it: we
think it's like that, but do not *know*. Othello (to use Russell's classic
example) was of the *opinion* that Desdemona loved Cassio, but
Iago, and Desdemona, *knew* that she did not. There are true and
there are false opinions; there is no false knowledge. This dichotomy,
still reflected in ordinary language, is fundamental to Aristotelian
as to Platonic thought. But the world itself, and our minds within it,
are so ordered, Aristotle believes, that the certainty of knowledge is
attainable within this perceptible cosmos itself. Or rather, in his own
terms, he *knows* that this is so.

Aristotle's confidence in the knowability of the cosmos, all the way from its humblest to its most divine ingredients, set its imprint on men's minds for centuries to come, and is ever again renewed as the proper guarantor of truth. Currently, for example, there is a lively renaissance of Aristotelian 'realism', directed both against the analytical and the existentialist traditions in recent academic philosophy. Both these lines of reflection seem to produce only philosophies of alienation, as Plato in his day had done. Aristotle's sound common sense, articulated with such elegance and finality in his metaphysics, seems to show us once more how to be at home in the world.

What I want to do here is to look at some of the features of Aristotle's conception of knowledge and its object, with two questions in mind. First, does he in fact offer us a source of certainty more plausible than Platonic recollection? And second, even if we cannot live our lives in the cosmos he pictures, can we nevertheless find in his account of knowledge some clues to help us in our own philosophizing? As with the *Meno*, so here, I am trying to use Aristotle's analysis as a starting point for my own, by no means Aristotelian, reflections; I am certainly not attempting to present a survey of the Aristotelian theory of knowledge. But there are two conceptions in Aristotle's account of our minds and its knowledge which plainly call for treatment in any epistemological context. These are: his theory of sense-perception and his concept of intellect or intuitive reason (*nous*), and I shall be dealing principally with these. Both these conceptions raise age-old cruces of Aristotelian scholarship which I am far from hoping to resolve; but I suspect that the ambiguity and obscurity of Aristotle's pronouncements about these matters reflects an ineradicable ambiguity and obscurity in the very nature of the subject-matter—and for that reason it may be rewarding to examine once more what he said about them. Aristotle was always precise and exact when he *could* be so, and when he was not so, one suspects that the very thing or process discussed forbids precision: to learn that would be something.

II

We may begin by going back for a moment to our previous starting point: Meno's question about learning, and looking at Aristotle's answer to the same question. The context is revealing. At the start of the *Posterior Analytics*, Aristotle is laying the foundation for the method of *demonstration*, by which the mind proceeds from true, appropriate, necessary, 'commensurately universal' premises, to true and necessary conclusions. (Commensurately universal premises are those which fit just this subject-matter and all of this subject-matter but no other.) In one of his usual introductory aphorisms, backed up by everyday observation, Aristotle remarks:

> All teaching and learning that involves the use of reason proceeds from pre-existent knowledge. This is evident if we consider all the different branches of learning, because both the mathematical sciences and every other art are acquired in this way. Similarly too with dialectical arguments, whether syllogistic or inductive; both effect instruction by means of facts already recognized, the former making assumptions as though granted by an intelligent audience, and the latter proving the universal from the self-evident nature of the particular. The means by which rhetorical arguments carry conviction are just the same; for they use either examples, which are a kind of induction, or enthymemes, which are a kind of syllogism.[1]

In the mathematical sciences, in other words, we start from axioms, definitions and so on which we *know* and prove the conclusions which follow from them. Argument in general, i.e., 'dialectical reasoning', however, as Aristotle understands it, lacks *necessary* premises. In dialectical argument we start from the opinion of our interlocutors and argue from what they accept to the conclusion *we* want. In inductive reasoning, we start from the perception of the particular and draw out of it the universal principle inherent in it. So from the observation of robins nesting, for example, I infer the universal 'oviparity' inherent in the life-history of each individual observed. Rhetorical arguments, in turn, are incomplete or condensed arguments of the previous dialectical or inductive kinds.

Now this is, it appears, an exhaustive classification of all instruction and all learning involving processes of thought or reasoning—in other words, of all learning with conceptual content and import, as distinct from purely practical learning of skills (though the 'arts', as productive sciences, the reasoned principles of the processes of making, are included). But if all such learning moves from pre-existent knowledge to its conclusions, then it would seem, the problem of the *Meno* is upon us. A man can only learn what he already knows. So Aristotle recognizes. But we must distinguish, he says, between the *kind* of knowledge possessed before or after the learning process:

> Unless we make this distinction, we shall be faced with the dilemma reached in the *Meno*: either one can learn nothing, or one can only learn what is already known.[2]

What is the qualification Aristotle has in mind: the difference between *prior* and *consequent* knowledge? The example he gives looks at first sight a strange one—and it is the same kind of example he has used earlier in the *Prior Analytics*, where he has also referred to

Plato's solution of Meno's problem: to the theory that learning is recollection. Let us look at the two passages together. In the *Prior Analytics*,[3] at the close of the analysis of syllogistic argument, Aristotle is sorting out various kinds of error in argument. These must result from some relation of ignorance or forgetfulness short of actual self-contradiction. A man cannot both know and not know the same thing in the same respect at the same time; but he *can*, for example, grasp a *universal* principle of which he does not know some *particular* instance:

> E.g., if A applies to all B and B to all C, A will apply to all C. Then if someone knows that A applies to all of that to which B applies, he knows also that it applies to C. But there is no reason why he should not be ignorant that C exists: e.g., if A stands for 'two right angles', B for 'triangle' and C for 'sensible triangle', because a man might suppose that C does not exist, although he knows that every triangle has the sum of its angles equal to two right angles; so that he will at once know and not know the same thing. For to know that every triangle has the sum of its angles equal to two right angles has more than one meaning; it consists either in having universal or in having particular knowledge. Thus by universal knowledge he knows that C is equal to two right angles, but he does not know it by particular knowledge; and therefore his ignorance will not be contrary to his knowledge.[4]

And this, Aristotle seems to think, is the situation Plato was misconstruing in the *Meno*:

> Similarly too with the theory in the *Meno* that learning is recollection. For in no case do we find that we have previous knowledge of the individual, but we do find that in the process of induction we acquire knowledge of particular things just as though we could remember them; for there are some things which we know immediately: *e.g.* if we know that X is a triangle we know that the sum of its angles is equal to two right angles. Similarly too in all other cases.[5]

In other words, the student who grasps a general principle seems, when he meets a particular application of it, 'to have known it all along'. But this is only a seeming, since the previous knowledge was universal, of triangles in general, and the present application is to *this* triangle in particular. This same distinction, between universal and particular knowledge, is used again to answer Meno's question in the *Posterior Analytics* passage, and the same type of geometrical example is used to illustrate the point:

> Recognition of a fact may sometimes entail both previous knowledge and knowledge acquired in the act of recognition; viz., knowledge of the particulars which actually fall under the universal, which is known

to us. We knew already that every triangle has the sum of its interior angles equal to two right angles; but that *this* figure inscribed in the semicircle is a triangle we recognize only as we are led to relate the particular to the universal. . . . Before the process of relation is completed or the conclusion drawn, we should presumably say that in one sense the fact is understood and in another it is not. For how could we know in the full sense that the figure contains angles equal to the sum of two right angles if we did not know in the full sense whether it exists? Clearly we apprehend the fact not absolutely but in the qualified sense that we apprehend a general principle.[6]

So, Aristotle argues, the student of geometry who already knows that all triangles have their angles equal to two right angles, but does not yet know that *this* figure inscribed in a semicircle is a triangle, learns for this case what he knew 'universally', for, learning that this figure is a triangle, he learns thereby that its three angles equal two right angles–which he did not know previously because he did not know that this particular figure existed. In this way a man 'in a sense' knows what he is learning and in a sense does not.

Surely there is something both trivial and wrong in this example of Aristotle's. Consider it in relation to the context of Meno's question, to which in both cases it is explicitly referred. Socrates, though ignorant of the nature of virtue, consents to continue seeking it, and Meno asks him how he can seek for what he does not yet know. Wherever there is genuine puzzlement and genuine search, wherever there is the peculiar union of understanding and bewilderment that constitutes the process of searching for something not yet known, there Meno's question arises. But the Socrates-Meno situation is clearly not what Aristotle is envisaging here. It is not the case that Socrates has a universal grasp of what virtue is, without knowing whether a particular instance of it exists. He is, professedly at least, wholly ignorant. True, the soul, he is about to argue, in a sense 'knows' all things and 'learning' only serves to evoke, through the particular case, our acquaintance with the object to be known. But that is in effect just what Aristotle himself is saying: what we know in general, we may yet have to learn to apply in the particular case. And it is just this principle which makes Plato's solution not a solution of the problem of learning, but a denial that learning exists. Yet at least Plato did, in the confrontation of Socrates the seeker with Meno's dilemma, pose the *problem* as a genuine one. Aristotle's solution is just as spurious, but he does not seem so much as to have recognized that a problem exists. So, taking the question in its original Platonic context, his answer seems irrelevant. Plato proposes an absurd solution to a substantial problem; Aristotle proposes a trivial solution to a trivial problem.

Does Aristotle really believe that this is Meno's problem and that he has answered it? I think he does, but he has taken it out of context and in a very limited sense. Plato has argued that learning is recollection; Aristotle now chooses an example of 'recognition' which *feels* like recollection–'we already knew this'–and shows that in a sense it *is* learning, since before we knew only universally, now in particular. So, he is arguing, not, as we should expect him to do, that learning is *not* recollection, but that 'recollection' is learning: in other words, that one kind of learning which appears to be recollection is in fact learning of an acceptable, common-sense kind, and so not recollection at all. He is in fact arguing rhetorically, by example, setting a counter-example against the geometry lesson of Socrates and the slave boy. For this, he must have believed, is the peculiar kind of learning process in which the illusion of recollection, and hence the ground of Plato's theory, occurs. But then in the other types of 'teaching and learning' that he has listed, one would infer, Meno's problem and with it Plato's queer answer do not come into question at all. To Aristotle it is quite plain, in these other cases, how pre-existent and posterior knowledge differ and how it is possible to move from the one to the other. There is nothing puzzling about it; only the trivial case he discusses would even appear from his point of view to generate the Meno problem.

What, then, is the account of learning, of the search for the not-yet-known, that Aristotle puts in the place of Meno's problem and Plato's reply? The answer is: no account at all. True puzzlement, search for the truly unknown, and, *a fortiori*, discovery, the *advance* of knowledge, have no place whatsoever in Aristotelian science. Aristotelian method, it has been rightly said, is one of *exposition* of knowledge already won, not of groping forward out of new puzzles toward new solutions. That is why Aristotelian method *had* to be rejected before modern science could begin—not because Aristotle was not interested in observation; he was, but because for him the world was such and our minds were such that learning was no more than the analysis and articulation of an order always already there, actually, in the forms of things themselves, and potentially in our minds, the 'place of forms', suited by nature to receive them. There is here no Socrates seeking in puzzlement what he does not yet know, stirring others to uncertainty of what they once thought they knew. There is only the sorting out into intellectual awareness and explicit statement of what is always already there: the orderly arrangement of the kinds that fill this limited, knowable, eternal, well-ordered world.

Look again at the catalogue of 'teaching and learning' with which the *Posterior Analytics* began. First, 'the mathematical sciences', or literally, 'mathematics among the sciences'. Mathematics, throughout the *Posterior Analytics*, serves as the paradigm case for demonstrative science, which in fact includes three branches: mathematics, physics, and first philosophy or theology. In all these we move, Aristotle believes, from necessary first principles, which we grasp by direct intellectual insight, to conclusions which are also certain, but less authoritative than the premises on whose self-evidence they depend. Surely this is no 'learning' in the sense of Meno's question. In fact, scientific demonstration in Aristotle's sense, the self-contained movement from certainties to certainties, is just the situation which, as Lachièze-Rey points out, should most directly evoke Meno's dilemma.[7] We are, in demonstration, only drawing out what the premises of our argument already contain, what, in effect, we already know. We are not seeking, but expounding.

That is all we can do, or need to do, in the Aristotelian world. That is, in the Aristotelian world, what 'learning' is. In that world, whatever there is is either a substance, an individual, independently existing thing, or an accident of a substance: a quality, relation, position, state or the like, dependent upon such a substance for its existence. Substances exist, moreover, in permanent, literally definable classes; our minds, when suitably trained, can formulate real, true definitions of these kinds, definitions grounded, in turn, in the mind's apprehension of their essential natures. There is nothing to do here but to sort things out properly, get the right principles in line for the right science, and demonstration follows. In this happy situation there is at bottom only a limited problem of correct arrangement; there are no radical uncertainties such as the Socratic *daimon* raises, no true unknowns to seek.

So much for 'learning' in the mathematical sciences, which stand here for the theoretical sciences in general. The 'arts', the disciplines of doing and of making, which Aristotle, here and later, contrasts with demonstrative science, proceed in the same fashion but with less accuracy. Their principles are rougher and less permanent because it is not permanencies they deal in, but 'things the principles of which can be or not be'. Nevertheless, the basic pattern is the same. For Plato, inspired as he was by Socratic criticism and by the moral genius of Socrates himself, the quest for knowledge is permeated by the inherent self-doubt and questioning of ethical self-scrutiny. For Aristotle, on the other hand, what is essential is the serene, self-confident knowledge of a stable nature; some of that serenity rubs off, so to speak, onto practical subjects. The arts, though demonstrative with lesser precision because their premises are less precise, still follow the same demonstrative schema. We define tragedy in the *Poetics*, or the end of action in the *Nicomachean Ethics*, and elicit from those definitions consequences in fact inherent in the definitions themselves. Here is no irony, no doubt, no conflict of real and apparent. We are only spring-cleaning, putting into good order for knowledge what is already there around us ready to be known.

And again, dialectic and rhetoric are simply inexact forms of demonstration: in this case so inexact as to be even uncertain. But again they only elicit, more arbitrarily, what is already there: what the dialectician or rhetorician wants to elicit. What he is doing is twisting others' opinions to his own ends; this is hardly learning or teaching in an important sense.

The one case that remains is *induction*, the movement from particulars to universals. Here, surely, it will be said, there is genuine learning, genuine resolution of problems. For is this not what scientists do: to move from what is visible in the world around them, to the formulation first of general laws, and then of theories explicative of those laws, and again confirmable, or at least refutable, in terms of their consequences, within the domain of the observable itself? Taking this admittedly inadequate schema as at least a very crude outline of scientific procedure, we can see that it differs from Aristotelian induction in two very important ways.

First, Aristotelian method does *not*, like modern scientific procedures, return again and again to the observed and observable. Aristotelian induction takes us from perceived particulars to universals, which in their turn form the premises of demonstration. But the conclusions of demonstration are also universal, and remain so: their whole credibility rests on the credibility of the premises from which they follow, *not* on the range of empirical or experimental verifications, or falsifications, they may suggest. Modern science moves continually, in both directions, between particulars and universals. Many philosophers of science have argued plausibly, though not, I believe, correctly, that, as William James put it, our general ideas are no more than railway tickets to get us around from one station in experience to another. But any such movement in Aristotelian science is strictly one-way. You must start with sense-perception, but the move to universals, once made, is permanent.

Secondly, and this is the more important difference in the present context, Aristotelian induction consists in drawing out the universal that is already clear—*dēlon*—in the particular. Induction as we understand it, on the contrary, is a daring, never-completed advance to the unknown. The transition from particulars to general laws, still more from general laws to explanatory theories, necessarily entails a leap: an interpretation of clues not inherent in the clues themselves. It is an achievement as much of imagination as of intellect. The mark of scientific originality is to find significant pattern where others could *not* see it. Aristotelian induction, in contrast, is an analysis of the seen, not a movement from seen to unseen. If it needs 'imagination' as distinct from its starting point, sense perception, and its terminal point, intellectual intuition, it is only the possession of memory images, Aristotelian *phantasia*, that is involved. One could almost say that the Aristotelian scientist is content with what Coleridge called 'fancy', while the imaginative power concerned in modern scientific induction is akin to the creative imagination of the poet. Indeed, in scientific discovery, as in poetry, that imaginative transcendence of the given which is inherent in all our consciousness is supremely evident. But Aristotelian science is analytical of the given; it cannot and need not leap ahead of it to an *unknown*. It is just this transcendence, however, that Meno's question asks us to explain. And in no one of the 'kinds of learning' Aristotle lists, induction included, is that question seriously faced.

III

Aristotelian induction, then, moves securely and permanently from a sense-perceived particular to an intellectually apprehended universal, and remains there. These two termini, as we said at the start of this chapter, are in fact the essential supports of Aristotelian certainty: of Aristotle's escape from the contradictions that faced his master–his escape from dialectic to something better. There is no error in either of them. Let us examine a little more closely the certainty afforded, in Aristotle's view, by each of these powers.

First, sense-perception. Aristotle asserts repeatedly, in the *De Anima*, that sense-perception is always true, or at least 'admits the least possible amount of falsehood'. That is one of the ways, for example, in which he distinguishes it from imagination, which is usually false. But before we can understand what this veridicity of sense entails, we must know what Aristotle means by sense-perception itself.

The Aristotelian doctrine of sense-perception is embedded in Aristotelian physics, that is, in the science of nature; and Aristotelian physics is embedded in Aristotelian metaphysics, in the doctrine of substance and accident. Again, everything there is, in Aristotle's view, is either a substance or an accident of a substance: that is, it is either an independently existent individual object or a characteristic-quality, relation or the like–dependent on such an object or class of objects. Real individual things, first substances, are fundamental to all else: without these, he says in the *Categories*, none of the others, none of the classes of things or characteristics of them, could exist.[8] Physics for Aristotle is the whole range of disciplines dealing with those substances that exist by nature, that is, which have within themselves an internal source of change. Again, only *substances* have *natures*. The condition of change in things is what Aristotle calls their *matter*, their capacity of being otherwise. The correlate of this is their *form*, the principle or order or organization or pattern that makes them essentially what they are. The kinds of change natural things can undergo are fourfold. They are born and die: this is substantial change, a change *of* a substance from non-being to being or, in death, the other way. Further, they change in place, they grow (change in quantity), and they alter in quality. In the *De Anima*, which, treating *soul*, the *form* of those substances we call living, falls within the physical sciences, all this is presupposed.

Soul, then, is the form, the principle of organization of living things. It is of three kinds, signifying three types of organic order, and each higher type presupposes the lower. Thus all living things have a nutritive soul, all animals a sensitive soul as well, and men alone a third kind of functioning, a rational soul, over and above the other two. Perception is a function of the sensitive soul; it is a *qualitative change* in which soul is affected by, or receives, the sensible forms of things. Now qualitative change, we have seen, is one of the kinds of change which substances undergo; yet perception is not a qualitative change like that, say, of a plant from green to yellow in a drought or dry to moist in wet weather. It is not a change in which the *matter* of the agent is transferred to the patient, as in nutrition, but one in which a certain pattern or formula in the sensible thing acts on the recipient sense-organ in such a way that it receives the corresponding pattern, but without the matter. So the coloured, in the medium of light, produces in the eye the perception: colour. The sounding thing, through the medium of air, produces in the ear the sensation: hearing. It is first and foremost in this direct, though mediated, contact of each special sense organ with its unique object, that the infallibility of sense-perception resides. When I see yellow, there is some yellow thing I am seeing. When I hear a tone, somewhere something is sounding. Of this there can be no doubt, or as little as possible.

Beyond this, Aristotle says, there are two sorts of sensory occurrence which are not indubitable. First, *incidental* perception, as he calls it, is liable to error. I see something white; this may be the son of Cleon. But perhaps not; perhaps it is not after all the person you were expecting. You see white; you see only incidentally the son of Cleon. You see yellow and taste bitter; that bile is both yellow and bitter cannot be the object of any one sense. If you suppose that this something yellow is bile and therefore also bitter, you may be wrong, for you cannot *see* the bitterness. So each sense confronted with its peculiar datum is unerring; the substance in which the seen quality seems to inhere may be 'seen' mistakenly, for it is only incidentally, not essentially, the object of sight.

When we look at this account of the infallible special senses contrasted with the fallibility of 'incidental' perception we may be reminded of modern descriptions of the relation between sensation and perception, or on the other hand between perception and judgment. Sensation, we know, is the apprehension of such data as hue, brightness, tone, bitterness, etc., and perception the seeing of objects, hearing of melodies, etc. Thus we all know that our visual field must be two-dimensional but what we perceive are three-dimensional objects. However we interpret this difference, we all recognize its existence. Now in the Aristotelian account, it is the proper receptivity of sense unified in its proper given that is the sole unerring core in the business of perception; the apprehension, *through* sense, of objects may well go astray. Aristotle has indeed only one word, *aisthesis*, to describe both kinds of occurrence. But is he in fact groping confusedly toward the distinction which modern terminology has enabled us to recognize? At least one recent historian of these matters, D. W. Hamlyn, argues that he was.[9] In fact, Hamlyn believes, Aristotle was caught between a view that sense is merely passive and a view that it is active and discriminatory: if he had worked this out all the way, he would have come to a modern sensation/perception theory. For the direct passive reception of a sensory datum cannot be anything but what it is; our active judgment of what it is, which we have built up into perceptions of things, may lead us astray. So Aristotle's view, if thus abstracted from its alleged confusions, would seem, so far, almost like that of a modern thinker such as C. I. Lewis, who believes that we have constructed upon a base of raw givens the interpretive framework through which we assess the reality or unreality of things.[10] In such a situation, it is indeed the case that sense cannot err, since, logically, it *is* just the immediate presence of qualitative data that constitutes sense. What is subjectively present is present; there is no more to it.

Such a theory, however, decidedly is not Aristotle's, as is plain from two considerations. First, on a sense-datum theory, sensation is in effect the possession of images, and sense can be distinguished from memory and imagination only by (1) the degree of vividness of the image or (2) the imposition of categories on a series of images through the exercise of judgment. The latter is the distinction made by Lewis, the former by Hume. Neither is Aristotelian. As to the first, Aristotle insists, as I have already mentioned, on the falsity of most of the contents of imagination as against the veridicity of sense: their difference is not simply one of degree of vivacity. And as to both distinctions: he in fact counts sense, imagination and judgment as *three* faculties. For the sense-datum theorist, however, there are at most two: sense, receptivity as such, and judgment, the activity of putting images–or sense-data–into their correct (or incorrect) conceptual pigeonholes. Thus, in Lewis's terms, givens, organized in one way, are judged to be real, in another, illusory. I cannot help seeing the mirage, but I know it to be sand, not water. There is no *tertium quid* of imagination, as there is for Aristotle.

Secondly, and more important, a sense-datum interpretation of the doctrine of the proper sensibles plainly contradicts Aristotle's own account of sense-perception. At the close of his discussion of the 'special sensibles' he makes, in summary, two points about sense in general. First, sense is:

> that which is receptive of sensible forms apart from their matter, as wax receives the imprint of the signet-ring apart from the iron and gold of which it is made; it takes the imprint, which is of gold or bronze, but not *qua* gold or bronze. And similarly sense as relative to each sensible is acted upon by that which possesses colour, flavour or sound, not in so far as each of those sensibles is called a particular thing, but in so far as it possesses a particular quality and in respect of its character or form.[11]

In other words, sense-perception is the core, so to speak, of an interaction between a certain functional principle in animals, what Aristotle calls the sensitive soul, and certain patterns or qualities of bodies. As the wax receives the imprint of the signet, so the sensitive soul receives the patterns of things as colour or flavour or sound, but without its receiving the matter which underlies the colour or flavour or sound of the things possessing those qualities. This is plainly not a statement about the direct, subjective awareness of sensible qualities, but about the impact of the qualities of things on organisms endowed with sensibility. And it is this sort of thing that Aristotle has been saying in the main in his whole account of the five senses. It looks as if, as the single term *aisthesis* suggests, he does not distinguish between sensation and perception, or if he does, the former is assimilated to its place within the full, physical, physiological ongoing of the perceptual process.

The second point he makes confirms this general impression:

> The primary sense-organ is that in which such a power resides, the power to receive sensible forms. Thus the organ is one and the same with the power, but logically distinct from it. For that which perceives must be an extended magnitude. Sensitivity, however, is not an extended magnitude, nor is the sense: they are rather a certain character or power of the organ. From this it is evident why excesses in the sensible objects

destroy the sense-organs. For if the motion is too violent for the sense-organ, the character or form (and this, as we saw, constitutes the sense) is annulled, just as the harmony and the pitch of the lyre suffer by too violent jangling of the strings.[12]

Soul in general for Aristotle is the principle of organization of a living being; sensitive soul is what we should call 'irritability', the characteristic mode of organization of animal life, and sensitivity is the power characteristic of this type of organization, a power located, so far as the special senses go, in special organs. In character the sense itself, a power of soul, is not to be identified with the material complex, the organ, in and through which it operates. But neither, on the other hand, would there be senses *without* sense-organs. It is not the inner feeling as such of, say, seeing red that interests Aristotle, but the whole physiological situation within which seeing red happens. It is, he says, a kind of mean, a principle of proportion of which, in the proper conditions, the sensitive soul is capable. This is borne out, he continues, by the contrast between plants and animals:

> It is evident, again, why plants have no sensation, although they have one part of soul and are in some degree affected by the things themselves which are tangible: for example, they become cold and hot. The reason is that they have no mean, no principle capable of receiving the forms of sensible objects without their matter, but on the contrary, when they are acted upon, the matter acts upon them as well.[13]

So far I have been talking about possible implications of Aristotle's account of *incidental* perception, the first of the two areas where error is possible in sensory occurrences. The contrast between Aristotle's conception and a modern sense-datum theory appears even more plainly when we look at the second field of possible error in connection with perception: what Aristotle calls the 'common sensibles'. Each sense has its peculiar object; but some sensible forms are perceived by more than one sense. Such, e.g., are motion, size, etc. These must be apprehended therefore not by *one* sense fitted to receive them—for there is no special sense added to the five—but by what Aristotle calls the common sense: i.e., the perceptive power acting not through specialized sense organs but on its own and as a unity. Now in the first place, the very existence of such a single power of all sensory performances is inconceivable in terms of sense-datum theory. And secondly, consider the common sense in relation to error. The operation of the common sense, Aristotle says, is most liable to error, even more than incidental perception.[14] Why? It may be because motion and so on are often perceived at a distance. But it is also, I believe, because, from the point of view of the theory of perception, the apprehension of common sensibles is *doubly* 'incidental', and therefore doubly liable to go wide of the mark. What sense *essentially* perceives is the distinctive object of each sense; incidentally it perceives this white as an accident of Cleon's son, and so incidentally perceives that individual. But incidental to that individual, already incidentally perceived, is the fact, e.g., that he is walking towards me. So we are moving here from the awareness of the accident of a substance, its colour, to the perception of the substance *through* its accident, to the perception of other accidents of that substance, not directly and uniquely the object of the sense from which we began. The immediate is non-erring; at each stage of mediacy a further risk of error enters.

But what we start from in this series is not, we must stress once more, a *subjective* immediacy. It is the immediacy of what biologists would call a specialized adaptation in the organic world. Each special sense-organ is so constructed as to discriminate the individual qualities peculiar to its power of apprehension: black from white, hard from soft, as the case may be.[15] The certainty entailed in perception is the certainty, not of detached, inner immediacy, but of the immediacy at the core of a well-ordered world where things are so made as to possess characteristic powers of causing perception and organisms so made as to possess characteristic powers of realizing the qualitative changes that constitute perceptions. In each case sense is a power, a potency, which is actualized by the effect, through the proper medium, of a change in the object upon the appropriate sense-organ in the subject. The apparent subjectivism of Aristotle's account is but the central core of a firmly realistic conception: grounded in a stable physical, physiological, metaphysical situation. There are *kinds* of things, eternal kinds, finite in number, including kinds of living organisms–in fact, first and foremost living organisms–so constituted that at the heart of their normal interactions with one another, in the appropriate circumstances, the reliable, unerring or at least minimally erring, awareness of the qualities of some by others follows.

Sense-perception, then, is the core of a physiological situation in a world of stable kinds such that in its normal functioning what is perceived *is* perceived, and has a relation, though not one itself infallibly perceived, to real things. In modern terms, again, perception is an aspect of the adaptation of the organism to its environment: resulting, however, most modern biologists would say, not from the eternity of mutually harmonious species, but from the negative force of 'natural selection'. In other words, were perception not effective in receiving the sensible forms of things around them, animals would not have survived: they would have mistaken their prey, their enemies, their potential mates–for all these must be sought and found successfully *through* sense–on pain of extinction. For Aristotle, there is no threat of extinction; the same kinds have always been and always will be. But the interpretation of perception as a specialized organic adaptation is the same.

Now all this may be so, a critic like Hamlyn might say, but it is not epistemology. Perhaps not, but it does have epistemological consequences: namely that perception is directed not to subjective sense-data, but to things in the real world, to *qualities* of things, but qualities of *things*. Merleau-Ponty, though far removed, philosophically, from the substance-accident base of Aristotle's theory, has put eloquently the same central point that perception is in, and with, the world:

> I give ear, or look, in the expectation of a sensation, and suddenly the sensible takes possession of my ear or my gaze, and I surrender a part of my body, even my whole body, to this particular manner of vibrating and filling space known as blue or red. Just as the sacrament not only symbolizes, in sensible species, an operation of Grace, but is also the real presence of God, which it causes to occupy a fragment of space and communicates to those who eat of the consecrated bread, provided that they are inwardly prepared, in the same way the sensible has not only a motor and vital significance, but is nothing other than a certain way of being in the world suggested to us from some point in space, and seized and acted upon by our body, provided that it is capable of doing so, so that sensation is literally a form of communion.[16]

For Aristotle sensory 'communion' is an achievement at rest, at home in a stable, finite world. For Merleau-Ponty, this achievement is forever caught up again in the movement of time. Because all awareness is history, it is always caught in the opacity of the past and the lure of the future. It has always, as the analogy of the sacrament suggests, an aspect of depth, of mystery. What matters here, however, is not this difference but the thesis common to both philosophers: that sensory immediacy has its directness, its reliability, not from its being cut off, 'in my mind', but from the very fact that it is out there: it is my most concrete, dramatic, pervasive manner of being in the world.

IV

Aristotelian science, we saw, is demonstrative science. The ground is laid for it by induction, the smooth transition from the narrow veridicity of sense-perception to the richer, intellectual truthfulness of the mind's grasp of the first principles appropriate to a particular subject-matter. In between, indeed, there is room for error: in incidental perception, in the common sensibles, in imagination, in judgment and opinion. In fact, Aristotle says, we spend more of our lives in error than in truth. Yet we *can* achieve intellectual certainty, e.g., in demonstrative argument. But more than this, and presupposed in it, are the principles from which such argument takes its start. The mastery of these constitutes the pre-existent knowledge entailed in mathematics and other theoretical disciplines, and it is this kind of knowledge that furnishes the most important certainty of all. But it is, once more, a certainty first and foremost *within* the world. It is not the Platonic philosopher practising death, turning away from nature, nor the rationalist inspecting inwardly some intimate illumination in his own mind, who achieves this certainty. It is either the mathematician, who abstracts from existing bodies everything *except* their quantity, and apprehends the first principles of quantity alone. Or it is the student of nature who starts by *looking* at the individual specimen of its kind and moves to the knowledge of the kind *in* the thing: who grasps intuitively and directly what it is for an octopus or an olive tree to be one of its kind. Or, thirdly, it is the 'first philosopher', the theologian, who moves, indeed, *from* natural things to the contemplation of separate mind itself existing as the *aim* of nature, beyond nature. Yet even the theologian grounds his argument firmly in the nature of motion itself in a finite universe and the need for a first and unmoved mover as the keystone of cosmic order. For were there no such first mover, we should be engulfed in an infinite regress of movements with no issue; and that cannot be the case, Aristotle is confident, in the definite, well-ordered, intelligible world within which we do in fact find ourselves. For each theoretical science, then, it is the limited, permanent natures which together constitute this unique universe, on which the certainty of mind's grasp of its object depends.

This is the most pervasive bearing of Aristotle's basic principle that *actuality* precedes *potency*. What is first both in time and in ontological rank is the wholly real thing with its whole essential character, from which the development to full reality of another thing can flow, and be understood to flow. Were this not the case, there could be no certainty. But this *is* so, and, secure in this knowledge, we can be confident that there is always a fully developed nature presiding over change, a *terminus a quo* to assure the fitting *terminus ad quem* for every process. Nature, says Aristotle, is like a runner, running her course from non-being to being and back again. The circle is possible because there is always some full being of each kind out of which the not-yet-existent being may take its origin. Oak tree succeeds oak tree, man is begotten by man. The understanding of development, of change, is tethered fast to the eternal fixity of the *kinds* of things. And it is these natures, *universalia in rebus*, which the mind comprehends in the defining principles from which scientific demonstration takes its start.

In other words, the foundation of the Aristotelian theory of first principles is the doctrine of real definition, the belief that human discourse is able to give expression to the essential nature of a given kind of real entity. And the foundation of the doctrine of real definition is the doctrine of the universal in the thing. Universals are not substances, Aristotle insists, they are not real as the individual is real, but the form of the individual can be *understood* as universal because it is *specific* form, the form of its *kind*. And rational soul is just precisely the power of grasping such forms in things: that is why Aristotelian induction has the happy, untroubled character it has, and why Aristotelian explanation is expository rather than exploratory, secure rather than in jeopardy. As sense confronted by the individual substance receives its sensible form, so mind confronted by the individual substance receives its intelligible form. Within the total confrontation of this man with this individual natural object, the progression from the sensory presentation to the intellectual presentation is not so much a progression at all as a series of stages in analysis. The whole nature of this man and the whole nature of this object, set in their proper places within the whole nature of nature itself, guarantee the success of the proceeding. It comes out like a puzzle, infallibly, once you have the knack. Yet it is not a 'knack' but an insight into the very heart of reality.

What can *we* make of this? Compare the sights and smells of any school chemistry laboratory with the equations, electron shells, and what not, invoked for the students' understanding of them. Is there here the same self-contained intelligibility of the individual, perceptible entity that Aristotle has claimed? And yet this is the most routine learning, the most routine understanding. Vastly more untethered, more unconfined, is the imagination of the discoverer, charting the unknown, guided only, as Norman Campbell put it, by his faith that somehow nature must conform to his intellectual desires. On the face of it, the antithesis between Aristotelian science and modern science—and therefore modern theory of knowledge, governed as it is by the authoritative status of science in our culture—would seem to be as deep and as wide as the progressives of the seventeenth century would have had it to be.

Nevertheless there is something we can learn from Aristotle about all knowledge, including scientific knowledge, and that is, in a word, its *realism*. Wilhelm Szilasi in a fascinating little book called *Science as Philosophy*, recalls the lesson Aristotle has to teach.[17] He is perhaps stretching Aristotelian concepts too far, but what he has to say is worth looking at. Ordinary experience, Szilasi points out, first, generally takes the things in its world as useful *for* this or that; science corrects this first and superficial perspective, but is still *ontological*, still directed to the *being* of things. It exhibits, in his terminology, objective *transcendence*.

Szilasi distinguishes three aspects of objective transcendence. First, all knowledge is seeking to elicit from the real entities and events of nature their *possibilities*, the lines along which they exhibit change or development. That, Szilasi argues, is what Aristotelian potency, *dynamis*, basically means. Perhaps so, if we take the Aristotelian interplay of act and potency as correlative, like form and matter–as indeed, for nature, they were meant to be taken. But it must not be forgotten that for Aristotle act always precedes potency–and here I think we must diverge from his ontology. Aristotelian potency is subordinate to the finite perfection of Aristotelian nature, to the fully actual which precedes and governs it. For us, it is real possibility that comes first. We *have* to try to imagine that man, life, earth, the universe once were not, might not have been, some day, if 'day' we can call it, may not be. For Aristotle this is inconceivable. Our natural laws are what Whitehead called laws of 'our cosmic epoch'. For Aristotle natural laws are eternal, necessary, incapable of being otherwise. For us, any law of nature, however necessary the internal structure of its consequences, is radically contingent: all truths of fact are contingent truths. This is a radical reversal of Aristotelian emphasis which must not be forgotten, and which those who would revive Aristotelian realism are often too willing to forget. But, conversely, those who try to cut knowledge off altogether from any hold on reality, who declare that scientists only contrive conventional shorthand for sense-data, only gadgets for prediction: they in turn forget that prediction must be met by something happening out there, by something real whose powers, whose ways of happening, the scientist is seeking to understand. Even if we accepted the whimsical slogan of Braithwaite's *Scientific Explanation*: science is a zero-sum two-person game with Nature, we should have to remember the existence of the other player.[18] It is the possible moves by nature that we are trying to anticipate. In this sense Aristotelian *dynamis* may be said to represent a fundamental aspect of natural knowledge. Better yet (because free of the correlate of actuality) to recall from ancient philosophy the Platonic thesis of the *Sophist* which defines being as *dynamis*: whatever has power, whatever can exert force or energy, is real–that is, whatever can make through change some impact on other realities, including among these realities our own power to receive such impact. Again, this maxim is feebly reflected in the positivist dictum about the *fruitfulness* of theories. But what is important to remember is that a theory is fruitful if the *world* bears it out, if *nature* exhibits its consequences even beyond those dreamt of by the theorist himself. The powers in being come out to meet the powers of our calculations; that is how there can be the adequation of minds and things that is truth. For us, as Szilasi also stresses, truth is open, for Aristotle it is closed and complete; but the meeting of minds with the powers of being itself must occur if there is truth at all.

The second aspect of objective transcendence can be described, Szilasi believes, in terms of another fundamental Aristotelian conception: substrate or substance with its range of predicates or properties. The beings we confront have their identity through the possession of a restricted range of characters or ways of acting. In 'definition' we delimit each kind from every other. But correlative of this defining activity is the indefinable, ineffable 'this-here', *tode ti*, the subject of our predication, which *is*, yet eludes our speech. Plato's really reals, which elude ultimate description, reside in a far-off world of their own; Aristotelian subjects are here, around us, safely *within* the circle of our discourse, but being themselves never predicates they cannot be *said*, they simply are. The third aspect of objective transcendence, finally, is *permanence*. Real things remain, we are confident, identical with themselves through change: we can see and say what happens to them, but they are still themselves, just as a friend seen after ten years' absence is still himself, however altered. All these aspects of objective transcendence, Szilasi argues, are inherent in the very calling of the natural scientist. He is forever reaching out toward the powers of underlying, self-identical realities.

Now in contrast, again, to the faith of positivism, these ontological claims are significant, and in a very broad sense Aristotelian too, but only in a broad sense. There are two difficulties. First: is the Aristotelian subject ineffable in the way in which Szilasi makes it appear so? First substances, this man, this horse, are not describable through predicates alone, but they can be named: they are Jim, Dobbin. There is so far, from Aristotle's point of view, no lurking mystery hidden in them. True, scientific knowledge deals in kinds, not individuals; so there is in a way a gap between the individuals who alone exist and the species and genera which alone the scientist knows. But that is the gap which Aristotle so carefully closes in *Metaphysics Zeta*. The individual is a unity of form and matter, but of these two aspects it is his *form* which is more truly substantial, more truly *what* he is. And the form is, as we have seen, the form of the species. It is the form *man*, not Jim, and it is specifiable through predicates. The subject, insofar as it interests the Aristotelian scientist, is the specific subject whose attributes can be exactly and finally stated, and in the neat closed organization of the Aristotelian cosmos the mysterious, inexhaustible real is all but buried within the order thus imposed upon it.

Further, form is identified in Book Zeta with each thing's 'being-what-it-is', or literally, 'being what it was', or 'what it was to be' that sort of thing. Szilasi makes much of the imperfect 'was' used by Aristotle in this puzzling phrase and links it with the German *gewesen* present in *Wesen*: essence is having-been. This is a trick familiar from Hegel, for whom essence is the negation of being and at the same time its conservation in a higher form. It is quite impossible in English, I believe, to make much sense of this. We can argue, indeed, as Whitehead and Merleau-Ponty have done, that awareness is always of the immediate past. When I hear a sound, it is the impact on my ear drums a moment past that has produced it, and the sound waves that produced this had in turn to travel, through time, from some more or less distant source. This is true and important, but it is, once more, the very reverse of an Aristotelian insight. Whatever the reason for the imperfect, 'being-what-it-is' is not a receding reality, not something slipping away into the past, but the most stable and permanent of reals. It is the firm and eternal *what* to which definition is directed, the equivalent of Plato's really real, but safely housed within the natural world. Time is irrelevant to it.

Yet there is something haunting about the image of the mind confronted with the being-what-it-is of each kind of thing: the unified configuration of [mind-defining-formula-being-what-it-is] expresses, as Aristotle believed it did, an aspect of knowledge which had escaped Plato and which escapes most modern thinkers. Perhaps we can discover something of what Aristotle is after by comparing his conception of the knowledge of each thing's being-what-it-is, with Polanyi's account of the knowledge of comprehensive entities.[19]

In the Aristotelian situation, the mind, working over the sensible forms received by perception, confronts and assimilates the intelligible forms inherent in the thing as perceived. This is not a construction by the mind, but a presentation to it, and the mind does not make the thing by its judgments, but *becomes* it. Mind, the individual human mind, is at birth nothing but a possibility of knowing. Yet it is potentially all things, since its activation consists in its identification with the objects of its knowledge. My mind *is* the forms I am engaged in knowing. There is also, for Aristotle, a 'separate' and 'impassable' reason, which contains no potency but is pure act; this, however, seems, so far as one can judge from the cryptic passage in *De Anima* III, 5, to be non-individual. We shall have more to say about this shortly; for the moment it is passive reason that concerns us. It is passive reason which comes first in the individual, and it becomes actual through identification with the forms it knows, with the being-what-it-is of things. We become what we know.

Polanyi's account of the knowledge of comprehensive entities makes the same point but with a difference which it is also essential to keep in mind. Polanyi's way of putting it is to say that knowledge of comprehensive entities, such as another living being, or a poem, or a game, is a kind of *indwelling*. When I recognize a face, I cannot necessarily specify the details of eyes, nose, quality of skin, etc., but my subsidiary awareness of such details serves as so many clues to my focal awareness of who it is: oh yes, it's Jim. I am *relying* on my awareness of all these details to *attend* to what they mean, the identity of the person recognized. Now it is of course somebody else's face I am aware of in these terms, not mine, yet I *dwell in* the features of his countenance as the means of recognizing him *out there*. The indwelling which is part of me and the out-thereness of which I am focally aware through it are inseparable aspects of a single structure. The *objective transcendence* of my recognition, to use Szilasi's term, its other-directedness, is at one with what we may call its *subjective immanence*, the foundation, assimilated to myself, upon which it rests. This analysis Polanyi has recently elaborated in reliance on psychological experiments on 'subception', which seem to confirm the significance of subsidiary factors in perceptual behaviour. In philosophical terms, one could equally well take the recognition of physiognomies in Polanyi's account of it as illustrating the existentialist thesis that our being is *being in a world*.[20] My awareness is not a separate subjective 'in-itself', but at one and the same time an assimilation of what is beyond and an extension of myself into the things beyond. This interpenetration of 'self' and 'world' is not only a central characteristic of mind; it is what mind is.

On the unity of mind and its object, then, Aristotle's account and Polanyi's are agreed. But there are three important points of contrast. First: in Aristotelian knowledge the result of the unity of mind and object is the achievement of explicit definition of the real nature of classes of things, which in turn can issue in explicit consequences demonstrated on the ground of such definitions. Secondly, such explicit knowledge is wholly impersonal, it is of eternal principles and is itself eternal, detached from the transient situation of the individual knower. For this reason also, thirdly, active reason *must* be non-personal, impassive and separate: the power which when activated is identified with the eternal ground of things cannot itself be subject to change and decay. Only its reflection in the individual is, with him, so subject.

What Polanyi is arguing, in contrast, is, first, the tacit ground of knowledge. He is proceeding from the fact that we know more than we can say, to show how knowledge is a process that builds what we can and do articulate on a foundation which we cannot tell and which we do not in the same sense know. As Aristotelian perception, we saw, receives the sensible forms of things, so Aristotelian mind receives their intelligible forms. With Polanyi there is a parallel analogy, but with a difference. As perception is rooted in subception, so is focal, explicit knowledge in subsidiary, tacit knowing. Aristotelian perception, as we have seen, is the unerring core of a stable physical-metaphysical situation; so is Aristotelian *nous*: the situation that there are eternal kinds of which we can apprehend the essential natures. Within this situation, what is *incidental* is implicit, but what is *essential* can be made explicit, held wholly at the forefront of attention and formulated once for all in a form of words. It is the distinction between substance and accident, and between the essential attributes of substance and its incidental characteristics, relations, and so on, on which the Aristotelian unity of knower and known rests. Without this distinction there would be no knowledge but only Heraclitean flux and Platonic scepticism of the natural world. But such a distinction is inconceivable for Polanyi or for any thinker whose work is grounded on the model of experimental science. Except for certain restricted branches of biology, science does not operate with substances in Aristotle's sense. It is *events* it deals with, and events are not so easy to classify. Nobody can ever say for certain about any experimental situation what properties are essential and what accidental. It always needs a sense of relevance, a sense of the bearing of clues on the solution to a certain problem, to support scientific knowledge. Therefore it is not possible ever wholly to detach such knowledge from its tacit base.

For the same reason, secondly, knowledge, in Polanyi's view, can never be wholly impersonal. Even the publicly confirmed and reconfirmed statements of science are rooted in the consensus of professional opinion, in the accepted conceptual framework of a given generation of those considered competent to judge. And thirdly, therefore, also, the knowing mind is always and inalienably the *whole* person, not a separate part of him. The achievement of insight does not cut us off from our whole psycho-physical nature nor rescue it from decay. Separate mind, as Aristotle briefly but definitely declares it to exist, is unthinkable in terms of the human situation as we know it. And it is unthinkable in terms of the metaphysical situation also. For if our knowledge of concrete individual aspects of reality is tied to our bodily orientation, to the orientation of our whole, ineradicably psycho-physical situation, so are our ultimate metaphysical beliefs. There are no fixed kinds of things whose essential attributes we could explicitly and unambiguously fasten on as qualifying fixed species of substances. Every 'substance', every individual, is a concretion of events, a centre on which we focus through our reliance on shifting and manifold clues. Either, through the subsidiary within, we focus on the surface out there, or, if we become aware of ourselves, it is, conversely, through reliance on perceptions pointing inward, through 'proprioception', that we turn in toward ourselves and make our bodily existence substrate for the mental.

What is true in Aristotle's account is that, as Szilasi emphasizes, there is no contrast here between apparent and real, but between one dimension and another of reality. The whole situation of comprehension, in which mind and its object are at one, is real. In objective transcendence we are in things, or events; and at the same time, in subjective immanence, the things or events are in us, nay, our participation in them, our being in the world, is what we are. But viewed in the light of the analysis of tacit knowing, this situation can never be wholly explicit, or wholly impersonal; nor can mind, so understood, even approximate to Aristotle's 'active reason', separate, impassive and immortal. For us, Aristotle's functional psychology applies to all of mind, to intellect as much as to sense or appetite.

Another comparison may make the difference clearer. I have mentioned already Aristotle's theory of universals. The general: man, dog, tree, circle, is not a substance, it does not exist as an *independent individual*, and these two criteria: *thisness* and *separability* are the indispensable marks of substantial being. But the mind in the grasp of first principles and in the scientific knowledge that flows from them understands the universal *in* the individual: grasps the essential nature of the species in the specimen. The universal in itself has a kind of vacuity compared to the rich reality of first substance; yet the mind, nevertheless, confronting the individual, understands, not the individual, which is fleeting and different in all kinds of incidental ways from other individuals of its kind, but the universal, which is actualized in this individual just as in every other of its kind. Compare this view with Polanyi's treatment of the problem of universals in an article in *Reviews of Modern Physics*.[21] He has been considering a number of examples of analyses of tacit knowing:

> (1) the analysis of skills by motion studies, (2) the characterization of a physiognomy by listing its typical features, (3) the giving of detailed directions for carrying out a test or using a tool, (4) the analysis of speech by grammar, and (5) the physiological analysis of perception.[22]

and he proceeds to show how the common structure of tacit knowing disclosed in all these instances illuminates a number of traditional problems. The example which figures most prominently in his analysis is the illusion described by Ames and Cantril, of the skew-shaped room which appears of normal shape, while the boy standing at the higher side appears taller than the man standing at the other and lower side of the room. 'In terms of tacit knowing', Polanyi writes,

> we would say that we rely on our awareness of numberless rooms seen before, and of the other elements of the framework within which the two figures are presented to us, and integrate all these particulars into the way we see the boy and the man on whom our attention is focused.[23]

The analysis of this optical illusion suggests a solution of the traditional problem of universals:

> The process by which the conception of a normal room is formed here, and a particular object identified as an instance of it, bears on an ancient problem of philosophy, the elucidation of which will throw further light on the powers of tacit integration and the limit set to a formalization of these powers.[24]

It is the difference of particular objects from one another, to begin with, that sets the problem:

> Plato was the first to be troubled by the fact that *in applying our conception to a class of things, we keep identifying objects that are different from each other in every particular.* If every man is clearly distinguishable from another and we yet recognize each of them as a man, what kind of man is this, as which all these men are recognized? He cannot be both fair and dark, both young and old, nor brown, white, black and yellow at the same time; but neither can he have any one of these alternative properties, nor indeed any particular property whatever. Plato concluded that the general idea of man refers to a *perfect man* who has no particular properties, and of whom individual men are imperfect copies, corrupted by having such properties.[25]

Polanyi contrasts this theory with traditional nominalism:

> That something so utterly featureless as the concept of man should have such a perfectly characteristic nature, presents great difficulties which have occupied philosophers ever since Roscellinus raised them close to 900 years ago. But his own view, that the word 'man' is but a name for a collection of individual men, leaves open the question how we can justify the labelling of a collection of different individuals by the same name—a question that is further accentuated by our expectation that we shall yet be able to subsume under this label future instances of men differing in every particular from any man thus labelled before. The difficulty is not eliminated by specifying the characteristic features of man, since in doing so we must again repeatedly use one name for instances of a feature that are different in every particular.[26]

Both theories rest, Polanyi continues to argue, on a common error:

> All these difficulties arise only because we are seeking *an explicit procedure* for forming collections of objects which can be justifiably designated by the same universal term. Let us watch instead the way in which perception identifies certain objects according to their nature. The illusion of seeing a skew room as normal should remind us of the fact that in thousands of other cases we have correctly seen normal rooms as such, however different each was from the other, and however different the angles were under which we saw any particular room at a particular moment. It also demonstrates that the identification of particular things goes on without naming them, which is confirmed by the fact that animals readily identify members of a class, though they have no language. What is at work here is a process, common to all manner of perception, in which we rely on our awareness of a great many clues to which we are not attending at the time, for seeing things in a particular way which is the meaning of these clues comprehended by us.[27]

Now this account is like the Aristotelian in that it shows how we apprehend the universal through the perception of the individual, without either positing a real universal beyond the world, or reducing it to a mere name. And it binds the knowledge of the universal firmly to the perception of the particular. We come to know what kind of thing this is, and what this kind is, without leaving the perceptible world either for some world of subsistence or some conventional realm of names. But look at the difference. Polanyi's starting point does not just happen to be from Plato's problem: it *is* Platonic.[28] For Plato starts from the *flux* of the sensible world: it is the fact that sensory particulars are indefinitely fluctuating, that every perceived particular differs in every respect from every other, that forms our starting point. Yet despite and through this kaleidoscopic variety we do focus on a unity which is the general concept to which those varying particulars are clues.[29] Aristotle, as a scientist in his sense of that term, is not concerned with such variability at all. The perceived particulars are clues to the individual in which they inhere, and this individual when properly understood by mind is a this-*such*: it is a specimen of its kind, we apprehend the kind *in* it. Its differences from its kind are merely the mark of its being enmattered, of its being, as a thing in the corruptible world, capable of becoming, within the limits of its class, other than it is. Socrates' snub nose is not quite the same as Theaetetus's, but it is possible to analyse out of each case, or either case, what it is that makes a snub nose snub rather than straight: concavity of flesh and bone; this is understood not only through and despite the differences between the particular snub noses of Socrates and Theaetetus, but in either one of them. There is no interesting diversity in the two cases. In Polanyi's account, on the other hand, we are focusing on a general concept achieved out of reliance on clues which are in themselves *contradictory* to one another:

> we are assuming here that our integrative powers can resolve the apparent contradiction involved in taking an aggregate of objects which differ in every particular, to be nevertheless identical in some other way.[30]

This again is analogous to the achievement of perception:

> We fuse the two different pictures of an object cast on the retina of our eyes by forming its stereoscopic image. Here perception resolves a contradiction by revealing a *joint meaning* of conflicting clues in terms of a *new quality*. A similar synthesis is achieved when we hear a sound as coming from a definite direction by combining its impacts that reach first one ear and then the other. This is also what happens in the formation of a general conception.[31]

But we must not overemphasize this difference; there is also a common theme. What is agreed in Polanyi's theory and Aristotle's is their acknowledgment that universals are part of our knowledge of *real* things, or real events, yet compared to the recognition of individuals, somehow *inferior in reality*. So in contrasting perception and concept formation Polanyi notes

> the curiously *unsubstantial character* of the joint meaning ascribed to a group of objects by a general term. Compared with optical illusions or stereoscopic images, general conceptions are abstract, featureless. The focus in terms of which we are aware of the members of a class appears vague and almost empty.[32]

Polanyi's description here is reminiscent of Aristotle's treatment of universals in Zeta. It is the universal that is known; science deals only with concepts, not particulars, yet the universal so understood depends for its reality on the particulars through which it is known.

This common theme is indeed a substantive one; yet in the last analysis the two accounts are deeply divergent. Why? Again, because of their different ontological foundations. Aristotelian universals are safely housed in the limited Aristotelian world of individual substances and kinds of substances with their eternal, explicitly definable essential attributes. Polanyian general concepts are concretions out of a world of flux. They are moments in a history, *claiming* universal validity, eternal rightness, yet always in danger of error, of the need of correction, because they are achievements of living individuals within a world that is radically engaged in change. To insist on subjective immanence as the correlate of objective transcendence is to insist upon immersing knowledge in history: to see the being not only of each of us but of man himself as temporal, not as a phase of eternal recurrence in an ungenerated, indestructible world where only inessentials change.

That is why, again, for Aristotle, discovery is wholly unimportant, and the problem of learning not so much as understood. For him, it is the grasp of general concepts at rest in the particulars, first of all, that counts, and then the exposition of systematic knowledge flowing demonstratively from such unique and appropriate first principles. The system is there in the things, in the being-what-it-is of each eternal kind, there all along, for us to sort out, and potentially, it is there in our minds as well. This is true, indeed, but are those 'things' Aristotelian substances? No, they are particulars grasped, in a world in process, by organisms in process. True, something of the stability Aristotle insists upon is also fundamental to science, since without the grasp of elementary regularities scientists could find no problems to solve, let alone theories by means of which to solve them. But Aristotelian *nous*, the correlate of Aristotelian perception and the end point of Aristotelian induction, is but the starting point of induction in the natural sciences as we have come to know them. So, for instance, to recognize the permanence of chemical compounds or the relative stability of plant and animal species is a routine presupposition of scientific discovery, but the most mediocre schoolboy can grasp this much of science. The advance of science, the power of science, depends on the imaginative grasp of *novel* concepts, on the original mind's capacity to find order where others did not dream of it. It depends on the synthesis of what on the face of it neither demands nor allows of synthesis. Aristotelian science stops wholly short of such problems and of their solution. Moreover, every routine induction, every routine learning process, seen in terms of tacit knowing, bears the same un-Aristotelian structure as does heuristic advance. In fact, the whole series, perception, routine induction, discovery, exhibits the same fundamental structure. Polanyi points this out in the article previously quoted:

> We must note here that the problems of how a universal concept is formed is part of the problem of empirical *induction*. All attempts to formulate strict rules for deriving general laws from individual experience have failed. And one of the reasons is again, that each instance of a law differs, strictly speaking, in every particular from every other instance of it. Such indeterminately variable experiences can indeed be subsumed under the same law only by relying on our awareness of them as clues to it. And just as for perception, many clues of empirical induction will be easily identified in themselves, while many will not be, and not all of them can be, identified. In other words, the scientist's 'hunches' may be based to a great part on subception. And just as a

keen eyesight enables one to discriminate objects that others cannot see, so does a gift of scientific discovery reveal natural laws in a scientific experience, which signifies nothing to others not so gifted.[33]

What Aristotle shows us is that this whole process is a continued immersion of our minds in reality. But the Platonic ground of the venture in the infinite diversity of particulars, and the ineluctable sense that it *is* a venture, a work in progress, never a concluded edifice, that constitutes knowledge: this is the necessary divergence from Aristotle and from Aristotelian certainty which we can never with honesty renounce. We are certain that we are in the world, that we are thrust into, indeed, that we *are*, the facticity, the ultimate contingency, of our situation in the world; but any special thus-and-so within this ultimate givenness can always, given time and the flowing of perspectives into one another, be called in doubt. Everything in the world rests, for Aristotle, on the necessity of eternal, intelligible, first things which could not be other than they are: these are not only what we call logical necessities, which are purely formal, but *ontological* necessities, reals which could not be otherwise. For us, on the contrary, the ground beyond which we cannot penetrate is the ultimate *that*, the certainty of the *non*-necessary, of the facticity in which and through which we have our being and our contact with being. The unity of mind and object, which comes to rest forever in Aristotelian *nous*, for us is forever in tension.

3 The Errors of Descartes

FOR ARISTOTLE, AS WE HAVE SEEN, CERTAINTY IS GIVEN US BOTH in the physiological root of our knowledge, in sense-perception, and in the direct intellectual apprehension of the essential natures of kinds of things which is the highest power of mind. Both these unique and particular certainties, I have argued, we in our situation must renounce. Confrontation, the out-thereness of what we know, our being, not as isolated spots of subjectivity, but as beings thrown into a world: this is the core of truth in Aristotelian certainty, but the flesh giving body and substance to the core, in our situation, is the texture of our conjectures, our hopes and disappointments, our advances, alternating between insight and trial and error gropings, towards the receding horizon of the world. Problems solved throw up new problems; problems wholly disposed of become dead lumber, at best 'bare facts'. It is learning that is the paradigm case of knowledge. Plato, we saw, found it a queer case and turned to recollection to account for it. For Aristotle it was a marginal affair; it was solutions, not problems, that he found of interest. My argument so far has tended to suggest that if we make discovery–the advance toward new knowledge–our central concern, we shall have to resign ourselves to uncertainties. The groping for the not yet wholly known, the criticism of what had in the past been uncritically accepted, will be our model for the situation of the knowing mind.

Yet the man who most conspicuously set his mark upon the modern intellectual temper, who represents the attitude to knowledge of modern science at its start, René Descartes, was indeed concerned primarily with problem solving, but at the same time with the certainty, the indubitable and permanent results which in his view could be obtained by that process if rightly conceived and rightly pursued. Descartes's method was one precisely of posing and getting rid of problems one after another and establishing at each step certainties never more to be overthrown. His philosophy for the first time puts discovery at the centre of the intellectual stage; it is a philosophy of heuristics. Yet it is the method he thought he had discovered, and the certainty on which it was alleged to rest, which we have primarily to combat and to overcome if we are to find, in his own words, a 'firm and lasting structure in the sciences'.[1] Before we leave the question of certainty and conjecture in knowledge, therefore, we must examine the Cartesian claims for our possession of indubitable truth.

They are, first and foremost, the claims of a great and original mathematical mind. Plato too relied on mathematics, demanded mathematical training for his philosopher-king, but mathematical knowledge was for him the step on the ladder previous to the highest, previous to dialectic, because it was hypothetical. Given a pair of straight lines, given a circle, says the mathematician, we then find . . . and so on. From such hypothetical givens he advances to conclusions dependent on these hypotheses, these constructs. But the highest knowledge must proceed *to* the Forms, the first principles of things, yet separate from them, and there come to rest. If, moreover, there are mathematical forms – the circle itself, equal itself – still it is the moral forms, justice, beauty and the like, that are Plato's initial concern. He is a moralist who has learned to use mathematical certainty as a prop in his search for independent, eternal moral standards. For Aristotle, too, mathematics is the paradigm case of knowledge, constantly appealed to in his analysis of scientific method; yet mathematics itself is only one among the three branches of theoretical science, and in no basic way fundamental to the others. Aristotle is a naturalist, again in his way leaning on mathematics as a model, because of the precision of its premises and the logical character of its arguments, but Aristotelian science is not primarily mathematical in character. Indeed, Galileo's maxim that 'nature is written in the mathematical language' was the warcry of the overthrow of Aristotelianism. In contrast to both the Greek philosophers, on the other hand, Descartes is a mathematician, first last and always, a mathematician extending the professional mark of his calling to knowledge as a whole. It is a 'universal mathematics' which his new method aims to achieve, and this in two senses. First, what he wanted was to clear a space *within* traditional philosophy in order to found a mathematical physics, a physics of geometry. Whatever was not germane to this enterprise, for example the Thomist framework of a divided but harmonious theology and philosophy, his famous programme of doubt left quite untouched. But, secondly, his 'universal mathematics' was not to be mathematical in the sense of being a universal science of quantity. It was not the modern positivist dream of a unified science equated with the quantitative formulations of physics that possessed him. It was a unified science, indeed, but guided by mathematics in that each component of it was to be equal in *clarity* and *distinctness*, and therefore in *veridicity*, to arithmetic and geometry. In the *Meditations*, taking the first steps in building his new edifice of knowledge, he brings us first to the knowledge of ourselves, in the *cogito*, next to the knowledge of God. Neither of these is for him in any sense at all a 'mathematical' concept; but they are both, he believes, thoroughly simple and lucid concepts, equal in their cognitive force to the conceptions of geometry and arithmetic. Neither of them contains, he argues, the least vestige of obscurity, neither of them is anywhere in any way open to doubt. 'Universal mathematics' is to consist wholly of insights on this level of total clarity.

The secret of Cartesian method, in turn, is to order such acts of understanding aright, so that we move in succession from the simplest to the less simple, on a single plane of indubitable truth. The unit of this series is the clear and distinct idea, or, as Descartes had at first called it, intuition, 'the undoubting conception of a pure and attentive mind', an intellectual act which in contrast to 'the fluctuating testimony of the senses', or 'the misleading judgment that proceeds from the blundering constructions of imagination', frees us 'wholly from doubt about that which we understand'.[2] If we confine ourselves to proceeding, one by one, along the proper series of such acts of understanding, we can not only arrive, Descartes believes, at *some* indubitable knowledge, but at the construction of a unified, all-embracing body of such knowledge. We can, in fact, within a couple of generations, solve all the problems that will ever confront the human mind. Descartes was expressing, in this hope, not his own arrogance—for any one, he thought, who would apply his method, could win through, 'however mediocre his mind', to the same successful issue.[3] He was expressing the supreme hope of his time in the uniform and eternal power of human reason. It was a hope that was to govern the political and social as well as the intellectual aspirations of the centuries to come, and its force is still felt in the peculiar union of idealism and despair, what one might call utopian disillusionment, that characterizes much of our own thought. It is a task, therefore, of practical as well as philosophical importance to examine it and come to terms with it at its source.

We may take as that source, for our purposes, Descartes's *Rules for the Direction of the Mind*, a fragmentary work, not published in his life time, written probably more than ten years before the *Meditations*, and stating more explicitly and plainly than he ever did again the nature of his method. For these are his rules for solving problems, one after another, without ever leaving the safe confines of certainty. Everything doubtful we leave behind before ever we take the first step, and ever after we make our way serenely along the luminous path traced by the light of reason alone. The technique, and the conception of our minds on which it rests, are made plain, in fact, in the first twelve rules, and of these the first three already indicate the Cartesian theses most essential for us both to grasp and to refute.

II

'Science in its entirety', says Descartes in Rule II, 'is true and evident cognition.' Subjects so difficult that there is room for doubt concerning them, he continues, we had best leave alone:

> we reject all such merely probable knowledge and make it a rule to trust only what is completely known and incapable of being doubted.[4]

This, it seems at first sight, will severely limit the scope of knowledge, for it will eliminate every field of knowledge in which two men have ever differed in opinion: whenever two men come to opposite conclusions about the same matter one of them at least must certainly be in the wrong, and apparently there is not even one of them who knows:

> for if the reasoning of the second was sound and clear he would be able so to lay it before the other as finally to succeed in convincing *his* understanding also.[5]

Note the inconceivability that two rational men can differ: human reason is so uniform that if guided aright it *must* lead to uniform conclusions. But is there any knowledge of this kind? As we have seen already, there is only mathematics:

> arithmetic and geometry alone are free from any taint of falsity and uncertainty,[6]

and this because they alone

> deal with an object so pure and uncomplicated, that they need make no assumptions at all which experience renders uncertain, but wholly consist in the rational deduction of consequences.[7]

What we conclude, therefore, is:

> not, indeed, that Arithmetic and Geometry are the sole sciences to be studied, but only that in our search for the direct road towards truth we should busy ourselves with no object about which we cannot attain a certitude equal to that of the demonstrations of Arithmetic and Geometry.[8]

In other words, as Rule III advises us:

> In the subjects we propose to investigate, our inquiries should be directed, not to what others have thought, nor to what we ourselves conjecture,

but to what we can clearly and perspicuously behold and with certainty deduce; for knowledge is not won in any other way.[9]

Descartes's alleged rejection of authority expresses the common temper of the progressives of his day; so for that matter does his rejection of probabilities. What is peculiarly Cartesian is his conception of what it is 'clearly and perspicuously to behold'; on this depends also his conception of 'deduction'.

What then is a Cartesian intuition, or, as he came to call it, a clear and distinct idea? It is, as we have seen, a *conception* of a pure and attentive mind so plain that no doubt remains concerning what is understood. What does this mean? Note, first, a *conception* of the mind. This is an *act* of understanding, something the mind does, not something that comes to us passively, as percepts and images seem to do. It is typically the frame of mind of a student of mathematics, who, confronted by a problem, has solved it. 'I've got it': what was dark is clear. And as *I* have solved the puzzle, worked through the proof, there can be no doubt about the outcome. It is my achievement; my clarity in viewing its issue is definitive. In the *Discourse on Method*, in recounting how he arranged his life in order to get on with his philosophical projects, Descartes remarked that a man of learning should never let himself depend on fortune, on anything that comes to him from outside and so could be capriciously whisked away. Let him be content with what depends upon himself alone. So, intellectually too, it is not what the world tells him but what he himself understands, from within himself, by his own rational volition, by the act of his own unclouded and attentive intellect: it is that which alone can furnish the indubitability he seeks. It is the subsequent change in the meaning of 'idea', with Locke's 'new way of ideas', from active conception to passive image, or quasi-image, that raises all the problems of empiricism. Whence do ideas come and what guarantees their fidelity to things? The Cartesian idea carries no such aura of uncertainty. It is self-guaranteeing because it is responsible, independent, an act of complete attention, resting self-sufficiently within the firm bounds of its own bright light: seeing clearly all that it sees and wanting nothing more.

But is not a Cartesian intuition then purely 'subjective', conventional, as many moderns think the 'insights' of mathematics are? Does not my confidence that $2 + 2 = 4$ rest in the last analysis on a decision to use these signs in a certain way? '$2 + 2 = 4$' gives me no information about the world; to 'know' it is to know nothing. The Cartesian clear and distinct idea, however, is not an act of conventional decision; it is an act directed to an object. That is the second point we must bear in mind about it. In it, 'no doubt remains concerning *that which is understood*'. On the other hand, its object is not necessarily nor always completely congruent with the nature of things. It is not, like Aristotelian *nous*, a direct unity of the mind with the being-what-it-is of some particular species. Indeed, there are for Descartes essentially only two 'kinds': minds and bodies. No, the clear and distinct idea is a unit, not directly of reality, but of *problem-solving*. It lies, uniquely, *between* mind and world. So, for example, Descartes points out in the *Rules*, I may, in dealing with the next problem on my path, have to order the relevant material in a fashion which I know, for the moment, to be arbitrary, in order to clarify my ideas and so discover thereafter how things really are. Thus in a physical problem, he suggests, I might order each colour to a given length of line: just temporarily to sort out somehow the class of things I am dealing with and run my thoughts clearly and in order over the range of my subject-matter. It is the ordering of what is before my mind, to make it accessible to understanding, that counts. If I have it so ordered, I can see over and through it, grasp it completely, keep it wholly within the light of reason, and so keep myself from straying into error.

For the clear and distinct idea, thirdly, is necessarily an act of a *pure and attentive* mind: the act of a mind unclouded by irrelevancies or obscurities, by the drift of imagination or the impact of sense. What is before it is *wholly* before it, wholly explicit. This does not mean necessarily explicit *statement*; Descartes is singularly indifferent to language, even mathematical language. But it is wholly explicit, wholly focal, *intellectual vision*. 'He who has a true idea', Spinoza was to say, 'knows also that he has a true idea.'[10] The self-contained clarity of a mind wholly and uniquely focussed on its object of understanding: that is the Cartesian ideal. Nor is it an ideal merely; Descartes believed it to be his daily stock in trade, accessible to all who would pursue the straight methodical course he had prescribed.

'Methodical': this brings us to a fourth aspect of Cartesian knowledge. For, again, it is the *order* of ideas that counts. And here we turn to 'deduction', the movement of the mind from one intuition to another. No finite mind can contain all it knows within the grasp of a single intuition; it must move, step by step, from one such self-illumined act of reason to another. There are, Descartes says, two possible orders, two directions of intellectual movement, which he distinguishes by the traditional names of synthesis and analysis. The synthetic method is the famous Euclidean one of demonstration from axioms and definitions; but this is not, for Descartes, the more significant method, since it is not the method of discovery. In synthesis we start from first principles, and the system simply elaborates the logical consequences of these principles. But this is not the natural starting point for the learner or discoverer. First principles are relatively complex and sophisticated; only the advanced student could comprehend them in their whole power and elegance. The beginner needs to start with something easier, indeed with the simplest possible concept. He needs to grasp an idea of his own measure: an idea that he can hold completely within the span of his attention. Such concepts must be *simple*, not analysable further into parts, and *absolute*, that is, such that they can be understood in themselves, not relatively to anything else. It is with such concepts that we should begin in analysis, in the process of discovery. When some of the critics of the *Meditations* asked why its author had not presented it *more geometrico*, he gave them in reply a sample of synthesis to contrast with the analytic method he had in fact used.[11] In the synthetic presentation, God, whose existence is proved only in the *Third Meditation*, would have come first, and the intuition first in analysis, the *cogito*, would have followed. But the synthetic method, though elegant, is not the proper method to use if we wish to make progress in finding indubitable truths, since it proceeds from the harder to the easier, and that way lies confusion. True, the ancient mathematicians, Descartes remarks in the *Rules*, liked to present their theorems in this demonstrative way. But Descartes is confident that they *discovered* them, all the same, by the method of analysis, moving step by step from the simpler to the more difficult; and then, he suspects, they threw away the account of their discoveries and devised the axiomatic method to enhance the effect of mystery and erudition. Descartes, on the other hand, in the *Meditations*, is seeking to guide all men along the right road of discovery: out of the dubitable to the first and easiest certainty, my immediate knowledge of my own existence as a thinking thing, which cannot be doubted at any moment when I am aware of it. From there he can then turn to the luminous knowledge of God, and thence to the knowledge of all other things of which the human mind can know, and, with respect to the things it cannot know, at least the indubitable knowledge that it cannot know them. This is the right way to solve problems, remaining ever within the light thrown by reason, along the path of certainties, building from the simplest of all through the less simple as far as the human mind can reach.

It may be instructive to compare Descartes's two methods with the two directions of Aristotelian inference: demonstration and induction. The former moves from what Aristotle calls 'the prior in nature' or 'prior simply', the other from 'things prior to us'.[12] At first sight this looks like the Cartesian distinction, synthesis starting with the simply prior, analysis with the pedagogically more appropriate starting point, things prior to us. And in the last analysis, demonstration and synthesis, both modelled on Euclid, are, if not identical, certainly akin. Descartes scorns the subtleties of syllogism; nor does his demonstrative method depend, like Aristotle's, on the right choice of a limited subject-genus. But demonstration and synthesis are both legitimate heirs of Euclid and ancestors of the axiomatic method; their differences need not concern us. What is important here, however, is the startling difference between the 'prior to us' as these two philosophers conceive it. For Aristotle, what is first for us is the concrete object grasped in sense-perception; through analysing out its essential character, we arrive, by induction, at the more difficult grasp of the first principles appropriate to the scientific knowledge of this kind of entity. But for Descartes what is first in the method of learning is already intellectual. Even the first step in analysis can be taken only by the rejection, or at least the suspension, of the crude and misleading information purveyed by our senses; even the first step is one of pure intellect: the confrontation of a wholly attentive mind with a wholly intelligible object, in fact, as it turns out, with itself. The mind's confrontation with itself, for Aristotle, on the other hand, is a late and difficult business. For Descartes, however, there is nothing easier, nothing more absolute, in his sense of that term, than the intellect's grasp of its own conscious existence in any conscious moment.

Further, the movement from step to step, 'deduction', for Descartes, is, *a fortiori*, wholly intellectual; yet it is not, in analysis, a *logical* movement, it is not the exhibition of conclusions as following validly from premises. Descartes calls it, in the *Rules*, indifferently *de*duction or *in*duction; whatever we call it, it is simply the passage from one clear and distinct idea to another, by whatever technique may offer itself as a guide. Look at some examples from Descartes's own practice. It is often objected to the Cartesian *cogito ergo sum*, for example, the first clear and distinct idea arrived at in the *Meditations*, that 'sum' does not properly follow from 'cogito'. But there is in the text of the *Meditations* no such formulation as 'cogito ergo sum', nor is the *cogito* intended as an argument in the logician's sense. The *Meditations* are meditations: the philosopher has schooled himself, in the first essay, to withhold assent from all his usual, merely probable beliefs, calling in the fiction of a Deceiving Deity to enable him to doubt even the truths of mathematics, to him the most certain of all. His mind, cleared of all this clutter, can turn to the intrinsic evidence of its own existence *whenever* it is thinking, even whenever it is doubting, and this immediate self-sufficient certainty no one, not even a Deceiving Deity if there were one, could destroy. 'I am, I exist', this is true whenever I pronounce it. The temporal qualification is essential. But no *logical* demonstration holds on

certain occasions only. Logical arguments are valid eternally, re-
gardless of circumstances. The *cogito* is not an argument but an
event, the act of a pure and attentive mind, the first, Descartes
believes, of a long chain of such acts, all equal in purity, clarity and
certainty.

So, again, in the next step: Descartes's first proof of the existence
of God, in *Meditation Three*, taken as a piece of demonstrative logic,
is very odd indeed. He is trying to prove that God does not deceive
him in order that he may henceforth be able to trust his clear and
distinct ideas, as before this he could not confidently do. But he uses
in his proof principles, like the causal axiom, which, he says, he
knows 'by natural light',–that is, as clear and distinct ideas. Again,
he has avowedly discarded all his former opinions in order to build
up anew a foundation for the sciences; yet the principles used in this
proof look, to us at least, very traditional indeed, just the sort of
maxims Descartes would have been taught to accept without the
initial critical doubt he so values–and he has by no means discarded
them. But if we look at the argument of the *Meditations* as an example
of Cartesian analysis, not synthesis, of discovery, not demonstration,
we see that what he is doing in the *Third Meditation* is to guide our
minds, by whatever devices he can invoke, to turn from the first
clear and distinct idea to the second, from the self to God. This is
not an argument, but *a movement of attention from one intuition to
another*. If we bring in principles not yet vouched for as parts of our
secure knowledge, they are serving as pointers, as helps to attention.
Turn your mind first from sense to your own conscious being, then
from your own conscious being to the idea of an Infinite Being which,
Descartes is sure, you innately possess: those two steps are what the
analytic movement of the first three *Meditations* aims to achieve. The
words, maxims, devices, on which they lean for this purpose, are,
relatively speaking, of small account. What is important is to move
securely from one intuition to another without straying beyond the
bounds of certainty.

Sometimes, it is true, one has to take a course rather more devious
than a simple step forward from clear and distinct idea to clear and
distinct idea. Such is the case, for example, in the *Third Meditation*,
when we classify the various contents of our consciousness–first,
ideas, volitions, judgments, then ideas as adventitious, factitious,
innate–in order to try to light on some one idea of which we can
know with certainty that its object exists. Such a procedure, like that
also, e.g., of classifying colours which we noticed earlier, Descartes
calls *enumeration* or *induction*. It is the only sideways movement, so
to speak, on the path of successive intuitions, that he allows, and it
has to be invoked where our span of attention is not adequate to do

without it. Our aim all along, however, must be the single, directly self-guaranteeing insights from which such procedures issue and in which they terminate. Science, again, is true and evident cognition, either what we perspicuously behold, the intuition itself, or the 'deductive' movement from one such act of vision to another. Whether in discovery or in the consequent, and subordinate, task of exposition, there is no act of mind which can produce knowledge but only these two.

III

How should we assess this conception of the method and nature of science? Any case study in the history of scientific discovery will tumble it in five minutes. Take just one very famous one. Joseph Priestley, known to every schoolboy as the 'discoverer of oxygen', clung so resolutely to the phlogiston theory of combustion in its death throes, that he refused to admit it was 'oxygen' he had discovered. He never believed in the existence of such a substance. It seemed absurd to suppose that stuffs when burned should take on something from the atmosphere, so plain that something is given off under heat, that for Priestley what we call 'oxygen' remained 'dephlogisticated air' to the bitter end. His was the achievement of first isolating the gas which Lavoisier christened oxygen, but its nature and role in combustion its 'discoverer' wholly misunderstood. Where in this story—which can stand here for many—are the 'clear and distinct ideas'? Where is the march straight forward from certainty to certainty? There is no such thing. In the advance of knowledge, the entanglement of truth and error, success and failure, are inextricable.

It may, indeed, be objected, that though this is true of the past, by now there is a hard core of certainty which science will never turn its back on. Philosophers, artists, statesmen, it is often pointed out, forever, disagree; but the results of science, once established, are agreed upon forever. True, classical mechanics now turns out to be but a particular case of a more generalized theory of matter; and with this greater generality some of Newton's presuppositions turn out to be not science but mistaken metaphysics. God, Newton believed, probably formed matter of solid, impenetrable particles. He did no such thing. But that error in metaphysics or theology by no means invalidates Newton's laws of motion or the inverse square law. Newton's discoveries have their once for all established truth, their certainty, upon which scientists of the future build, or ignore if they are no longer interesting, but can never again deny. It is true, even now, that in the process of discovery error and groping and guesswork happen; but the results are irrevocable. The framework, the surrounding concepts, may be called in doubt, but not the established facts. It was a matter of controversy in the seventeenth century whether the blood circulates; it is now a fact. To deny it would be as silly as to say that the earth is flat. Scientists, day by day, are most concerned with the problems still to solve; naturally, that is what research is. But what makes it *scientific* research, it is claimed, is the knowledge that the problem has a solution, that it is possible to get out an answer which, once accepted by the consensus of competent opinion, will never again be questioned, because it is *so*. This is just the model of problem-solving which Descartes and his contemporaries believed in, and they were right in its issue, if not in its step by step technique. That is why science differs from, and excels, every other effort in the history of the human mind.

There are several objections to this claim. Granted, that the advance of modern science is unique in the intellectual history of mankind. But first, and that is the main point here, as a proceeding, as a way of getting from one insight to another into the nature of reality, science is not the track along a line of pure intellectual certainties that Descartes thought it to be.

Secondly, the established 'facts' of science, however unquestioned, are still held in being by the same intellectual passions that first discovered them: they are still conjectures so amply and confidently attested that no one 'in his senses'–that is, no one who accepts the authority of competent scientific opinion–would call them in doubt. At any stage, on its way or in its routine and authoritative acceptance, science, as the late Professor Franck put it, 'is either something scientists are doing, or it is nothing at all'.[13] But nothing any human being does has the wholly assured, wholly self-evident character of Cartesian method. The truth of this statement for the structure of scientific knowledge is massively demonstrated in the argument of *Personal Knowledge*; I shall not try to recapitulate it here.

But remember, thirdly, that even the best-established conjecture, the 'fact' which will never again be called in doubt, bears the certainty, not of the logically necessary, of that which could not be other, but of sheer fact: it is like historical 'certainty', the sheer *that* which might have been other but is not. The inverse square law is a contingent fact of our cosmic epoch, just as the outcome of the Battle of Waterloo is a contingent fact of nineteenth-century history. Those who glory in the march of science may stress the once-for-all nature of such facts; those who are concerned with the structure of knowledge itself must still insist on the want of logical certainty, of Cartesian self-evidence, characteristic of even the least doubtful of established truths. A probability approaching the value 1 is still a probability, a conjecture however unquestioningly accepted is still conjecture, a strand of our being-in-the-world so firmly woven into the fabric that we cannot think it would break. Yet we and the world and the fabric are one in such a way that we can never withdraw from the whole nexus one item of 'information' and say of it, this, all on its own, is so luminous, so firmly established, that it could not conceivably be otherwise. It is an aspect of our 'Geworfenheit',[14] of the world into which we are cast, and we forget at our peril its ultimate contingency.

Even in mathematics, finally, from which it took its origin, Descartes's dream of method has faded. There are several points to notice in this connection. First, look at the modern analogue of mathematical certainty: the conception of mathematical truth as analytic. The great achievement of mathematical logic at the turn of this century was, it seemed, to reduce mathematics to pure logic and thus plainly to exhibit its logical necessity. The statements of mathematics, it was held, are analytic statements, or, as some said, tautological: they are all reducible to the form 'not both A and non-A', and their contradictory would be a contradiction. There is no need here to refer to Descartes's intellectual 'indubitability', let alone 'natural light' or any such lingeringly scholastic concept. It is simply impossible that a self-contradiction should be true, for if it were, everything would follow from it including its own negation. But on the other hand, the truths of mathematics so conceived are true precisely because they are empty. They assert only the denial of contradiction, they convey no information about anything. Applied to science, they function, in Hempel's metaphor, as theoretical juice-extractors, magnificent machines, indeed, but no part of the beverage they help to produce.[15]

What, on this theory, would be said of Descartes's 'universal mathematics'? The criticism of Descartes would be, first, that he has unnecessarily psychologized mathematical certainty, which is in fact that of an inference machine or computer, not that of a thinking mind, and secondly, that he has wrongly extrapolated mathematical certainty to the domain of experimental science, which is properly that of probabilities only, not of certainties. This second criticism is unanswerable. What of the first? It is, at any rate, an ironic trick of the history of thought. It was Descartes who most persuasively sketched the model of mechanistic explanation, the machine set in sharp contrast to the mind that understands it. But the modern version of the story makes the intellectual certainty of the mathematician itself mechanical. Instead of a great natural machine spread out in space and, over against it, the mathematician's mind intent on grasping clearly and distinctly its order and working, we have the spread of space-time events in nature and over against these their mapping, equally mechanically, in axiom systems which are themselves machines. In fact, the certainty of axiom systems conceived as networks of tautologies is exactly the certainty provided by a metal inference machine, by a computer. In the conflict between the cyberneticist's identification of mind with machine and the Cartesian dualist's insistence on the existence and identity of a non-mechanical mind, the modern conception of mathematical certainty appears as anti-Cartesian. There are only machines, whether constructed of nervous tissue, paper and ink, or steel, it is all one. Thus, even within mathematics, the Cartesian quest for an assured self-evidence in the sciences has destroyed itself. The only reliable intuitions, it turns out, are not intuitions but mechanical certainties. What makes an axiom system dependable is not that you grasp its processes mentally, indubitably, step by step, but that you need not comprehend it at all. Whatever is put in, it extracts automatically in another shape; but the *raison d'être* of the transformation need not concern you. It is the very *un*intelligibility of the proof that guarantees its objective validity, its mechanical reliability that proves its excellence. It may be said, of course, that meta-mathematics, the theory *of* mathematics, depends on intuition; but from the point of view of orthodox axiomatics, this is a regrettable fringe case, and indeed the meta-mathematical system could itself be axiomatized and so mechanized, leaving as ragged fringe an intuitive meta-mathematics, and so on. But a residue of intuition receding into an infinite regress is scarcely intuition as Descartes intended it.

Strictly speaking, moreover, modern mathematics can no longer claim even this mechanical certainty. If mathematics were certain, we have just been saying, it would have to be so, not as a series of Cartesian intuitions, but as an inference machine. Our reliance on a machine, however, depends upon our ability to specify and delimit its parts. The corresponding specification in a mathematical system would be represented by a consistency proof. But such a proof, it has been demonstrated by Kurt Gödel, is ruled out, and it is ruled out because in any formal system it is always possible to construct an indefinite number of indemonstrable sentences, theorems formally permissible in the system but not demonstrable on the ground of its axioms or theorems. Therefore we never have in any formal system a perfect machine. The system is always open-ended, and so we can never prove the consistency of the whole.[16]

This is a formal admission which is philosophically of the greatest importance, but it is only a hint of what we find, fourthly and finally, if we look not at the structure of axiom systems, not at Cartesian synthesis, but at what interested Descartes himself more: at analysis, at mathematics in motion, at the mathematician at work. In an important series of articles, Dr. Imre Lakatos has illustrated by means of a single case history the structure of what he calls 'situational mathematics', or mathematical heuristics: the processes involved–essentially involved–in mathematical discovery and the advance of mathematical knowledge. The problem he considers is one in solid geometry:

> Is there a relation between the number of vertices V, the number of edges E and the number of faces F of polyhedra–particularly of *regular polyhedra*–analogous to the trivial relation between the number of vertices and edges of *polygons*, namely that there are as many edges as vertices: $V = E$?[17]

The problem was first noticed by Euler, in 1750, and the answer he suggested was $V - E + F = 2$. The conjecture is persuasive, but the attempted proofs and refutations of these proofs take us through a century and a half of mathematical speculation and criticism without a conclusive outcome. I shall not attempt to summarize here Lakatos's brilliant display of the many techniques that come into this story; suffice it to make two points.

First, the study of mathematical heuristics, far from exhibiting a clear path of certainty, demonstrates that hunches, the imaginative use of example, definition and redefinition, sheer irrational preference or prejudice, enter essentially and centrally into the reasonings of mathematicians just as they do in any other process of learning or discovery. The fact that mathematical concepts are simpler and more precise–or less imprecise–than more everyday concepts does not mean, as Descartes thought it did, that in mathematics one has left the plane of fallibility, of gropings, of half-lights, of puzzles wrongly solved and tried again, for some unique utopia of infallible truth. There is no such place. True, the propositions asserted by mathematicians *claim*, like all universal propositions, universal validity. But the claim, however strong, is always rooted in the confidence of those who make it. Mathematicians, like other people, are trying to make sense of an aspect of experience: trying to find a pattern in what is otherwise disorder. Admittedly, theirs is a very rarefied, a very abstract kind of experience; and because their situation, *qua* mathematicians, is a situation built of high abstractions, their successful solutions of problems, or even their conjectures, have great generality and scope, often providing immensely powerful techniques for the assistance of those puzzled by more concrete disorders, more practical puzzles. But in their strange ethereal world they are still groping, seeking, and finding understanding: not *the* truth, but a claim to truth, still anchored in their personal intellectual situation, in their orientation in the world.

The second point of interest in the present context is that Lakatos's story starts from a conjecture–by no means an 'intuition'–of Descartes himself. For though it was Euler who first published the suggested formula $V - E + F = 2$, Descartes had, in a sense, already reached the same result. Lakatos writes:

> It has been recently generally accepted that the priority of the result goes to Descartes. The ground for this claim is a manuscript of Descartes (ca. 1639) copied by Leibniz in Paris from the original in 1675–6, and rediscovered and published by Foucher de Careil in 1860. The priority should not be granted to Descartes without a minor qualification. It is true that Descartes states that the number of plane angles equals $2\varphi + 2\alpha - 4$ where by φ he means the number of faces and by α the number of solid angles.[18] It is also true that he states that there are twice as many plane angles as edges (*latera*). The trivial conjunction of these two statements of course yields the Euler formula. But Descartes did not see the point of doing so, since he still thought in terms of angles (plane and solid) and faces, and did not make a conscious revolutionary change to the concepts of 0-dimensional vertices, 1-dimensional edges and 2-dimensional faces as a necessary and sufficient basis for the full topological characterization of polyhedra.[19]

Thus, Descartes, who scorns all that is not wholly clear and distinct, all that is not self-contained lucidity, has originated not even what was to be Euler's conjecture, but, in a crude and inappropriate form, two parts of it, lacking the concepts which would make it clear and distinct, even as conjecture. It is a hunch still wanting the conceptual reform to make it a viable hunch, like 'mesmerism' before the introduction of the concept of hypnosis. What is the dealer in certainties doing with thoughts like these? He is doing what every creative mathematician does, and the very reverse of what he claims to do : making, by a kind of intellectual instinct, tentative advances into the unknown. He who remains within the clear light of reason goes nowhere and has nowhere to go.

IV

We shall deny, therefore, with assurance, Descartes's affirmation that 'science is true and evident cognition'. But to deny it will not show us *why* it is false; we shall understand this, and be able to present a tenable alternative, only if we look more closely into Descartes's reasons for his claim. What is the conception of man and his knowledge in which his claim is imbedded, and what theses of his led him astray?

There are four theses, which, taken together, constitute the core of Descartes's theory of knowledge and method; we have already talked about three of them, but it is the fourth, which is mentioned merely by the way in the argument of the First Rule, which underlies all the others. We may call these four theses: the principles of (1) indubitability, (2) self-evidence or total explicitness, (3) the unity of science, (4) the duality of man. These four principles are not isolated; they form a structure. There is knowledge which is incapable of being doubted because there is knowledge which is self-evident, self-contained; the sum of evident knowledge is wisdom, which is the same everywhere; and both the evidence and the unity of knowledge are possible because, and only because, knowledge is the work of the intellect alone. Were the mind not cleanly and essentially separate from the body in nature and function, the whole programme would collapse.

The foundation of the method in mind-body dualism is plain from the text of the First Rule. The rule itself sounds innocuous enough:

> The end of study should be to direct the mind towards the enunciation of sound and correct judgments on all matters that come before it.[20]

But look at what follows:

> Whenever men notice some similarity between two things, they are wont to ascribe to each, even in those respects in which they differ, what they have found to be true of the other. *Thus they erroneously compare the sciences, which entirely consist in the cognitive exercise of the mind, with the arts, which depend upon an exercise and disposition of the body.*[21]

It is the separateness of mind which makes science different from the acquisition of the arts, and it is the failure to make this distinction that has kept men from embarking on the programme of universal mathematics which Descartes is here about to undertake:

> They see that not all the arts can be acquired by the same man, but that he who restricts himself to one, most readily becomes the best executant, since it is not so easy for the same hand to adapt itself both to agricultural operations and to harp-playing, or to the performance of several such tasks as to one alone.[22]

Skill with the plough and the harp demands the exercise of different muscles, different nervous reactions, different physical temperaments. And knowledge, too, men have supposed, must be cultivated in particular ways, through particular training, like other skills:

> Hence they have held the same to be true of the sciences also, and distinguishing them from one another according to their subject matter, they have imagined that they ought to be studied separately, each in isolation from all the rest.[23]

But in this, Descartes argues, they were quite mistaken. Knowledge, he holds, is not diversified like skills, since, as we have just seen, he considers science to consist in the 'cognitive exercise of the mind', independently of the 'exercise and disposition of the body', which are necessary to the cultivation of the arts. Science is the activity of intellect, the cultivation of pure unsullied intellectual vision, and this has no compartments, no varieties, but is everywhere the same:

> For since the sciences taken all together are identical with human wisdom, which always remains one and the same, however applied to different subjects, and suffers no more differentiation proceeding from them than the light of the sun experiences from the variety of the things which it illumines, there is no need for minds to be confined at all within limits; for neither does the knowing of one truth have an effect like that of the acquisition of one art and prevent us from finding out another, it rather aids us to do so.[24]

Practice in geometry will not stop a man from understanding medicine, it will, in Descartes's view, aid him in doing so, in contrast to practice in ploughing, which will plainly spoil the hands of a harpist, should he decide to engage in that rougher form of work. Minds are not coarsened, as the harpist's hands would be, by a change of labour, because there is only one proper work of mind, the pure exercise of the pure light of reason itself, which is everywhere and always the same. Hence, Descartes claims, we are justified in bringing forward this as the first rule of all, since there is nothing more prone to turn us aside from the correct way of seeking out truth than this directing of our inquiries, not towards their general end, but towards certain special investigations. Instead of this dispersal of our attention,

> we must believe that all the sciences are so inter-connected, that it is much easier to study them all together than to isolate one from the others.[25]

What we are seeking, therefore, and are confident that we can find, is a unified intellectual discipline in contrast to the diversity of bodily skills: a science which is equivalent to human wisdom, the pure illumination of reason itself:

> If, therefore, anyone wishes to search out the truth of things in serious earnest, he ought not to select one special science; for all the sciences are conjoined with one another and interdependent; he ought rather to think how to increase the natural light of reason, not for the purpose of resolving this or that difficulty of scholastic type, but in order that his understanding may light his will to its proper choice in all the contingencies of life.[25a]

Even practical problems, questions of medicine or of morals, will find their rational solution if we proceed in this way: for the mind, first cognizant of itself and its own separate nature, will turn in clarity of vision to arrange and solve the problems both of the nature of bodies and of the nature of the collaboration of mind and body peculiar to the course of human life. The unity of knowledge, and its self-guaranteeing certainty, both these depend, in the last analysis, on cutting off the being and essence of the intellect from the implications of its associations with a body, an association intimate and inevitable in the 'contingencies of life', but irrelevant and misleading in the cultivation of truth.

It may be objected, of course, that Descartes when formulating his method did not yet know, in terms of his own procedure of analysis, the nature and the separateness of *res cogitans* and *res extensa*. I have tried earlier to defend him against the charge of circularity in the arguments of the *Meditations*; now we find that the method itself depends upon the mind-body dualism which it will eventually establish. In this larger sense Descartes's philosophy does indeed rest on a circle: without the duality of body and mind, no method; without the method, no knowledge of the substances, thinking and extended, which constitute the Cartesian world. This fact on its own, however, would form no valid objection to Cartesian metaphysics. Every comprehensive theory, every vision of the universe, is necessarily circular: it forms a closed system, a universe of discourse, within which the mind of the thinker dwells. It is the breadth and inclusiveness, or exclusiveness, of the circle, not its circularity, that makes us challenge it.

In Descartes's case, we must challenge all four fundamental principles, and once again, in terms of an alternative theory to which the denial of the fourth principle is basic. First, all knowledge is on principle susceptible of doubt, of criticism. It is so, secondly, because it is never wholly explicit, but is always rooted in an act of tacit knowing, in which we attend from certain clues to the meaning of those clues upon which our attention is focussed. A change of focus can always bring to the level of attention, and to criticism, what was previously unquestioned because submerged.[26] Moreover, because of this balance of tacit and explicit aspects, thirdly, knowledge is always a clarification in and of a particular situation; however comprehensive, however inclusive, it can never be wholly unified into the one all-embracing system, since, at the least, the aspects which are subsidiary in one context may become focal in another. Since they can never be all explicit at one time, in one act of pure attention, there is no one universal 'wisdom'. Finally, knowledge has inescapably this dual, and therefore diversified, structure because it is *personal*, because it is an achievement of the whole, inalienable psycho-physical person, making sense of one aspect or another of his situation, of his world. It is not the work of a disembodied intellect. We must therefore assert, against Descartes, the principles (1) of criticism, or the possibility of criticism, as essential to all knowledge, (2) of the pervasiveness of a tacit component in all knowledge, (3) of the diversity of the sciences, and (4) of the unity of man, not indeed in the sense of reduction to mere matter or distillation to pure mind, but in the sense of *personhood*, which can entail immense complexities of organization, many levels of being and achievement, but is never cut off from its contingent, local, bodily root.

We have already had occasion to mention, in one context or another, all four of these anti-Cartesian principles. Let us look at them once more, in conclusion, and compare the view of knowledge they entail with the Cartesian view, and by implication with the residuum of Cartesian methodology still inherent in contemporary thought.

First, criticism versus indubitability. Descartes, in common with most philosophers before him and many after him, was confident that knowledge, which is certain, is a nobler and higher achievement than mere opinion, which is only probable. Thus, when it comes to assessing grades of cognition, the possibility of criticism is the mark of an inferior brand. Moreover, what marks off man from the brutes is not just his power of making judgments as such (though this too in the Cartesian view is restricted to the human species), but Reason, which in its essence is natural light, the unerring grasp of truth. We err, Descartes argues, only when we let our will outrun the limits of our understanding, when we assent in judgment to an idea or complex of ideas which lacks the clarity and distinctness symptomatic of truth. So long as reason guides us, so long do we remain unerringly within the bounds of truth. True, in terms of knowledge, animals attain neither truth nor error; they are automata. But what characterizes men uniquely among creatures is that in addition to following the directives of bodily behaviour they have minds: they know. That is their proper condition; to err, to need to correct and criticize their opinions, is a privation, a falling away from the proper path of undeviating certainty.

How different from this is the situation as we see it now. Doubtfulness, the possibility of error: this is the mark of the higher, not the lower powers of mind: 'a concept-possessing being', says Price 'is one who can make mistakes',[27] and earlier he has concluded his account of what he calls 'primary recognition' as follows:

> . . . if primary recognition is incapable of being erroneous, this is only because it is a mental occurrence so primitive and elementary that the

antithesis of correct and incorrect does not apply to it. There is nothing particularly grand about such inerrancy, and there is no occasion for taking off one's hat to it. On the contrary: it is the fallible forms of recognition, secondary recognition and recognition of individuals, on which we should congratulate ourselves (and the lower animals too) if we are in the mood for congratulations. Let us rather take off our hats to any creature which is clever enough to be caught in a trap. It is the capacity of making mistakes, not the incapacity of it, which is the mark of the higher stages of intelligence. The whole importance of primary recognition, both biologically and epistemologically, consists in this, that it is the indispensable basis for the higher, and fallible, levels of intellection.[28]

And when we distinguish man from other animals, it is not the certainty we alone achieve, but the possibility of *reflection*, of criticism, even of negativity, that seems to mark our kind off from other creatures as unique. It is hard to believe that many people who have worked with animals could ever have accepted the Cartesian theory of the *bête-machine*. But by now experimental psychology, ethology, evolutionary theory have all added to the weight of ordinary experience the well-authenticated fact that animals do reason in much the same way, fundamentally, that we do: rats in mazes, jackdaws counting, apes using tools–the instances are too numerous and too familiar to need repetition here. And their inferences are sometimes correct, sometimes mistaken, as ours are. What distinguishes our reasoning is the vast range and power resulting from speech, and what this produces is neither infallible insight on the one hand nor mere verbal behaviour on the other, but the ubiquity of the power to criticize. We can store up our inferences for re-consideration, improve or reject them, build vast systems of them, still subject to rejection or correction. We have, through language, detached reasoning from its natural environment and given it the power of turning back on itself, of reflection. Speech, as Merleau-Ponty says, is the surplus of our existence over natural being.[29] This is what Plessner calls man's 'natural artificiality':[30] it belongs to our natures to set ourselves over against being, over against the world; there is a gap, a nothingness, which articulate thought has introduced between ourselves and things. Our concepts are indeed concretions of experience, but also other than experience. We can always compare them again with the next experience, we can always find we have been mistaken. And if we set this right we may still find the same again.

Hence, for example, both the obvious correctness of the so-called 'correspondence theory of truth' and the difficulty of giving it adequate formulation. A statement is true if things are as it states them to be. But we know things only, or chiefly, through our concepts of them, and through our statements in terms of these concepts. However we refine and revise our concepts, they are still at one remove from the reality they are meant to describe or explain. How can we tell if things and statements 'correspond' or not? If we try to 'verify' our statements, our formulation of the result still retains the artificiality of our symbol-systems, their selectivity and abstractness. We are in the world, yet not of it; our immersion in it is mediated by the very instruments through which we understand, or misunderstand, it. We are always reaching through thought to reality, but since mediation is always inherent in the process, there is always the chance we may have gone astray. There is always room for doubt. It is the very possibility of doubt, of self-criticism and correction, that makes the power of the human as distinct from other animal minds.

Nor is there a higher power of certain understanding beyond the middle range of conjecture, a Reason at the top of the scale no longer open to doubt. The higher we go in the complexity of intellectual processes, the greater the risk of error. It is the humbler, subjective awarenesses, as of great pain or intense pleasure, that are least susceptible to error. Vast-ranging theories tell us incomparably more about the world but may so much the more easily lead us astray. The power of criticism, the responsibility of criticism, once accepted, is never again to be laid aside.

Secondly, Descartes's indubitability was psychological. As we have seen, it was the total luminousness of the act of understanding which was to guarantee the truth of its content. But there are no such acts. On the contrary, it is because *no* knowledge is wholly focal, wholly present all in one to the knowing mind, that it is always capable of reassessment. I have already referred to Polanyi's account of the structure of tacit knowing and shall have occasion to do so again, but it may help us at this stage to understand the contrast in question if we compare the analogy with perception implicit in Cartesian 'natural light' and the analogy between perception and more advanced forms of knowledge in Polanyi's epistemology.

What the mind 'sees', Descartes is confident, it sees all at once: the intuition as act has its whole content, the same intuition as object, wholly present to itself. It is a wholly focal act of attention. If I understand that $2 + 2 = 4$ or that the sum of the angles of a triangle equals two right angles, I grasp this whole state of affairs in one act of attention, I *see* it through and through. Knowledge here is *theoria*, vision in the sense of complete illumination. This analogy between understanding and vision, the keenest of the human senses, is of course an ancient one, going back to Plato and the neo-Platonic tradition. And the same analogy is basic to Aristotelian thought: the sensible 'species'—*eidos*—that which is plain to be seen—is grasped in sense-perception, the intelligible species in the rational insight that apprehends first principles.

Now it is true that there is a fruitful analogy to be drawn between perception and the higher forms of knowledge. Judgment, inductive inference, the understanding of theoretical explanations: they all display a homologous structure, which in fact, like the homology of the vertebrate limb, suggests a common origin. But the analogy we should draw today suggests that knowledge is not like the Cartesian or neo-Platonic theoria, but very different. Looked at in its physiological context, to begin with, vision is a complex and indirect achievement. A two-dimentional upside-down image on my retina *I see* as a three dimensional right-side up tree outside the window. How do I do this? By attending *from* the excitation of my retina, cortex, etc. *to* an object some yards away, in which, by such attention, I dwell, to which my being is extended, and which is correspondingly interiorized to become part of my experience, of my world. Seeing is an achievement by which I make sense of an aspect of the world, of my world – for it is a 'world' only as organized by the accommodations and adaptations of organisms.[31] There is not an object, this tree, a this-such, passively present to my view, but there are given me a set of clues which *I* relate to one another in such a way as to achieve the perception of this tree.

This fundamental situation is repeated, developed and elaborated in higher learning processes; but it is still essentially the same kind of process. For perception, as W. H. Thorpe suggests, is already a primordial act of learning, that is, of the acquisition of knowledge: since it is temporal and spatial relations that are ultimately dominant in perception, perception itself is essentially a learning process – for obviously the perception of relations must involve comparison, and comparison in its turn involves memory and expectation, and so is clearly a form of learning.[32] And in the more developed forms of learning, the reliance on subsidiary knowledge from which we attend to that which we focally know: this two-level structure is everywhere maintained. Even the most precise, the most explicit knowledge in pure mathematics or the exact sciences depends for its comprehension on knowing what its symbols mean, and this knowledge, as distinct from the symbols themselves, is necessarily tacit. It may either be subsidiary, when we attend to the manipulation of the symbols themselves, relying on their meaning; or focal when we attend from the symbols to what they mean. But if we focus wholly on the symbols in themselves without relying on what they mean, they become empty; the achievement of *knowing* what they mean is gone. In biological, medical, literary or artistic knowledge, the unspecifiable, subsidiary aspect is more massive than in the exact sciences, but it cannot be absent if there is to be meaning, and so knowledge, at all. And it is for this reason that, as we have seen, knowledge is always subject to reflection and revision. For the clues may alter, what was submerged may become central, and so on. And conversely, no subject matter, no concept, however precise, can be, as Descartes thought it, wholly at the centre of attention, and for that reason no subject, no concept is ever self-evident and indubitable.

This conclusion holds for allegedly explicit knowledge in general. There is one item of Cartesian intuition, however, which we should also mention particularly, and that is Cartesian *self*-knowledge. If the mind purely and with complete attention confronts the object of its knowledge, then it would seem reasonable to hold that the object closest to it and clearest to it, *itself*, should be most clearly and certainly known in this wholly explicit way. This is a cardinal point of Cartesian thought and one in fact which few modern philosophers have questioned. The knowledge of *other* minds, in the Cartesian and the empiricist traditions alike, has proved a thorny problem, but philosophers seem to have swallowed complacently the Cartesian thesis that my *own* mind is what I know directly, luminously and without difficulty. Hume, indeed, as we shall see, recognized that on his principles no such knowledge was possible; but empiricism in general, operating within the confines of Cartesian epistemology, has taken it for granted that I know who I am, but that I must reason somehow by analogy to the existence of others.

But is this in fact the case? Through their actions, expressions, statements, I know others. As I recognize a friend's face by relying on familiar features which I could not itemize or even draw from memory, so I know *him* also through the clues to his existence, to his mind, which his behaviour affords me. He is the focus to which I attend from the particulars manifested in speech, look, writing, etc. But can I do the same with myself? I may misunderstand my friend's character and be deceived in him, but can I even *try* to read my own character in the same way? To do so, I should have to detach myself from myself, to be not myself but another. In fact, it is our *self*-knowledge which comes more often than not at second hand, from the reflected impact of ourselves on others. In the main, the self comes to itself only indirectly, and each self is known primarily, through the double structure of subsidiary and focal knowledge, to other selves within whose horizon its effect is felt.[33]

In its denial of this truth, the *cogito* is one of the great falsehoods of philosophy. Other selves, even sticks and stones, are known to me before and better than I myself am known. True, I am 'within' my own experiences and not some one else's; but this 'insideness' is mere subjectivity, not knowledge. To suffer pain, to feel cold, is immediate and unquestioned, and 'within', but it *is* simply, it is not knowledge. To *know* is to interpret clues of which I am only subsidiarily aware, perhaps even wholly unaware, in terms of the entity or event upon which they bear – to see *through* them what they mean. Only because of this indirectness can such insights be conveyed, indirectly, to others, be publicly substantiated, become knowledge rather than a blind given. But this sort of mediation is just what I cannot perform upon myself, precisely because what should be focussed on, attended to, is already subsidiary, part of what I dwell in, of my own reality, and the proper clues to knowledge of myself are accessible in countenance and tone of voice, in turn of phrase or speed of reaction, to others more readily than to me. They are part of my bodily existence, so interiorized already that I can project from them only outward, not inward. Let us have done then with the pretence that I am pellucid to myself. I live in a world of human beings most of whom pass by unknown, some of whom I understand a little, a few perhaps well, but I myself, being myself at the core of this knowing, am, to myself, essentially a mystery.

So much for our second thesis: the two-level, focal/subsidiary structure of knowledge against the wholly lucid, explicit intuition of Descartes. Thirdly, moreover, it was because knowledge, as he believed, was wholly explicit that it could be unified. Science, he held, is everywhere simply the light of reason and as such is one, in contrast to the multiplicity of arts or skills. But again, analogously, we shall insist that just because it always has a tacit core, is always rooted in my reliance on all possible clues available at all levels of awareness, even of non-conscious excitation, through which I strive to make sense of my world, knowledge is, on the contrary, essentially skill-like, and, like skills, therefore necessarily diversified. If skill in ploughing will not make me a good harpist, neither will practice in botanical taxonomy make me a good mathematician nor excellence in theoretical physics make me a good diagnostician of nervous diseases. The basic analogy here, as I pointed out earlier, is tool-using. If I am beginning to learn to knit, I notice the position of the needles, the way I hold the yarn for knit and purl and so on. When by practice I can use these implements and materials I can no longer tell, if I ever could, just how I do it, but pay attention through the accustomed movements to the pattern I am working. The scientist uses abstract tools, concepts and maxims, on which he relies to spy out the hidden pattern he is seeking. His tools, his materials, his manner of working with them, are by no means identical in different contexts. He can only face one kind of problem, find himself in one situation, at a time, and to become a competent practitioner of one such skill he must change himself into *this* kind of performer, not another kind, and certainly not all kinds at once. Even a single problem may admit of many approaches. A problem in learning theory, for example, may be approached through psychological experiment in the laboratory, through ethological observation in the field, through cybernetics and the study of computers, through sociological analysis. Yet this is a single problem. The question, say, of the cosmological significance of the 'red shift' or the mapping of a crystal, will rely on very different tools and techniques from any of those germane to the analysis of learning. Nor is this just the result of 'overspecialization': specialization in the sense of devoted puzzlement, of groping toward the solution of *this* problem, *your* problem, not just any one's problem, –though the solution if successful will be every one's–such 'specialization' is essential to the development of any skill, however abstract and generalized, however intellectual.

This is so, finally, again for the very opposite reason to the reason for Descartes's opposite principle: that is, once more, because knowledge is an achievement, risen, both phylogenetically and individually, from its roots in the learning process of perception itself, an achievement of the whole person, not, as Descartes would have it, of a cogitating mind divided in nature and substance from the extended body in which it happens to be housed. Knowledge begins with the child's acquisition of a spatio-temporal orientation and develops into further and further dimensions of mental, emotional, spiritual as well as bodily orientation, but always of the total, psycho-physical being whose orientation it is. The world of a human being is infinitely richer in directions and levels of reality than that of an amoeba, but in the last analysis the exchange of action and reaction, of adaptation, has essentially the same foundation in the situation of the living thing as such: in a centre of appetites, curiosities, gropings, satisfactions in which inside and outside, subjective and objective, mental and physical are inextricably intertwined. There is no such thing as a mind by itself; there is no such thing in the living world as a body by itself. It is from this cardinal metaphysical error of Descartes that his epistemological errors, with all their misleading consequences, flow.

Let us take our contrast, however, in conclusion, one stage deeper into metaphysics. Descartes's world, of spatial relations on the one hand and the geometer's understanding of them on the other, is atemporal. Time for him was a series of independent instants such that it needed the concurrence of the Divine Will to keep the world in being from one such moment to the next. And his failure to understand the unity of our psycho-physical nature can be traced to his failure to acknowledge the ultimate reality of time. For it is from our existence as temporal beings, as histories, that our nature derives its strange ambiguous unity. Samuel Alexander, in his space-time cosmology, called time 'the mind of space'.[34] That is perhaps too sweeping a statement; but in the animal world at least it is the structure of temporality that determines the character of psycho-physical existence. Perception is a pervasive power of animal life, and perception, we have seen, has been found to be at bottom the grasp of spatial and temporal relations. Even the perception of spatial relations, however, is temporal in its occurrence. It takes the time of stimulation and response, it takes the ongoing apprehension of the organism, to produce it. All living beings beyond the simplest level, certainly all bisexually reproducing organisms, are four-dimensional entities, stretching within a certain niche in nature from their birth to their death. And it is that stretch, taken in itself, in its intensity, which, though inseparable from its extension, from its embodiment, is the organism's mind. For Descartes, however, there is no *stretch* of time, there are only the instantaneous beads of it, each independent of the other. That I am now entails neither my past nor my future: God may have made me a moment ago and fail to re-make me a moment hence. It is on the one hand my present consciousness and on the other the present map of the extended world that *are*. This is, again, the geometrician's vision, the vision that was needed to lay the groundwork of Newtonian mechanics, the recurrent vision, perhaps, of the triumphant mathematicizing intellect. But it is false, not only to the insistent facts of organic development, of evolutionary change, of heuristics, of history; it is false to the root structure of experience as lived. This is beautifully put by Merleau-Ponty in the *Phenomenology of Perception*:

> It is in my 'field of presence' in the widest sense–this moment that I am spending working along with, behind it, the horizon of the day that has elapsed, and, in front of it, the evening and night–that I make contact with time, and learn to know its course. The remote past has also its temporal order, and its position in time in relation to my present, but it has these in so far as it has been present itself, that it has been 'in its time' traversed by my life, and carried forward to this moment. When I call up a remote past, I reopen time, and carry myself back to a moment in which it still had before it a future horizon now closed, and a horizon of the immediate past which is today remote. Everything, therefore, causes me to revert to the field of presence as the primary experience in which time and its dimensions make their appearance unalloyed, with no intervening distance and with absolute self-evidence.[35]

But this 'presence' is not the discrete Cartesian instant:

> It is here that we see a future sliding into the present and on into the past. Nor are these three dimensions given to us through discrete acts: I do

not form a mental picture of my day, it weighs upon me with all its weight, it is still there, and though I may not recall any detail of it, I have the impending power to do so, I still 'have it in hand'. In the same way, I do not think of the evening to come and its consequences, and yet it 'is there', like the back of a house of which I can see only the facade, or like the background beneath a figure.[36]

The reference to background and figure recalls Polanyi's account of focal and subsidiary knowledge, and indeed, Merleau-Ponty's analysis of the mind at work is strikingly congruent with the epistemology of personal knowledge. But he is here setting the tension inherent in tacit knowing into its foundation in the tension of passing time. So he continues:

Our future is not made up exclusively of guesswork and daydreams. Ahead of what I can see and perceive, there is, it is true, nothing more actually visible, but my world is carried forward by lines of intentionality which trace out in advance at least the style of what is to come (although we always wait, perhaps to the day of our death, for the appearance of *something else*). The present itself, in the narrow sense, is not posited. The paper, my fountain-pen, are indeed there for me, but I do not explicitly perceive them. I do not so much perceive objects as reckon with an environment; I seek support in my tools, and am at my task rather than confronting it.[37]

Merleau-Ponty draws, here as elsewhere, on the phenomenology of Husserl:

Husserl uses the terms protentions and retentions for the intentionalities which anchor me to an environment. They do not run from a central *I*, but from my perceptual field itself, so to speak, which draws along in its wake its own horizon of retentions, and bites into the future with its protentions. I do not pass through a series of instances of now, the images of which I preserve and which, placed end to end, make a line.[38]

That would be the intellectualized Cartesian model; the case is rather that

with the arrival of every moment, its predecessor undergoes a change: I still have it in hand and it is still there, but already it is sinking away below the level of presents; in order to retain it, I need to reach through a thin layer of time. It is still the preceding moment, and I have the power to recapture it as it was just now, I am not cut off from it, but it would not belong to the past unless something had altered. It is beginning to be outlined against, or projected upon, my present, whereas it was my present a moment ago. When a third moment arrives, the second undergoes a new modification; from being a retention it becomes the retention of a retention, and the layer of time between it and me thickens.[39]

It is the structure of time, in fact, which generates that 'natural light' which Descartes held to be so self-contained and eternal. But if reason, if self-consciousness, is essentially temporal, then knowledge is never finished, never at rest in 'manifest truth'. We are always beyond ourselves in the venture of knowing, the task of finding and giving as best we can significance to our world, the world which is always beyond us at the horizon, but whose concrescence, whose interpretation, whose meaning we are. Knowledge is an achievement, but like every living achievement a stage in history, neither an end nor simply a beginning, but a 'stage on life's way'. The ideal of wholly explicit, wholly certified truth, ignoring this insight, falsifies at once the nature of the knower and the known, of mind and the world. Against the Cartesian string of bead-like instants, the world without process, the mind over against it free of aspiration or desire, we shall set the acknowledgement that there is no aspect of our lives which is not essentially process:

> time is the foundation and measure of our spontaneity, and the power of outrunning and of 'neantiser' which dwells within us and is ourselves, is itself given to us with temporality and life. Our birth, or, as Husserl has it in his unpublished writings, our 'generativity', is the basis both of our activity or individuality, and our passivity or generality–that inner weakness which prevents us from ever achieving the density of an absolute individual.[40]

We are not pure cognitions absurdly attached to a machine,

> we are not in some incomprehensible way an activity joined to a passivity, an automatism surmounted by a will, a perception surmounted by a judgment, but wholly active and wholly passive, because we are the upsurge of time.[41]

Part Two
The Structure of Experience

4 Hume's Premises

SO FAR WE HAVE BEEN EXAMINING SOME VERSIONS OF THE AGE-OLD dream of certainty, and seeking, through our critical encounter with them, some clues towards an account of knowledge consonant with our own intellectual aspirations and the demands made on us by our recognition of mind's limitations as well as its powers. It is of course nothing new to recognize the limitations of knowledge, or of the power to know. The modest, probabilistic mood in epistemology goes all the way back to ancient scepticism, to Plato's heirs in the Academy, who, despairing of their own capacity to face the dazzling brilliance of the Forms, contented themselves with moving about, from conjecture to conjecture, in the shadowy world of mere opinion. Yet, for us, as it is the Cartesian model of certainty which we have most urgently to wrestle with, so it is the post-Cartesian insistence on the limitations of our intellectual powers which presents, for our situation, the most pressing problem. In fact, the Cartesian programme itself was intended both to establish a method of certain knowledge and to establish the certainty of ignorance where, by the nature of mind and the world, no such certainty can be had. For Descartes, this technique was safe enough: it was only a transformation of the Thomistic claim to secure 'truths of faith' for revelation, safe from the depredations of philosophical scepticism. But with Locke's version of the 'new way of ideas', the concept of the mind's *limitations* became the triumphant theme of philosophical reflection. The insistence on abolishing scholastic nonsense, of sticking to common sense−in modern phrase to 'ordinary language'−had its way with traditional concepts both of mind and nature, until in the heel of the hunt there was neither nature left to know nor mind to know it.

It is Newton who is the key figure in this story. Deeply influenced by Descartes and imbued like him with the confidence of mathematical genius in the rational mind's ability to the grasp truth of things, he nevertheless believed at the very same time that this mathematical insight could be read not from the mind itself, but from the perceived *phenomena*. Yet in the Cartesian universe, as we have seen, there is nothing, except the will of God, to hold these two, mathematicizing mind and extended matter, together. This paradox at the very root of what is roughly called 'scientific method', haunts us still. Its character and history were eloquently described by Whitehead in his lectures on 'Nature and Life'.[1]

Whitehead starts his account of what he calls the 'Hume-Newton' situation by referring to the 'common-sense notion of the universe', crystallized in men's minds about 350 years ago. Looking at its destiny since then, he discovers that, on the one hand, every item in it has been abandoned, and that on the other hand, practical thinking, even the underlying conceptions of science in general (though not the particular concepts of special disciplines), still rely unthinkingly upon it. The common-sense notion was what we have been describing as Cartesian: 'the grand doctrine of Nature as a self-sufficient meaningless complex of facts–the doctrine of the autonomy of physical science'.[2] What were the items progressively abandoned from it? First, secondary qualities: 'the colour and the sound were no longer in nature. They are the mental reaction of the percipient to internal bodily locomotions.'[3] This, Whitehead argues, was 'a severe restriction to Nature', but in fact a justified one, for sense perception, or better, 'presentational immediacy', as he elsewhere calls it, is in his view 'artificial'. That is, in it we relate sensations felt in us to the 'spatiality which is the grand substratum of Nature'.[4] So:

> when we perceive the red rose we are associating our enjoyment of red derived from one source with our enjoyment of a spatial region derived from another source. The conclusion that I draw is that sense-perception for all its practical importance is very superficial in its disclosure of the nature of things.[5]

That is why, he continues, there is always a kind of *delusiveness* about sense as such, as when we perceive stars long since vanished, single images with our double vision, reflections in mirrors, and so on. Once we come this far, moreover, we recognize the important fact that sensory awareness *never carries its own interpretation*. This is Hume's great discovery and the reason why, Whitehead believes, every philosophy since must build on Hume's foundations. But this is at the same time one side of the contradiction in which modern science has left us. The other side comes from the nature of the Newtonian synthesis, and then, to make matters worse, the consequent abandonment of the remaining items in the original common-sense picture, leaving only its gaping and incongruous frame.

The Newtonian synthesis concerned primarily the common-sense doctrine of space and local motion. But, Whitehead writes,

> the forces which he introduced left Nature still without meaning or value. In the essence of a material body–in its mass, motion, and shape–

there was no reason for the law of gravitation. Even if the particular forces could be conceived as the accidents of a cosmic epoch, there was no reason in the Newtonian concepts of mass and motion why material bodies should be connected by any stress between them. Yet the notion of stresses, as essential connections between bodies, was a fundamental factor in the Newtonian concept of nature. What Newton left for empirical investigation was the determination of the particular stresses now existing. In this determination he made a magnificent beginning by isolating the stresses indicated by his law of gravitation. But he left no hint why in the nature of things there should be any stresses at all. The arbitrary motions of the bodies were thus explained by the arbitrary stresses between material bodies, conjoined with their spatiality, their mass, and their initial states of motion. By introducing stresses— in particular the law of gravitation—instead of the welter of detailed transformations of motion, he greatly increased the systematic aspect of nature. But he left all the factors of the system—more particularly, mass and stress—in the position of detached facts devoid of any reason for their compresence. He thus illustrated a great philosophic truth, that a dead nature can give no reasons. All ultimate reasons are in terms of aim at value. A dead nature aims at nothing.[6]

From now on, the fundamental paradox is with us:

> Combining Newton and Hume we obtain a barren concept, namely a field of perception devoid of any data for its own interpretation, and a system of interpretation, devoid of any reason for the concurrence of its factors.[7]

In fact, as I have already remarked, this paradox was inherent in Newton's own method; it was for Hume to draw out the logical conclusion of its phenomenalist aspect. Now in the intervening centuries, finally, the progress of physics has exacerbated our plight by rejecting both absolute space and the isolated bits of matter moving in it, in short, every item of the common-sense Newtonian cosmology, yet insisting on retaining in its conception of method the presuppositions of that cosmology. It has retained, in other words, a conception of its own method which *would* have been appropriate to a Cartesian-Newtonian, merely extended nature if nature were really like that:

> The result is to reduce modern physics to a sort of mystic chant over an unintelligible universe. This chant has the exact merits of the old magic ceremonies which flourished in ancient Mesopotamia and later in Europe. One of the earliest fragments of writing which has survived is a report from a Babylonian astrologer to the King, stating the favourable days to turn cattle into the fields, as deduced by his observations of the stars. This mystic relation of observation, theory, and practice, is exactly the present position of science in modern life, according to the prevalent scientific philosophy.[8]

Such a situation, Whitehead concludes, is a *reductio ad absurdum*, and unacceptable as a foundation for philosophical reflection. The main developments of modern philosophy in the generation since he delivered this lecture have nevertheless continued, in the main, to base themselves on this inadequate foundation, and in so doing have amply borne out his conclusions.

Philosophically, the nature of this impasse appears most plainly in Hume's application of the new 'experimental method' to the problem of knowledge. What I want to do here, therefore, is to look at the outlines of Hume's empiricism and to see how it persists in contemporary philosophy. Later I shall return to Hume's theory to consider what we must alter in it to adapt it to our own conception of knowledge as stabilized conjecture, as learning, as the elaboration, phylogenetically and ontogenetically, of the primordial power of perception which we share with the whole animal world.

II

Hume's *Treatise of Human Nature* fell, according to himself, 'dead-born from the press', yet it has turned out to be the most influential – or perhaps one should say the most fundamental – philosophical document in English, for it stated definitely the plain, common-sensical view of the human mind which seemed, and still seems, to be sponsored by the authority of science. It is a conditioned-reflex sort of mind in which associative mechanisms generate roughly satisfactory habits of belief. These habits have no logical guarantee – everything that holds together might fall apart – but they work out well enough since they have the sanctity of being grounded in sensation. Separable sense impressions, their imagined and remembered counterparts: these are the elements which build themselves up by a sort of mental chemistry (the 'gentle force of association') into a workable, worka-day world.

What is so satisfactory about this rather humdrum universe? Principally the fact that there is no nonsense about it. 'Superstition and enthusiasm' have been banished. The pretensions of theology, metaphysics, even political myth are brushed away, and the everyday wants of decent, sensible people are allowed to work themselves out as nature and its shadow, custom, provide. This is still the prevailing temper of modern empiricism. Lord Keynes, in his essay, 'My Early Beliefs', recalled its dominance in his own Cambridge circle, notably in the case of Russell:

Bertie in particular sustained simultaneously a pair of opinions ludi-crously incompatible. He held that in fact human affairs were carried on after a most irrational fashion, but that the remedy was quite simple and easy, since all we had to do was to carry them on rationally.[9]

For a Humean mentality these are two sides of a single coin. The irrationality of other people is due to the ridiculous prejudices and violent emotions by which they let themselves be carried away; one's own rationality is due to the absence of these. Indeed, it is not so much rationality in any metaphysical or transcendental sense as it is naturalness. So Hume writes:

> While a warm imagination is allowed to enter into philosophy, and hypotheses embraced merely for being specious and agreeable, we can never have any steady principles, nor any sentiments, which will suit with common practice and experience. But were these hypotheses once removed, we might hope to establish a system or set of opinions, which if not true (for that, perhaps, is too much to be hoped for), might at least be satisfactory to the human mind, and might stand the test of the most critical examination.[10]

The gist of this attitude is: get rid of all the insanities, and what is left is sane.

This common-sense, habit-governed world is constructed in Hume's *Treatise* with brilliant simplicity and rigour on the ground of three principles which he states in Part One of the first book. We may call these: (1) the Genetic Principle; (2) the Atomic Principle; (3) the Associative Principle. Hume states them as follows:

(1) *The Genetic Principle*: 'All our simple ideas in their first appearance, are derived from simple impressions, which are correspondent to them, and which they exactly resemble.'[11]

(2) *The Atomic Principle*: 'There are not any two impressions which are perfectly inseparable.'[12]

(3) *The Associative Principle*: The assertion of a 'gentle force, which commonly prevails (sc. to unite ideas), and is the cause why, among other things, languages so nearly correspond to each other, nature, in a manner, pointing out to every one those simple ideas, which are most proper to be united into a complex one'.[13]

The genetic principle is Locke's 'new way of ideas' taken seriously. Cartesian ideas understood as images, as passive mental content, first come 'into' the mind from outside: in Cartesian terminology, they are all 'adventitious'. Even the 'factitious' ones—like the idea of Pegasus—must have come from somewhere: they must be put together of bits originally derived from experience: as the idea, in this case, of a horse, with the wings clipped off a bird attached to its back. But what of the originals themselves, which Hume calls 'impressions'?[14] Images are images *of* something, and the Lockean idea is basically representative, as was the Cartesian.[15] Ideas (if = images) do, like photographs, in the main imitate their objects. Must we not then, in turn, derive, genetically, impressions from the things *they copy*? Locke, with his ideas of sensation, had tried to do this, and he was in fact confident that some of his ideas, those of primary qualities, do resemble their originals. The relation between secondary qualities and their subjective counterparts, however, he could not specify; and the things themselves, the extended substances possessing both primary and secondary qualities, were no more than a necessary but unknown X underlying these. Our knowledge of substance and of real existence, he found, goes but a very little way. And that little way–the step from my idea to *something* containing the quality it has copied–Berkeley was able to block effectively, demonstrating that primary and secondary qualities are alike cut off from any substrate to which they inevitably point. He showed plainly (though he failed to follow his own showing) that a rigorous empiricism must start from the data of experience themselves, not seek, speculatively and uncritically, to probe behind them. Hume, therefore, retaining the Lockean genetic method after this Berkeleyan catharsis, asks only: from what original units of *experience* do my ideas spring?, not: whence my original impressions, whence those units themselves? For impressions are the neutral originals, beyond which, if I really stick to experience, to the 'phenomena', I *cannot* question. I could indeed build up a physiology on a Humean basis and place my account of perception itself within it. That is in effect what a behaviourist like Quine has done in *Word and Object*.[16] But this would not be, for Hume, a philosophically honest beginning. It is true that he sometimes uses terms like 'object' rather than 'impression', but impressions *are* the neutral objects with which he begins. Behind these it is, at the beginning of an empiricist epistemology, impossible to inquire. Hume is determined to build up an account of experience out of the units of experience itself. The Cartesian clear and distinct idea with its elastic passive-active character, its suspension between mind and world, has been transmogrified into a precise, delimitable image, a unit of passive immediacy, and it is out of such units and such units alone that all knowledge must be built. Any idea which presents itself must show its passport, but a passport from original experience only. Behind this surface no one can penetrate, no common sense person would want to penetrate. As with Aristotle, so with Hume, the task of philosophy is not to push forward into the unknown, but to rearrange and sort out what is there; only for Hume all that is there is the immediate, the sensed quality, the feeling, the sheer subjectivity of experience itself.

The idea as image, secondly, is discrete. It is an atom of experience.

If mental contents are literally images, each one in its purity is plainly delimited from every other. A recent snapshot of a friend may or may not bring to mind his appearance ten years ago, but the two images are quite distinct. By Hume's third principle, one may recall the other, but by the second, neither can entail the other. In the case of the snapshot, it is the *resemblance* between the two images which leads me to recall my friend's former appearance. The other 'natural relations' which usually occasion this associative process are *contiguity*, as when, meeting an acquaintance, I recall the play I saw him performing in last week, and *causation*, as when, hearing a noise in the kitchen, I go to see who is rummaging in the refrigerator. This last associative agency in turn depends, it will turn out on 'constant conjunction'–in this case between kitchen noises and refrigerator rummaging. All these lines of association sum up in the last analysis to the force of habit. It is custom that makes Hume's world.

But, one may argue, if all our experience is just a matter of custom, of blind habits built up by a sort of mechanical conditioning, so is Hume's philosophy. Why should we believe it, rather than some other philosophy which by *our* habits of association we happen to believe? Are Hume's habits of belief better than any one else's? It's all very well to talk of getting rid of insanities, but who can judge the sane and the insane, and by what right? Hume is brilliantly consistent in dealing with this question. He recognizes explicitly that every theory which gives an account of human knowledge must include itself in the knowledge it legitimates; and so, meditating on the habit-forming associations of the human mind, he seeks no securer sanction for this meditation. He who is induced by habit to believe, habitually believes that he is so induced to believe. This is just a harmless habit of his own, built up associatively by the same kind of lucky accident as all his other beliefs. 'Nature has determined us to judge, as well as to breathe and feel,'[17] and in this determination David Hume is avowedly in the same case with all the rest of us.

Moreover, if we feel uneasy about this purely irrational success of 'reason', we may take comfort from our likeness in this to other creatures, as well as from the likeness of our own powers to one another. In theory and practice, reason and will, in the constructs of experimental science or the generation of the moral sentiment out of sympathy, everywhere we see at work the same habit-building mechanisms–and in animals as in men. Thus Hume puts a section on 'reason in animals', 'love and hatred in animals', and so on, at the close of each part of the *Treatise*: for this hypothesis of his, in imitation of the method of the incomparable Newton, is strengthened by the fact that it accounts for many phenomena (including, as we have just seen, itself) rather than for only a few. So he says (and this is an instance of the application of his own method to itself):

> When ... we see other creatures, in millions of instances, perform like actions, and direct them to like ends, all our principles of reason and probability carry us with an invincible force to believe the existence of a like cause.[18]

Should anyone suggest an hypothesis with as broad a range, he will consider it equiprobable with his; but as most philosophical theories have prided themselves precisely on separating men from brutes, and theory from practice, they are not likely, by this analogical canon, to offer serious competition.

I shall return later to these two principles, of epistemological circularity, and of confirmation by analogy; we shall see what becomes of them when we examine the modern heirs of Hume. But let me finish my sketch of Hume's common-sense world before proceeding to look at its modern counterparts.

It is, as I have said, a world with no nonsense, yet it is a world with no sense either, and that for one principal reason: that there is nobody in it. Herein, not in his critique of causation, lies Hume's real scepticism. The self, he says, is a bundle of impressions, and though that is one of his more devastating expressions, there is quite literally, on his principles, nothing else for the self to be. Associative mechanisms cannot make a person. If there is, on Hume's view, no logical necessity to what I know, neither is there any responsible agent to assent to my knowing it. Habits just happen: sets of sense-data looked at one way make physical systems, looked at another, physiological or psychological ones. None of it is anyone's fault, or anyone's risk, or anyone's success. Hume himself in the Appendix to the *Treatise* acknowledged this limit of his own system. The mind is capable only of perceptions; all perceptions are separable; how shall we account for the togetherness even of that bundle of them which we may designate a 'mind' or 'self'? 'For my part', he concludes, 'I must plead the privilege of a sceptic, and confess that this difficulty is too hard for my understanding.'[19]

Yet this admission of scepticism is not an admission of defeat on Hume's part. The edifice he has constructed rests squarely on the tension between scepticism and common-sense, a tension which his concluding concession only draws a bit tauter. Looked at one way, the structure is not, theoretically, sound; but it holds up and we live in it, and the demands of life are such that we simply can't worry too much about these things most of the time. The 'propensity to feign'[20] carries us through. We know that our knowledge is, if more elaborate, very like that of Pavlov's dogs who expect food when the bell rings.

The togethernesses of which we have made a world are no more logical or objective than those canine conjunctions. Yet our irrational hunches work and we rely on them.

But if we know this, we know too that they cannot carry us *beyond* common experience, whether of bells and food, or of falling bodies and acceleration, to abstruse and unconfirmable questions of Mind or Matter, of God or Immortality. Thus Hume's scepticism consists, not in vacillation between credulity and incredulity, but in a steady habit of seeing all mental operations and the mind itself as pure percepts, of admitting differences in degree of vividness or intensity as the only type of distinction between classes of percepts, and association as the only connection between them, and of confining philosophical explanation to the extremely limited area permitted by this restriction. As applied to the uncharted and unchartable seas of theology, the whole case is put most beautifully by Philo the sceptic in the opening of the *Dialogues Concerning Natural Religion*:

> So long as we confine our speculations to trade, or morals, or politics, or criticism, we make appeals, every moment, to common sense and experience, which strengthen our philosophical conclusions, and remove (at least, in part) the suspicion, which we so justly entertain with regard to every reasoning, that is very subtle and refined. But in theological reasonings, we have not this advantage; while at the same time we are employed upon objects, which, we must be sensible, are too large for our grasp, and of all others, require most to be familiarized to our apprehension. We are like foreigners in a strange country, to whom everything must seem suspicious, and who are in danger every moment of transgressing against the laws and customs of the people, with whom they live and converse. We know not how far we ought to trust our vulgar methods of reasoning in such a subject; since, even in common life and in that province, which is peculiarly appropriated to them, we cannot account for them, and are entirely guided by a kind of instinct or necessity in employing them.[21]

This is a wonderfully self-consistent, if self-limiting system, whose inconsistencies, if they are such, are at its edges. But for Hume himself these inconsistencies were only just and reasonable limits. He could approach and look beyond them without a trace of metaphysical nausea. Let us see how, within these limits, he used his theory in morals, politics, religion.

It may seem difficult—and has seemed so sometimes to subsequent empiricists—to apply this delightfully simple conditioned-reflex view of mind to moral matters. But it was for their sake that Hume embarked on his investigation: the purpose of the *Treatise* was to introduce the experimental method into moral subjects. And here again the result is a brilliantly consistent–and rigorously self-limiting–system. Once more it all depends on limiting the activities of mind to perception (in Hume's sense of passive units of felt experience). Our sensations of pleasure and pain are accompanied by feelings: loves, hatreds, in short, passions, some calm, some violent. These form associative patterns, as our ideas of objects do. Thus the pleasure we derive from an individual's society causes us to love him; but this love in turn produces a new, associated pleasure at the sight of the loved object, again increasing our love, and so on. We can even, since there is no metaphysical person and no rigid boundary in the experience of 'mine' and 'thine', feel, if less intensely than our own, the pleasures and pains *of* a loved person. And less intensely still, when we allow the prevalence over our minds of calm, not violent feeling, we can feel with assent or aversion the pains or pleasures of anyone insofar as they are involved in the habits or actions of himself or anyone else. Thus the gift of sympathy (which, again, we share with animals) becomes, when attenuated and generalized, the taste for virtue, the perception of vice: the moral sentiment. It is by no means the principal motive of action, if a motive at all; but it is a kind of reflective imagination turned, from a Lucretian eminence, on the characters of our fellow men.

Yet somehow morals must be authoritative. How can the calm passions exercise authority over the violent? The answer: as the burnt child shuns the fire–by custom and association. Moral taste is, like causal generalization, a self-confirming custom. For the moral sense is a 'calm general determination of the passions founded on some distant view or reflection',[22] which approves whatever disposition is useful or agreeable to the person judged, or to any person affected by it, and disapproves the contrary. And it is precisely the calm as against the violent passions which are, by this moral sense, judged to be useful or agreeable, etc. Thus:

> when we enumerate the good qualities of any person, we always mention those parts of his character which render him a safe companion, an easy friend, a gentle master, an agreeable husband, or an indulgent father.[23]

What a world is in that list of adjectives! What confidence, what equanimity, what innocence! One is reminded of Fanny Price's fear that her adored Edmund might, in his infatuation with Mary Crawford, 'cease to be respectable'. For it is indeed a world in which the worst imaginable evil would be to cease to be respectable: a world in which, though we recognize the capriciousness of human nature, and the selfishness of most actions, yet

... the intercourse of sentiments ... in society and conversation, makes us form some general unalterable standard by which we may approve or disapprove of characters and manners. And though the *heart* does not always take part with those general notions, or regulate its love and hatred by them, yet are they sufficient for discourse, and serve all our purposes in company, in the pulpit, in the theatre, and in the schools.[24]

The moral sentiment, then, is generated by self-perpetuating habits on the ground of feelings common to all men :– or at any rate, as it may seem to us, to most cultivated British gentlemen of the eighteenth century. But it is confirmed also, in Hume's case, by his own disposition. In the same chapter ('Of Benevolence') from which I have just been quoting, he gives himself away. 'Men naturally, without reflection', he says,

approve of that character which is most like their own. The man of a mild disposition and tender affections, in forming a notion of the most perfect virtue, mixes in it more of benevolence and humanity than the man of courage and enterprise, who naturally looks upon a certain elevation of the mind as the most accomplished character. This must evidently proceed from the *immediate* sympathy, which men have with characters similar to their own. They enter with warmth into such sentiments, and feel more sensibly the pleasure which arises from them.[25]

Gentleness was Hume's besetting virtue, and he read human nature somewhat in his own likeness. Of course he knew that the violent passions often overcome the calm : witness, for example, his colourful account of the Irish Insurrection of 1641.[26] Yet he found this often the result of priestcraft and fanaticism generated in the many by the bad influence of the few. There was no reason in the nature of the case why the gentle passions should not sometimes of themselves prevail 'according to the *general* character or *present* disposition of the person'.[27]

In fact, this benignity of his forms the deepest root of his sceptical system. In his experience as an historian, and before and beneath this, we may guess, in his childhood experience of the Scottish Kirk, he learned to associate theological speculation with fanaticism, and fanaticism with cruelty. And as, in his untroubled good nature, he hated cruelty, so he distrusted militant religion and its ally, militant metaphysics. Wholly pre-romantic in temper, he could look at hills purple with heather as so much loss to industry and profit. And philosophically, too, he preferred the well-kept lawns and gardens of an amiable society to wild moors of mystery inhabited by prophetic brigands or murdering saints.

From this disposition springs also, again with entire consistency, what has seemed to some the paradox of his Tory politics. Somehow, sceptics and empiricists are always supposed to be liberals. But Hume, as Whig as politeness demanded in his own day, and decorously applauding 1688, became as an historian increasingly sympathetic to the Stuarts. He was particularly devoted to Charles I, in his view an amiable and virtuous prince, victim of the rampant enthusiasm of his time, which 'being universally diffused, disappointed all the views of human prudence, and disturbed the operation of every motive which usually influences society'. Faced with the zealous frenzies of Covenanters or Roundheads, Hume's very scepticism could not but strengthen such Stuart sympathies: read, for instance, his account of the outbreak in Scotland over the liturgy, or of the ruse by which Fairfax was got to pray for enlightenment at the very moment of the king's execution–what man of moderate humanity but would react with aversion to such unnatural admixtures of piety, violence and fraud?[28] No love of abstract liberty–and Hume loved no abstractions–could outweigh such living arguments. Even when writing of his own time, while he praises the judicious balance of the British government, he not only thinks the tide turning slightly toward the monarchy, but holds it more desirable (since 'death is unavoidable to the political as well as to the animal body')[29] that the British constitution should terminate in an absolute monarchy than in a popular government. Once more, it is not an abstract question 'concerning any fine imaginary republic, of which a man may form a plan in his closet'.[30] But out of the British government as it is, Hume suggests, there might come either a tyranny of the Commons issuing in civil war and coming to rest at last in absolute monarchy, or absolute monarchy peacefully established from the start–the latter being therefore 'the easiest death, the true *Euthanasia* of the British constitution'.[31]

On the other hand, the very principles which made him mildly conservative in his politics–or better, the character in which those principles were lodged–made him at the same time a radical sceptic in religion. For the passion in him that came nearest to violence was the hatred of 'priestcraft and fanaticism'. It has sometimes been argued that it is Cleanthes, the scientific deist, who speaks for Hume in the *Dialogues Concerning Natural Religion*. But this posthumous work, which had held Hume's attention at intervals over a period of twenty-five years, puts a very weak case for deism. It is the agnosticism of Philo the sceptic which is enforced blow by blow in this, the most perfect piece of rhetoric in our philosophical literature. What is so magnificent is not simply the overwhelming series of hypotheses by which Philo turns the tables on Cleanthes with his analogical argument; or the classic argument on evil by which the lamentations of the pious Demea on the wickedness and misery of men are turned to Philo's sceptical purpose. What is most astonishing is the way in which Hume-Philo, from his safe niche of common-sense reliance on common experience, surveys the hypotheses which bolder spirits have adopted to explain the origin of the universe. Has any philosopher ever looked with such clarity beyond the limits of his own mentality, ever seen so plainly what he does not see? A great array of alternative hypotheses is spread out before us : the Epicurean theology, the world soul of neo-Platonism, Spinoza's rational necessity, Plato's *Timaeus* (the world as an eternal living creature), even, in anticipation, the cosmology accepted by some of Hume's empiricist descendants–the world originating in a vast explosion, now slowed down to an orderly rate 'so as to present an uniformity of appearance, amidst the continual motion and fluctuation of its parts',[32]–the adaptation of animals and plants to their environment being due to what we now call natural selection. This last alternative would seem most sympathetic to a person of Hume's inclinations and beliefs; yet as they are all, to him, equally flights of fancy, they are all sketched with the same skilful pencil as so many *un*likely stories to which the man of sense, *and* therefore of scepticism, will attach no serious weight.

No wonder Hume's friends advised him against publishing the *Dialogues*. As it was, his contemporaries felt vividly enough the force of his reflective detachment from religious issues. Especially was this clear in the mood with which he faced a painful death. Forty years earlier he had written:

> The annihilation which some people suppose to follow upon death, and which entirely destroys the self, is nothing but an extinction of all particular perceptions; love and hatred, pain and pleasure, thought and sensation. These, therefore, must be the same with the self, since the one cannot survive the other.[33]

Now he faced what on his own theory must be annihilation with all the good sense the theory had originally been intended to support. Poor Jamie Boswell, who called in to see David Hume, 'just a-dying', recorded with horror his imperturbable equanimity. When his visitor, 'he knew not how', brought the subject round to immortality, Hume in both wit and logic so outargued him as to evoke, in Boswell's phrase, 'a sort of wild, strange, hurrying recollection of my excellent Mother's pious instructions', as well as of 'Dr. Johnson's noble lessons'.[34] For Hume's friends the same mood only confirmed their admiration. Adam Smith wrote:

> Upon the whole, I have always considered him, both in his lifetime, and since his death, as approaching as nearly to the idea of a perfectly wise and virtuous man, as perhaps the nature of human frailty will admit.[35]

III

Such was the most amiable of British philosophers, who was, at the same time, the compleat empiricist. What has become of his philosophy? His eighteenth-century self-confidence, his implicit and unargued faith in the simple uniformity of human nature, even the eighteenth-century turn of his benevolence–all these belong to a vanished world. Yet the First Book of his *Treatise* is still the canon for the principal practice of philosophy in Britain and America. The axioms which were, as he expressed them, intrinsically inherent in that lost world and in himself, its offspring, have shaken loose from their setting and, in strange isolation, dominate the direction and confine the scope of philosophical inquiry. Thus the scepticism which in Hume was the consequence of a positive aim and character has become in itself a dogma, doubt of which is held to be dangerous, if unintelligible, dogmatism. Moreover, this sceptical orthodoxy is still grounded in a completely Humean assessment of the nature and limits of our intellectual powers. Percepts organized by habit: that is still, and more than ever, for contemporary philosophers, the acknowledged pattern of the mind.

This holds not only of thinking modelled on the crude be-behaviourism of the twenties–which is obviously Hume decivilized–but of many shades and varieties of scientifically oriented thought. Russell, for example, in the *Inquiry into Meaning and Truth*, explains that he is simply translating Hume's epistemology into the language of modern logic.[36] Professor Braithwaite in his *Scientific Explanation* admits as his aim the assimilation of the complex deductive theories of modern physics to Hume's 'constant conjunction' pattern.[37] Von Wright in *The Logical Problem of Induction* is wrestling with Hume's argument–and so on.[38] Even when Hume is not explicitly invoked, the debt is obvious. John Dewey's pragmatism was wholly dependent on Hume's principles; logical positivism was an attempted formalization of them; recent analytical philosophy tries to repair this rigidity and make them again more flexible. The result of this last effort, however, has been to confine still further the scope of philosophical reflection. Linguistic usage, which is now so popular a theme for philosophic discourse, is but a subspecies of Humean custom. It is a particularly useful subspecies–for when one comes up against an uncomfortably serious problem one can turn it into a question of the use of words and so evade it. This trick–supported by a superficial pretence of putting verbal habits into the context of other habits–is used over and over, with admirable virtuosity, to bestow an air of problem-solving on what is at bottom a technique of problem-dodging. Hume, in his securer world, could complacently survey the traditional riddles of philosophy and let them be. The Humes of our uneasier day must avoid at all costs such embarrassing confrontations; and that is just what their linguistic about-face manoeuvre enables them to do. Thus a philosophy already limited has become more limited still. Stripped of its flesh and blood, the skeleton of Hume's system, its bare, unattractive, conditioned-reflex logic, presides over the trivialization of philosophy.

Two examples of modern empiricist thought may help to substantiate this sweeping statement: they are examples of what we may call unhappy and happy empiricism respectively, but they both illustrate the impasse to which philosophers in the Humean tradition are inevitably driven. The first of the two is Russell's *Human Knowledge: its Scope and Limits*,[39] and the other Braithwaite's *Scientific Explanation*.[40] Both writers, as I have already mentioned, acknowledge their debt to Hume; although it is in the *Inquiry* that Russell's acknowledgment is explicit, in *Human Knowledge* he still follows the same empiricist principles.

We can see in the latter book both how exactly Russell follows the principles of the *Treatise* and where they come to grief, how they lead, in fact, to the self-contradiction of empiricism.

The Genetic Principle is stated by Russell in his account of ostensive definitions or of 'minimum vocabularies' in science[41] or in his version of the correspondence theory of truth.[42] For brevity's sake I shall quote it in a passage which affirms the Atomic Principle as well. The passage begins:

> Hume's scepticism with regard to the world of science resulted from (a) the doctrine that all my data are private to me ...

This is another form of the genetic principle: i.e. all my data are sensations, or in Hume's terms impressions. Russell continues:

> together with (b) the discovery that matters of fact, however numerous and well-selected, never logically imply any other matter of fact. I do not see any way of escaping from either of these theses. The first I have been arguing; I may say that I attach especial weight in this respect to the argument from the physical causation of sensations.[43]

This argument, of course, is not strictly Humean, but depends upon the superimposition of a physicalist theory upon Hume's phenomenalist base. It by no means contradicts Hume, however, but lends to his basic position the prestige of scientific support. Russell proceeds:

> As to the second, it is obvious as a matter of syntax to any one who has grasped the nature of deductive arguments. A matter of fact which is not contained in the premisses must require for its assertion a proper

name which does not occur in the premises. But there is only one way in which a new proper name can occur in a deductive argument, and that is when we proceed from the general to the particular, as in 'all men are mortal, therefore Socrates is mortal'. Now no collection of assertions of matters of fact is logically equivalent to a general assertion, so that, if our premises concern only matters of fact, this way of introducing a new proper name is not open to us. Hence the thesis follows.[44]

Russell is loyal to Hume, moreover, in his atomistic interpretation of this thesis. For although he pays lip-service, both here and in the *Inquiry*, to gestalt psychology, his eagerness to treat gestalten as aggregates of Humean atomic data is clear, for example, from his exposition of what he calls 'complexes of compresence':

> We may agree with Leibniz to this extent, that only our ignorance makes names for complexes necessary. In theory, every complex of compresence can be defined by enumerating its component qualities. But, in fact, we can perceive a complex without perceiving its component qualities; in this case, if we discover that a certain quality is a component of it, we need a name for the complex to express what it is that we have discovered. The need for proper names, therefore, is bound up with our way of acquiring knowledge, and would cease if our knowledge were complete.[45]

In other words, instead of the shorthand offered us by the apprehension of gestalten, and their designation by proper names, we should have strings of remembered or imagined atomic qualities exactly copied from the qualitative atoms of sense. This is still the world which Berkeley thought an algebraically minded God had devised for us out of little separate bits of red, green, hot, sweet, hard, loud, etc., but with the Divine Mathematician removed.

And instead of Berkeley's God we have Hume's Associative Principle, which, again, Russell seems faithfully to follow. For instance:

> I give the name 'animal inference' to the process of spontaneous interpretation of sensations. When a dog hears himself called in tones to which he is accustomed, he looks round and runs in the direction of the sound. He may be deceived, like the dog looking into the gramophone in the advertisement of 'His Master's Voice'. But since inferences of this sort are generated by the repeated experiences that give rise to habit, his inference must be one which has usually been right in his past life, since otherwise the habit would not have been generated. We thus find ourselves, when we begin to reflect, expecting all sorts of things that in fact happen, although it would be logically possible for them not to happen in spite of the occurrence of the sensations which give rise to the expectations. Thus reflection upon animal inference gives us an initial

store of scientific laws such as 'dogs bark'. These initial laws are usually somewhat unreliable, but they help us to take the first steps toward science.[46]

But he goes even further when he says, a little later:

> Scientific method, I suggest, consists in eliminating those beliefs which there is positive reason to think a source of shocks, while retaining those against which no definite argument can be brought.[47]

And so, all the way through to the most creative or most sophisticated inferences of science, the Humean description is adhered to: the not-quite chance generation of self-perpetuating habits of association accounts for all the activities of the human mind.

So much for Russell's adherence to the principles of the *Treatise*. What of its method: that is, the canons of analogy and of epistemological circularity by which Hume thinks his argument should be judged? First, it is clear from the passages already quoted that the analogy with animals looms large in Russell's exposition. It is the conditioned-reflex pattern, applied to man and beast, that is basic. The very phrase 'animal inference' makes this clear. Or take the following analysis of 'belief':

> I suggest that what really constitutes belief in a general proposition is a mental habit: when you think of a particular man, you say, 'yes, mortal,' provided that the question of mortality arises. . . If this is granted, we can allow a preverbal form of a general belief. If an animal has a habit such that, in the presence of an instance of A, it behaves in a manner in which, before the acquisition of the habit, it behaved in the presence of an instance of B, I shall say that the animal believes the general proposition: 'Every instance (or nearly every instance) of A is followed (or accompanied) by an instance of B.' That is to say, the animal believes what this form of words signifies.[48]

The other passage already quoted, about scientific method and the avoidance of shocks, is even stronger: we go on habitually reinforcing those habits not shocked out of us and eliminating those habits which shock does eliminate. That is how rats learn in the learning experiments psychologists set for them, and how scientists learn in the experiments they (habitually) set for themselves.

The question still remains, however, whether the philosopher reflecting on all this is content to reduce all empirical inference, including his own philosophical reflection, to animal habit. Is he willing to rest within the epistemological circle? The answer in this case is 'No'. Russell can and often does describe all knowledge in these terms; but he is not satisfied with this. He wants not only to describe empirical or inductive inference, but to *justify* it, and that is what in one way or another all empirical philosophers since Hume (and back to Protagoras) have wanted, and still want. Some of them nowadays, like Feigl, Kneale, or for that matter, Braithwaite, in effect justify it, as Hume did, by pointing to practice.[49] Since the 'inductive policy', as it is now the fashion to call it, works, we continue to use it, whatever its theoretical deficiencies. Others, like Carnap, try to construct an elaborate deductive justification of it, which already presupposes its justifiability, and so begs the question.[50] So do the 'inductive policy' advocates in one way and another, which I shall not try to enumerate here. But Russell—and this is what seems to me so important about his book—openly and honestly acknowledges that on Hume's principles induction both needs justification and is unable to get it. Thus the passage I quoted on the genetic and atomic principles continues:

> If we are not to deduce Hume's scepticism from the above two premisses, there seems to be only one possible way of escape, and that is to maintain that, among the premisses of our knowledge, there are some general propositions, or there is at least one general proposition, which is not analytically necessary, i.e. the hypothesis of its falsehood is not self-contradictory. A principle justifying the scientific use of induction would have this character. What is needed is some way of giving probability (not certainty) to the inferences from known matters of fact to occurrences which have not yet been, and perhaps never will be, part of the experience of the person making the inference. If an individual is to know anything beyond his own experiences up to the present moment, his stock of uninferred knowledge must consist not only of matters of fact, but also of general laws, or at least a law, allowing him to make inferences from matters of fact; and such law or laws must, unlike the principles of deductive logic, be synthetic, i.e. not proved true by their falsehood being self-contradictory. The only alternative to this hypothesis is complete scepticism as to all the inferences of science and common sense, including those which I have called 'animal inference.'[51]

In other words, induction makes sense, or is knowledge, rather than just blind self-conditioning, only if we *know* some principles *not* inductively derived, which validate it.[52] This, however, makes the empirical theory of knowledge itself which Russell is expounding formally self-contradictory.

That is easy to see. Let us call the logical product of Hume's three principles for short E, for empiricism—and I think that on the historical evidence one may fairly make this equation. Now it is a necessary consequence of this doctrine that all meaningful assertions, or propositions, or indicative sentences, if one prefers the more grammatical sounding and less controversial name, are of two forms: *analytic a priori* or *synthetic a posteriori*. That is, they are, on the one hand, like the propositions of pure mathematics, such that their denial is self-contradictory: they assert 'A or non-A', or, to put it positively, they are tautologous, and assert in some form 'A is A'. These are the statements which are described by Hume as arising from the examination of ideas themselves, and are such that they necessarily change when the ideas change. They are necessary but empty. Or, on the other hand, propositions are synthetic, that is, they bring together concepts not amounting to a logical identity, and this can happen, on empiricist principles, only *a posteriori*, i.e. as a result of experience. In Hume's terms, ideas which are not perfectly inseparable have habitually got themselves connected together to form an 'inductive' judgment. There is in fact no other way in which Hume's psychological atoms could form judgments. This disjunction therefore is exclusive and exhaustive. All statements are either necessary but empty, or have content but are based on experience, not logical necessity. Let us call this disjunction: S. We may then assert:

If E, then S.

or conversely, by the *modus tollens*,

If non-S, then non-E.

But, Russell says, if empiricism is to make sense, we must know something beyond, and before, experience, which is not analytic, that is, 'whose denial is not self-contradictory', and yet this principle cannot in turn be derived from experience, since 'deriving from experience' depends on it. In other words, it must be a proposition which is both synthetic (non-analytic) and *a priori* (pre-inductive). But then there will be at least one proposition which is neither *analytic a priori* nor *synthetic a posteriori*. In that case it is false that all statements are *a priori analytic* or *synthetic a posteriori*; that is, if we want to justify E, we must assert non-S: or

If E, then non-S

But as we have already seen,

If non-S, then non-E.

So we have:

If E, then non-S

If non-S, then non-E,

or:

If E, then non-E,

or: E is self-contradictory.

This is a bald and simple argument, but it is borne out by the continuing uneasiness of empiricist philosophers about induction, and also by a wave of doubts on the part of philosophers and logicians about this very division of statements into analytic and synthetic. Professor Quine in his famous essay 'Two Dogmas of

Empiricism' showed that it is only the very narrow context of artificial languages (like those constructed by Carnap) which permits the distinction to stand at all.[53] It operates in so-called 'natural languages' (including the technical ones of science) only as a distinction of degree. As a distinction of kind it must be abandoned, according to Quine, along with the equally artificial dogma of 'reductionism' (which is Hume's genetic principle). What is left after this double banishment Quine still calls 'empiricism', but if it is (and I do not understand what it is), it is certainly not traditional empiricism, which Quine himself has shown to be not only, as Russell in effect admits, theoretically invalid, but, far from the practical prescription it is thought to be, a highly artificial and abstract construction with no practical relevance to support it. And indeed a self-contradictory theory cannot be of much practical assistance, since it says both everything and nothing. A recipe which said: 'Beat the whites till stiff and dry, and do not beat the whites till stiff and dry', might be very subtle, but it would be of little use.

Yet–to go back to Russell–what is the way out of this impasse? He surely would not revert to the Kantian escape into *synthetic a prioris*, and whatever wisdom we may find that Kant has to offer us to help us toward a new form of philosophical reflection, the Kantian *a priori* as they stand are, in the light of non-Euclidean geometry and post-Newtonian physics, untenable. Nor, incidentally, am I suggesting that he might resort to some other form of intellectualism: relying on Aristotelian *nous* or Hegelian Reason or the Popperian dismissal of the whole inductive context, to rescue the stranded probabilist. For none of these systems bears any relation to Hume's problem, and however one answers Hume, one cannot, or ought not to, ignore him.

In fact, then, Russell remains an empiricist but an unhappy one, who concludes:

> But although our postulates can be fitted into a framework which has what we may call an empiricist 'flavour', that is, by reference to animal inference, it remains undeniable that our knowledge of them, in so far as we do know them, cannot be based upon experience, though all their verifiable consequences are such as experience will confirm. In this sense, it must be admitted, empiricism as a theory of knowledge has proved inadequate, though less so than any other theory of knowledge. Indeed, such inadequacies as we have seemed to find in empiricism have been discovered by strict adherence to a doctrine by which empiricist philosophy has been inspired: that all human knowledge is uncertain, inexact and partial. To this doctrine we have not found any limitation whatsoever.[54]

Professor Braithwaite appears, in his *Scientific Explanation*, a more cheerful empiricist. He is just as explicitly as Russell a follower of Hume, taking as pattern for scientific laws Hume's constant conjunction model and showing with great care and precision how the much more sophisticated deductive theories of modern science can be cut to fit it. Moreover, he follows, more closely than Russell, Hume's mood in appraising the aims and success of science. Russell would like to think that scientists are trying to gain knowledge of nature, to understand something if only inaccurately and partially. It is this aspiration which leads him to contradict himself: for Hume's interpretation of science excludes the knowledge of anything, it excludes understanding with any degree of probability as much as it does certainty. But this does not worry Braithwaite. He is a pragmatic man, he makes on behalf of science no claim to knowledge, certain or probable; he takes for granted the Baconian principle that the purpose of science is 'to predict and control the future'. Now this view (as is clear, for example, from Braithwaite's own painstaking and painful argument on induction)[55] begs philosophic questions wholesale: so much so that once safely inside it one can proceed merrily without the sort of discomfort that faces Russell.

Yet Braithwaite too reaches a point at which the limits of Hume's position become apparent: here he too becomes uncomfortable—and his discomfort is just as significant as Russell's. It is this discomfort to which I want to call attention here. The difficulty arises in connection with probability statements and their role in science. The occurrence of statistical judgments in science, notably in quantum mechanics, has presented a peculiar problem for the 'constant conjunction' empiricist. All meaningful factual statements, which are after all just associations arising out of experience, must be confirmable in experience. Yet, by Hume's atomic principle, they are never really confirmed. The reliance of the empiricist is therefore not on such confirmation, but on its opposite, on Russell's 'shocks'. In other words, statements of fact can be *falsified*—and it is this possibility which is really the heart of the so-called verifiability theory of meaning or of truth. The laws of science are reliable because, if they were not so, experience would falsify them; we should be shocked out of them. This could happen, it is true, only at what one might call the sensory root of a theory; but it could happen. But no single experience can decisively and univocally falsify a statement of probability. Physicists assign a mathematical value to the probability that, under given experimental conditions, an electron will have such a location. Supposing it doesn't: the probability is unaffected. Braithwaite puts this by saying that the 'fit' of a theory to experience is looser for statistical theories.[56] One can also put it logically by saying that a probability statement asserts a disjunction: it says 'A is likely but non-A is possible', that is, 'A or non-A'. The occurrence of non-A cannot prove this disjunction false.

And of course the same want of shock–which *is* a shock to Hume's associative reflection on associative reflection–is apparent not only in the remote recesses of theoretical physics, but in all the statistical correlations on which both the natural and social sciences depend. What makes a correlation *significant*? Or, as Braithwaite puts it, what makes it sufficiently *wanting* in significance so that we can reasonably reject it? Not the fact that experience has shocked us out of it–or could shock us out of it. Doubtless experience would gradually wear us down if we constantly picked useless and disappointing correlations; but out of the infinite number available, how are we to pick 'significant' ones and avoid the others? Is it just a question of lighting upon a pretty, straight or curving graph instead of a wobbly one? But what have such irrelevant aesthetic considerations to do with 'predicting and controlling the future'? There are of course some statistical 'laws' like grading curves, to which, once we have set them up, we ourselves can make adjustments; but such self-referent systems are both exceptional and–in the 'control' they offer –trivial. Theoretical statisticians, notably Sir Ronald Fisher, the inventor of the 'null-hypothesis',[57] have worked hard at elaborating precise and 'objective' criteria for 'significance', and Braithwaite has worked hard at stating a criterion not unlike Fisher's, which he calls the 'k rule of rejection' for non-significant statistical hypotheses.[58] 'k', however, is a constant not discovered in nature, but *chosen*–as Fisher's figure of 5 per cent for the falsification of the null hypothesis is chosen. And 'k' may be chosen at one figure or another. The strictness with which we reject possible hypotheses will depend upon the 'k' we choose. Thus if we choose 'k' very large, we may reject hypotheses which it will later turn out (if somebody else chooses them) we ought to have chosen; and if we are more easy-going in our 'k' we may clutter up our minds with a lot of hypotheses of no use at all. Yet choose we must, says Braithwaite: and in choosing we must weigh the advantages accruing from the hypothesis if we do accept it against the chance that it is false. This choice we have to make, freely and responsibly: no gentle force of association can do it for us.

I shall not go into the mathematical aspect of Braithwaite's theory; but I think some light is shed on his view by the use he makes of the theory of games elaborated by von Neumann, which describes 'a rational policy for playing a general zero-sum two-person game.' Such a policy, Braithwaite says,

is, so far as the method for selection is concerned, exactly the same as the prudential policy expounded for selecting a strategy for preferring one statistical hypothesis to another. The prudential policy for this choice corresponds to the prudential policy for playing a zero-sum two-person game in which player B (corresponding to Nature) has a choice of only two possible moves and player A (corresponding to the scientist) has a choice of 2^{n+1} possible moves, where n is the number in the observed sample.[59]

Thus, in general, he continues,

> we can treat every problem of choice between m alternative statistical hypotheses H_1, H_2 ... H_m on the basis of the observation of n instances on the analogy of a zero-sum two-person game in which player A (the scientist) has the choice of m^{n+1} possible moves and player B (nature) the choice of m possible moves, and we may use any of von Neumann's mathematical methods or results which may be of service to us.[60]

To play this game with nature, moreover, we need not assume her intent to cheat us, but only our ignorance of her next move. With no anthropomorphic assumption of a Deus Deceptor, but with no hope of providential assistance either, we go ahead, indifferent to nature's caprices, to follow the prudential policy of maximizing our minimal gains.

We must notice, moreover, that this policy, devised for the problem-child statistical judgment, is really the one we have to follow for ordinary, old-fashioned unambiguous theories as well. Once we take statistical judgments into account, we assimilate 'universal judgments' to them as statements whose probability is 1 or 0: and all science, not only its statistical portion, assumes the character of a game between the scientist and nature. In fact, the purely predictive interpretation of science allows no other view: it is all a question of strategy.

A strategy, however, – and here is Braithwaite's embarrassment – has to be chosen, and it has to be chosen on the ground of evaluation of prospective advantages, of goods and evils: of, in Braithwaite's words, 'the sort of future we want'.[61] Thus we cannot avoid, he says apologetically, the intrusion of an ethical element into induction. This is, from Braithwaite's point of view, a sort of imprecision at the boundary: a rather disturbing but not *very* distressing intrusion of *oughts* where, strictly speaking, *oughts* ought not to be. Yet the grounding of induction in evaluation constitutes just as fatal a contradiction to Hume's associationism as does Russell's discovery of the non-empirical premises of an empirical theory of knowledge. Evaluation demands a responsible person to evaluate: choice demands an agent. But the *denial* of a more than associative person is, as we have seen, essential to Hume's system: indeed, it can be argued that it is the heart of it. In his zeal against zealots, his gentle anti-fanatical fanaticism, it was the theological and metaphysical person–for him the hated Calvinist puritanical person–whom he most of all wanted to depose. And so the practical as well as the (so-called) theoretical behaviour of the mind is shown to be passively, associatively formed by the habitual cohesion of pleasures and pains. Now this sort of utilitarian chemistry can perhaps–if one doesn't look closely–'account' for the everyday behaviour of people whose needs are obvious and 'natural'. But for the 'evaluating' of mathematical hypotheses, which depends on the very complex kind of appraisal involved in weighing alternative statistical judgments, the crude automatic calculus of pleasures and pains is glaringly insufficient. Such evaluations do not make themselves: the scientist has to make them. But who is he? A chain of associative mechanisms proceeding by habit–unable to stop, evaluate, and choose.

If, then, we follow through the speculative side of Hume's empiricism and try to find out what we know on empirical principles, as Russell does, we find the limit of this position in the acknowledgment of non-empirical principles which alone could make empirical practices meaningful. Or if we follow through, as Braithwaite does, the purely pragmatic aspect, we find in the light of the study of statistical method that we are not simply acting associatively, but are driven to make appraisals of significance, and are acting always on the basis of such appraisals. Thus empirical procedures, whether interpreted intellectually or pragmatically, are philosophically inadequate in the sense that they cannot on their own principles account for themselves. In both cases (i.e. both Russell's intellectual and Braithwaite's pragmatic interpretation) they presuppose an appraisal of significance, if not, as for Braithwaite, in the technical statistical sense then, as for Russell, in a broader epistemological context. But such an appraisal is, on the empiricist's own principles, nonsense. In one case it is the significance which is found wanting, and in the other the appraisal; yet both wants are lethal; nor are they, as we shall have reason to see, so far asunder as they may at first appear.

Meantime we can only conclude that empiricism followed through on its own principles leads to its own demonstration of its own inadequacy. In short, in the consistent and rigorous expression of Hume's principles we have achieved a null-point philosophy from which, within the Humean tradition, there is no egress. What path is left to us? To reflect afresh on the character of human knowledge, and in particular of the mind as knower–and so to accept Hume's challenge. For after confessing the profoundest difficulty of his own position: that his account of mind or person is 'very defective', he continues, in the paragraph from the Appendix already quoted:

For my part, I must plead the privilege of a sceptic, and confess that this difficulty is too hard for my understanding. I pretend not, however, to pronounce it absolutely insuperable. Others, perhaps, or myself, upon more mature reflection, may discover some hypothesis that will reconcile these contradictions.[62]

They will not discover such an hypothesis, however, within the framework which Hume's principles allow them.

5 Kant: The Knower as Agent

I

THE CONCLUSION OF THE PRECEDING CHAPTER AMOUNTS TO THE maxim: no knowledge without a knower. Purely passive contents of experience could not build themselves up into systems of knowledge, unless given shape and significance by the *person* whose experience they are. But classical empiricism, whether in its eighteenth- or twentieth-century version, possesses no theory of the person, and so breaks down as a theory of knowledge. It was this direction, indeed, that was given, or should have been given, to philosophy by Kant's Copernican revolution. Kant recognized in Hume's scepticism the logical conclusion of the attempt to derive knowledge from the mind's receptivity alone. If we try simply to list what comes *into* the mind from out there, as Locke had, in his half-hearted way, begun to do, we must finish with the negative conclusion of Hume: no knowledge, no general, systematic structure of information about the world, is or can be so derived. 'Things in themselves' do not get themselves conveyed somehow into our subjective experience. Let us try, then, Kant argued, much as, he supposed, Copernicus had done for the solar system, to revolve reality around the spectator instead of the spectator around reality. Let us ask what we as knowers contribute to the objectivity of our experience. By this reversal of direction, Kant believed, he could demonstrate the possibility of a knowledge which, on Hume's premises, had appeared beyond the reach of human minds.

Kant's task was made easier for him by his optimism about the uniformity of the human mind–an optimism which in fact he shared with the sceptic Hume. That ways of human thinking, or in Hume's terms, of human habit formation, might differ among themselves in important ways, neither Kant nor Hume imagined. On the other hand, Kant's task was made more difficult by the demand for *certain* knowledge, a demand which, again, he shared with Hume as with the major philosophical tradition. In looking for the mind's contribution to our knowledge of reality, he was looking for contributions in the form of *necessary* truths.

Kant's argument in the *Critique of Pure Reason* is one of the most obscure in the history of philosophy and at the same time one of the most instructive. It is obscure partly because of the tension character-istic of Kantian thought. His argument moves on the one hand through altering, as radically as he claims to do, the very direction of philo-sophical thinking, through probing adventurously into recesses of human thought which other thinkers seem to have left untouched. And at the same time his thought is as cramped and confined as even the most 'scholastic' of scholastic philosophers can ever have been by the demands of a 'technical' vocabulary, a rigid superstructure of artificial professional distinctions. Worse still, Kant himself is slovenly in the extreme in applying his own 'technical' terms: words in his hands fail to keep the strict meaning he has so solemnly given them. But Kant's argument is difficult not only because of this weakness on his part, because of his passion for schematizing, for multiplying technical phraseology, and then failing to use it consistently. It is difficult also for a good reason: that is, because, like most fruitful philosophical arguments, it moves on more than one level. That is at the same time why it is so instructive. For Kant is progressing dialectically through a nexus of interrelated questions in such a way that the implications of his questions, and their answers, open up vistas in a whole range of directions. If one once enters sympatheti-cally into the movement of Kant's critical thought, it may take one unexpectedly into some quite new direction of philosophical reflec-tion–and the points of entry and of further reflection are as many as Kant's readers. Kant, like Plato, is a philosopher who can be fruitfully interpreted anew by every generation, and every student.

What I want to do here is to look at one strand of Kant's argument in the first *Critique*, at what seems to me its central strand, to see if and how Hume's scepticism has been answered, or how we in turn must modify the Kantian synthesis to get *our* answer. When we have done this, we can look back at Hume's premises and see how we should revise them in the light of the lessons learned from Kant.

II

We must first keep in mind the starting points of Kant's philosophy, in the sense not of the questions he put, but, before that, of the beliefs he never doubted: they form the unquestioned framework of his inquiry. The philosophy for which Kant is famous is called *critical* philosophy; it questions the alleged power of the mind to know ultimate reality, and sets definite limits to the powers of reason to achieve knowledge. Kant was opposing to the dogmatism of school metaphysic, not indeed a scepticism like Hume's, but nevertheless a powerful critical analysis with what seemed to his contemporaries, and indeed to his successors, a devastatingly negative outcome. But this critical enterprise took place on the ground of certain accepted premises which he shared with more traditional thinkers, and the tenor of his criticism can be understood only on the ground of these unquestioned assumptions.

First, he never doubted the existence of God. Kant's religious background, his relation to the Pietist movement, is well known. The fact that he put paid, as he did, to traditional arguments for God's existence by no means makes him, where religion is concerned, a sceptical thinker. As he himself says in the introduction to the *Critique of Pure Reason*, he was clearing a space within the field of Reason in order to make room for faith. If fallacious arguments are used by clever scholars to defend religion, Kant believed, they cannot, indeed, shake the faith of the common man, but they can do harm by obscuring the secure, if more limited, truths which the human mind is genuinely fitted to understand. The arguments of Hume's *Dialogues*, which appear to the non-believer to dethrone traditional theism from our lives as well as from our minds, had for Kant no such issue. It has been shown that he had read the *Dialogues* before he composed, or at any rate completed, his own attack on the traditional proofs of God's existence; but for him it would have been both impious and impossible to uproot the faith in their creator from the hearts of men. Such faith, secondly, was not simply an addendum to the truths of reason: it was, for Kant, the necessary foundation of those truths. For he was entirely confident that the God in whom he, and all men, believed, had created man with certain fixed, inalienable endowments as well as certain inalienable weaknesses. We live, Kant believed, in two worlds at once: that is how God made us. We live as fallen creatures in the world of sense: we grasp the being of things not directly as an infinite mind would do but always through the mediation of appearance, the mediation of our perceptions of things in space and time. But at the same time, made as we are in God's image, we live in a supersensible world: we are in contact with ultimate reality at two boundaries of our lives. First, we 'know' absolute reality in the experience of duty, in moral experience. This experience, again, Kant never doubted to be uniform and unalterable in ordinary unspoiled 'natural' men. Respect for the inner, moral law, grounded in our 'knowledge' of ourselves as free, responsible agents: this was, he believed, a universal human experience which all men can recognize and acknowledge. Such 'practical' knowledge of morality, Kant insisted, is independent of faith, though it is supported by it in our hope of immortality and our confidence in God's goodness. Secondly, in faith itself, in our acknowledgment of God's existence, we stand as his creatures before the ground of our being and of all being. We cannot *know* him rationally and scientifically through demonstration and experiment as we know the laws of nature or the theorems of geometry; but we 'know' him in worship and prayer as creator and redeemer. And it is, in the last analysis, through this unshakeable faith that we can rest assured of the validity of our human powers, limited though they are. The one system of reason, through which we apply orderly rules to our perceptions and so make of them knowledge of the phenomenal world, and the one law of morality, through which we order our wills as responsible agents in the practical contingencies of life: these two aspects of our being are secure, each in itself, and in ultimate harmony with one another, because, as we believe, as even the fool in his heart believes, God made us so. Kant's critical arguments were intended to elucidate, never to obscure or cast doubt upon, the order and harmony of God's creation.

Further, the stability of the Reason God has given us was confirmed, for Kant, as for many of his contemporaries, by the recent achievements of natural philosophy. This parochial restriction, which identified the structure of *the* human mind with the structure of contemporary science, limited Kant's perspective in the theoretical sphere, much as his Pietist faith limited his conception of the problems of morality. Kant's insistence on the activity as well as the passivity of the knowing mind is the theme we shall be pursuing through the central argument of the *Critique of Pure Reason*. In both aspects, passive and active, however, the mind as he sees it is, in historical fact, the mind of a Newtonian scientist. The principles of Newtonian mechanics were, in his view, the principles of the human intellect as such. They were the rules by which the mind has always already organized experience. These principles, moreover, rested in turn on the foundation of uniform, Euclidean space and smoothly flowing measurable time. The Newtonian postulate of 'absolute true and mathematical space and time' indeed, Kant was to deny, but neither could he accept the Leibnizian conception of space and time as purely relational. If only as the universal form of our perceptions, Newtonian, that is Euclidean, space, and Newtonian time must remain as the groundwork of all human thought in so far as it can issue in knowledge. Thought not so grounded would be, for a human mind, empty speculation. I believe we must accept these historical limitations of Kant's philosophizing and try to see how, within and despite these limits, he develops an argument with implications reaching far beyond them.

Let us see, then, where the central argument of Kant's critical inquiry, so far as it concerns theoretical knowledge, arises and where it leads us.

III

The *Critique of Pure Reason* as a whole is directed to the problem: is a science of metaphysics possible? It was the failure of metaphysics to enter the steady path of a science which first set for Kant his critical problem. Seeking, as it is bound to do, the key to ultimate mystery, to the being of the world, of God, and of the self, human reason comes again and again to contradictory conclusions. Is the world finite or infinite? Is there a least part of matter or is matter infinitely divisible? Are all events determined by rigorous causal necessity or is there somehow causality also through freedom? Can we or can we not argue validly to a necessary being who is the ground of nature and of ourselves? From such conflicts it seems impossible for our reason to escape: to any argument on either side of these 'antinomies' there is an equally valid–and equally invalid–counter-argument. Yet we have by nature a deep-lying need to answer these vexing questions. Can we put these conflicts to rest and establish once for all a science of metaphysics, or must we be content, if not with total scepticism, at least with some restriction of our intellectual aspirations?

We can answer this question, Kant tells us, if we examine the sciences we *do in fact* have, and discover *the grounds of the possibility* of their existence as sciences. Then we can tell whether similar grounds exist for a possible science of metaphysics too. The preface to the second edition, of 1787, provides a useful starting point to show us how Kant set out the framework of his problem. That three branches of theoretical knowledge were securely and unalterably established, he was convinced. They were (1) logic, (2) arithmetic and geometry, and (3) the fundamental principles of natural science. In the case of logic, its character and even, it seemed to Kant, its content were established once and for all in the form given it by Aristotle. Since then, he says, logic has taken neither any retrograde nor any forward step: it seems to be complete. But for logic, he continues, this achievement was easy: it is the very narrowness of the subject which permitted its once-for-all formulation. Logic is concerned only with the pure *form* of thought. It 'abstracts' Kant says, 'from all objects of knowledge and their differences, and so in it the intellect is concerned with nothing but itself and its form'.[1] If, as Kant believed, the human mind is uniform and stable, this form once established will never alter. But, he continues, 'it was naturally much harder for reason to take the sure road of science when it had to do with objects'.[2] Thus logic, as propaedeutic, 'constitutes as it were only the vestibule of the sciences'.[3] When it comes to knowledge, in the sense of information about a given subject-matter, we do indeed, Kant argues, presuppose logic in our assessment of such knowledge, but we must acquire it 'in sciences properly and objectively so-called'.[4] Such sciences, however, in so far as they are rational, must contain some portion of *a priori* knowledge, that is of knowledge whose validation does *not* depend on the evidence of experience. Here Kant accepts Hume's sceptical conclusion about 'experimental reasoning'. All generalizations from experience, he admits, are probable only, and therefore, by Kant's criterion, they are *not* science. They are fumblings, guesses which have not the necessity, universality and certainty required for rational knowledge.

Kant puts this point formally in terms of the distinction between *analytic* and *synthetic* and *a priori* and *a posteriori judgments*. Following the traditional analysis of propositions, he takes it that every judgment, in other words, every assertion of a proposition by the mind, consists in uniting a predicate with a subject. All judgments can be analysed in the form: *S* is *P*. In some cases, 'P' is already contained in 'S'. For example, the judgment 'All bodies are extended' simply specifies in the predicate a characteristic already contained in the concept 'body'. A non-extended body, that is to say, a body which did not occupy space, simply would not *be* a body at all. Such a judgment Kant calls *analytic*. On the other hand, the judgment 'All bodies are heavy' adds to the subject 'body' a predicate, 'having weight', which was not contained in the concept 'body' itself. There could conceivably be (and are, in outer space), weightless bodies. Such a judgment, which adds to the subject a predicate not already contained in it, Kant calls *synthetic*. So far, so good. But as rational beings we make judgments, not arbitrarily, but for some reason. How do we *justify* bringing P to S to form the judgment 'S is P'? In the case of *analytic* judgments no justification is needed, for to assert that S is P in this way is merely to reassert a part of S. We do not need to look beyond the judgment itself, to consult practice, or experience, for its validation. All analytic judgments, therefore, are self-justifying; they hold good, of themselves, prior to experience, that is to say: *a priori*. Such in fact are all the propositions of pure logic. On the other hand, these judgments, though necessary, are trivial. They cannot in Kant's view form a substantive part of knowledge itself.

What about *synthetic* judgments? These, since they bring together a predicate and a subject not internally connected, need some validation from beyond themselves. The place to look for it would seem to be *experience*. Synthetic judgments, one would suppose, are *a posteriori, after* experience. And there is indeed a vast body of such judgments. But this is just where Kant's problem arises. They are all, Hume has demonstrated, guesses. It is custom and custom alone which impels us to unite with any subject a predicate found to pair with it in our past experience. Experience alone can generate only subjective compulsion, not rational necessity. But knowledge, to be knowledge, must be necessary, universal, rational. Hume's conclusion, in effect, therefore, is that there is no knowledge: for analytic judgments, stating the internal relations between ideas, are trivial; and synthetic *a posteriori* judgments, bringing ideas together by the mere force of habit, are not truly necessary but compelled by custom alone. If there is any knowledge worthy of the name, therefore, it must consist of a body of *synthetic a priori* judgments. Are there such judgments and if they exist how can they be justified? If we may not, for their validation, refer to some past experience, how can we justify, rationally and necessarily, bringing to *S* a *P* not analytically contained in it? If Kant can show *how* this happens in areas where, as he sees it, it plainly *does* happen, he can then discover whether it can happen in the field traditionally described as metaphysics, and so can answer his leading question: is metaphysics possible?

Where, then, are we to find synthetic *a priori* judgments which we can question as to their justification? *A priori* knowledge, Kant says, can be related to its object in either of two ways, two ways which distinguish the *theoretical* from the *practical* exercise of reason:

> . . this knowledge may be related to its object either as merely *determining* it and its concept (which must be supplied from elsewhere) or as also *making it actual*. The former is *theoretical*, the latter *practical* knowledge of reason.[5]

Here, however, we must also introduce a further distinction: between the *pure* portion of these *a priori* disciplines, and the balance of the science in question. The *pure* portion, 'however much or little it may contain', Kant says, is 'that part in which reason determines its object entirely *a priori*',[6] that is, with no admixture of empirical content. This part must be expounded first, he warns, in order to separate it clearly from the empirical content which may afterward be added. Thus in describing the pure portion of natural science, for example, Kant will include such principles as the conservation of substance or the law of causality, but not, say, the laws of motion. Movement has to be perceived; it is an empirical concept. And even though we may derive certain laws concerning it *a priori* from the initial, pure principles of natural science, we have to add empirical content, even though not empirical procedures, to our original principles in order to derive such laws from them. To know clearly what we are about, therefore, we must so arrange our exposition that we put the pure *a priori* first, then the further *a priori* judgments derived from these by the addition of empirical concepts. Otherwise, Kant admonishes us, we run into danger of confusing what is wholly *a priori*, the pure part of our science, with concepts derived from other sources. And this would be dangerous:

> For it is bad management if we blindly pay out what comes in, and are not able, when the income falls into arrears, to distinguish which part of it can justify expenditure, and in which line we must make reductions.[7]

We are here concerned, in the First Critique, with theoretical reason only; so we are looking for those areas in which pure reason *determines* its object prior to experience, not referring to experience to justify its judgments, nor, so far as is possible, using concepts derived from experience. Are there any such areas? Kant is convinced that there are two, one wholly pure, the other partly so:

> *Mathematics* and *physics* are the two disciplines in which reason achieves theoretical knowledge, and which have to determine their *objects a priori*, the former doing so quite purely, the other at least in part purely, but then also in accordance with sources of knowledge other than reason.[8]

How does Kant know for certain that these two 'pure *a priori*' fields of knowledge exist? The answer, as he gives it in the introduction to the second edition, in fact indicates clearly the direction in which his own 'Copernican' revolution has moved. Like all original thinkers, he sees the past in terms of the ideas which are in fact his own achievement. Compare, for instance, Kant's account of the past here with Descartes's. Descartes, at the beginning of his new enterprise in method, had pointed out that men have disagreed down through the ages about almost every subject, and therefore had only opinions, not knowledge about these matters. To this scene of universal confusion, only mathematics has formed an honourable exception. Why? Because in mathematics alone were men dealing with matters so simple that they could grasp them by means of clear and distinct ideas. Only for such limited and simple problems were they capable of acts 'of a pure and attentive mind', so clear that no doubt remained concerning the object of thought.[9] Descartes hoped to achieve the same clarity and hence the same certainty in a unified science, and in the first instance, in mathematical physics. By Kant's time, in turn, many people had come to believe, not perhaps that Descartes had succeeded, but that, in their somewhat different way, Galileo and Newton had done so: there was, or seemed to be, a science of nature possessing the same kind of completeness and certainty that was thought to obtain in mathematical knowledge. For Kant, therefore, there were two fields in which scientific certainty had in fact been achieved, and they were both recognizable by the abrupt cessation of disagreement, or, as Kant calls it, of groping or fumbling. Suddenly, in each case, the discipline in question had moved from the opinion-mongering, tentative stage to 'the sure path of a science'. But his account of *how* this happened is different from the Cartesian. Let us look at what he tells us about it.

For mathematics, the change took place already in antiquity:

> From the earliest times to which the history of human reason extends, among that admirable people, the Greeks, *mathematics* had already entered upon the sure path of science. But we must not think that it was as easy for mathematics as it had been for logic, in which reason is dealing with itself alone, to happen upon, or rather to build for itself, that royal road. On the contrary, I believe that it long remained, especially among the Egyptians, in the groping stage, and that the transformation must have been due to a *revolution* brought about by the happy thought of a single man in an experiment–an experiment after which the road that must be taken could never again be missed, and the sure path of a science was entered upon and signposted for all time to come and into the infinite distance.[10]

What was this unique 'experiment', so revolutionary in its results? It was the first geometrical *construction*:

> A light flashed upon the mind of the first man ... who demonstrated the properties of the isosceles triangle. The true method, he found, was not to inspect what he discerned either in the figure, or in the bare concept of it, and from this, as it were, to read off its properties; but to bring out what was necessarily implied in the concepts that he himself had formed *a priori*, and had put into the figure in the construction by which he presented it to himself.[11]

Thus it was the constructive achievement of ancient geometers which produced the certainty of their science, and which brought about the transformation from fumbling and guesswork to the straightforward, cumulative, undeviating course of true scientific knowledge. In short, what that great unknown discoverer discovered was that:

> if he is to know anything with *a priori* certainty he must not ascribe to the figure anything but what necessarily follows from what he has himself put into it in accordance with his concept.[12]

It is then, for Kant, not the direct, intuitive, Cartesian act of apprehension that transforms opinion into science, but the constructive activity of mind, which imposes on a material of its own an operation performed by itself.

For science the development, though slower, was similar:

> Natural science was much longer in entering upon the highway of science. It is, indeed, only about a century and a half since Bacon, by his ingenious proposal, partly initiated this discovery, partly inspired

fresh vigour in those who were already on the way to it. In this case also the discovery can be explained as being the sudden outcome of an intellectual revolution.[13]

Kant proceeds to enumerate some of the events which, in the experimental sciences, brought about this striking and irrevocable change:

> When Galileo caused balls, the weight of which he had himself previously determined, to roll down an inclined plane; when Torricelli made the air carry a weight which he had calculated beforehand to be equal to that of a definite column of water; or in more recent times, when Stahl changed metal into calx, and calx back into metal, by withdrawing something and then restoring it, a light broke upon all students of nature. They learned that reason has insight only into that which it produces after a plan of its own, and that it must not allow itself to be kept, as it were, on nature's leading-strings, but must itself show the way with principles of judgment based upon fixed laws, constraining nature to give answer to questions of reason's own determining.[14]

That, for Kant, is the lesson of intellectual history: that we have certain, universal knowledge, a fund of synthetic *a priori* judgments, only insofar as our mind contributes to nature the concepts through which we understand nature:

> Reason, holding in one hand its principles, according to which alone concordant appearances can be admitted as equivalent to laws, and in the other hand the experiment which it has devised in conformity with these principles, must approach nature in order to be taught by it. It must not, however, do so in the character of a pupil who listens to everything that the teacher chooses to say, but of an appointed judge who compels the witnesses to answer questions which he has himself formulated.[15]

Thus it is the constructive aspect of the experimental method to which physics, too, like geometry, owes its definitive revolution. Nature will answer only such questions as we ask her. True, we must not invent the answers; these, nature must provide. But she can provide nothing certain and stable except in terms of the questions we set and the conceptual scheme we provide to contain the answers. It was, Kant insists, to this insight, and to it alone, that physics owed its entry upon the high road of science, after so many centuries of mere random groping.

Here again, then, like Descartes, Kant sees science as having entered in modern times upon a new and revolutionary path, and, like Descartes, he sees this as a repetition of the similar achievement of Greek mathematics. Before, we had groping; now we have certainty. But this revolution, for Kant, was not the revolution of the clear and distinct idea, it was the revolution of the *synthetic a priori*: the revolution in which man, or a man, suddenly saw that he could be certain, in effect, *only about his own constructions*. Thus his historical sketch foreshadows both the questions he will proceed to ask and the lines along which he will give his answer.

From this historical excursion, let us return to the main line of Kant's argument. Apart from the formal discipline of logic, we have found two areas of securely established knowledge, *mathematics* and *natural science*. So we have to ask: (1) what are the grounds of the possibility of mathematics; (2) what are the grounds of the possibility of pure natural science, and (3) given these answers, is a science of metaphysics possible? These questions are answered in the three main sections of the *Critique*: (1) the Transcendental Aesthetic; (2) the Transcendental Analytic; (3) the Transcendental Dialectic.

The answer to the third question need not concern us here, at least not directly, nor are we concerned primarily with the answer to the first, for the aspect of Kant's argument which is germane in the present context is carried forward into the part of the *Critique* which answers the second question: how is pure natural science possible? It is in answering that question that Kant replies to Hume and in so doing revises the concept of *experience* itself so as to include a necessary reference to the mind's activity.

Let us see, in the larger context of the critical inquiry as such, how this comes about. All three questions are what Kant calls *transcendental* inquiries. This means: that given something we in fact have, we look for the grounds of the possibility of this given something. Three qualifications must be added to this general description. First, if we have A, and ask what X we must presuppose to make A possible, the X we discover will be admissible not 'in itself', but only *as* the ground of the possibility of A, and only as far as A reaches. We can never, in a transcendental inquiry, cut loose our presuppositions from that which they make possible and assert them unconditionally on their own. We may note in passing that this principle already prejudges the issue with respect to metaphysics: since we do not already possess a science of metaphysics as a fact, we could hardly establish its existence by this method. And Kant does in fact forego the hope of a scientific metaphysic in the traditional sense. What he does is to establish the transcendental principles of natural science as a metaphysic of a restricted kind: a metaphysic tied to the phenomena whose scientific study it makes possible and reaching only as far as they. But that is by the way.

Secondly, the presuppositions Kant is looking for in his transcendental inquiry are necessarily contributions by the *mind*. It is not some underlying substrate of nature we are seeking, but the structure of the human mind itself. It is this which constitutes Kant's Copernican revolution in philosophy: instead of turning the knower around the world, we change our direction and move the world around the knower. We ask: what Reason contributes to knowledge. As we have seen from Kant's historical sketch of the origin of mathematics and of natural science, it is only by this method that we *can* arrive at *a priori* knowledge. With our finite powers, and tied as we are to the mediation of sense for all our knowledge of reality, we cannot hope to come out of our own thought to the grasp of things as they are; but turning inward to the structure of reason itself we can analyse out and elucidate the principles which constitute the forms through which things appear to us as they do.

This is to say again, thirdly, that what we are asking is: how in certain fields *synthetic a priori* judgments are possible. Now every synthetic judgment, we have seen, brings to an 'S' a 'P' *not* inherent in it, and so what, in effect, we are asking is: by what right does the mind perform such syntheses? In *a posteriori* judgments, it is some particular experience or group of experiences which 'justifies' the synthesis. Yet this justification never achieves necessity. For synthetic *a prioris*, in contrast, there must be some 'third', that is a 'third' in addition to S and P, which will justify the synthesis *prior* to experience. We are tied to experience, to the phenomenal world. We cannot reach out to the essences of things in themselves to find our justifying third, nor can we pull it down from some far-off Platonic heaven of really reals. Yet no particular experience either will give us what we want. In the case of mathematics, Kant discovers in the Transcendental Aesthetic, it is the pure sensuous forms of space and time which provide the needed foundation. Thus the proofs of geometry, he argues, depend on the visualization of spatial relations: a visual presentation (*Anschauung*) prior to and underlying all experience. And the propositions of arithmetic depend on the operation of counting, which takes *time*: again, a *form* in which and through which our consciousness, prior to any given content, is always organized. These two passive contributions by mind, the spatial organization of all our perceptions and the temporal organization of all our awareness, whether in perception, imagination or feeling, are the *a priori* foundation, Kant finds, on which geometry and arithmetic come to rest.

There is, as I have already suggested, little to be said for Kant's view of mathematics. But that all our experience is temporally organized, and all our outer experience spatio-temporally organized, is both true, and essential as the cornerstone of Kant's further, and central argument. For the examination of the principles of pure natural science, in the Transcendental Analytic, moves from time as the form of inner sense *to* objects in space and time, exhibiting, in effect, spatialization not only as passive and sensuous but as the necessary product of conceptualization as well. The argument is a dialectical one, taking the passive forms of time and space established in the Aesthetic as the *terminus a quo* and the *terminus ad quem* of the investigation of the grounds of pure natural science. It is this argument which we must now examine and criticize.

IV

The synthetic *a priori* judgments of mathematics, Kant has argued, are made possible by reference to the media of space and time, the pure *a priori* forms of all our sensuous presentations. Experience, however, is not purely passive; our confrontation with reality, our grasp of it as it appears to us, but as it appears *objectively*, as an organized world of *objects*, is always mediated by concepts as well as presented through sense. It is made what it is, not only by the receptivity of sense, but by the activity of thought. Thoughts alone, Kant declares, are empty, percepts alone would be 'blind'. And the examination of his second question, how pure natural science is possible, is in effect an examination of the contribution of mind's activity to the constitution of an *objective* world, a world *of objects*. Thus the question: how natural science is possible, is also the question: how nature is possible, or how nature as experienced, how the experience *of* nature, is possible. It is, in fact, the principles of pure natural science which make nature possible.

But is not this a circular argument? Kant sets out to seek the grounds of the possibility of pure natural science, and what he finds is pure natural science as the ground of the possibility of something else, or even of two other things: of experience and of its objects. Yet conversely, just because it is the ground of their possibility, they in turn, justify it, and so are the grounds of its possibility, which we were seeking. That is so. All transcendental arguments are circular, yet not viciously so. They are comprehensive, exhibiting the all-embracing structure of the conceptual framework that constitutes our world. They come to the confines of that world and turn again inward upon themselves. They are not, strictly, proofs, but probings within a structure already given. They exhibit, not formal circularity, but the self-containment of an organized whole. In the present case, the circle involved may be further elucidated as follows.

The synthetic *a priori* judgments of mathematics were justified by reference to the forms of space and time. Those of pure natural science must have some similar referent, some 'third' to justify the subject-predicate syntheses in question. This cannot be some particular experience, nor can it be a 'thing in itself', to which, as finite minds, whose knowledge is mediated through perception in space and time, we have no access. What then is it? The 'third' which justifies the principles of pure natural science is a *possible experience as such*, or *all possible experience as such*. The principles of pure natural science are valid for all possible experience, and only for possible experience, because without them organized experience as experience of objects, would be impossible. But we do have such experience. And here is where the circle comes in. For in discovering how pure natural science is possible we are also discovering how *experience* is possible, since the principles of natural science which we have taken as given are in fact the principles which underlie and make possible experience. We could as well be inquiring, and are in fact inquiring, how *objects* as experienced are possible and discovering the principles of pure natural science as the ground of the possibility of the objects of experience. This is in fact the leading principle of Kant's investigation of the 'principles of pure understanding', that is, the principles of natural science: *The grounds of the possibility of experience as such are at one and the same time the grounds of the possibility of the objects of experience.*[16] On both sides it is, in Kant's view, the principles of pure natural science which constitute these 'grounds of possibility'. So they, as something we in fact have, are justified *by* their necessary existence as justifying something else we in fact have, namely experience as experience of objects. They are held validly prior to all experience and are valid for all objects of experience because without them experience would not *be* experience of objects at all. They are the contribution of mind's activity to objective experience; they legislate into being its objectivity.

Let us look a little more closely at the argument in which Kant shows how the activity of mind makes experience possible. The basic argument is that known as the 'Transcendental Deduction of the Categories'. Kant has already shown, in the Aesthetic, that the pure forms of space and time contain and determine, on the passive side, the way things appear to us. But our knowledge is always passive *and* active, sensuous *and* intellectual, at once. Kant now proceeds to examine the activity of mind, the range and limits of our powers of *reasoning*. In terms of his three initial questions, it is the principles of pure natural science that he is seeking. Principles, however, are judgments formed by uniting concepts; so he must first find his pure *a priori* concepts, if such there be. The search has two parts. First, Kant looks at the basic concepts offered by traditional logic, and with some readjustment contrives to find four sets of three, which he calls after Aristotle, *categories*. Kant was plainly fascinated by this neat cataloguing, and pursued it sometimes to absurdity. In the next part of the argument, however, he relaxes his grip on the rigid framework of the twelve, and seeks, in the Transcendental Deduction, to justify not these categories, but categories, in his sense, as such. He asks, in other words, about the possibility and nature of the mind's active contribution to experience in general, and lays the foundation for the more detailed argument on the principles of pure natural science, which the next section of the text will elaborate.

The Transcendental Deduction, in turn, has two branches, which Kant first states separately and then combines. These are the *objective* and the *subjective* deduction. Each argument has the characteristic transcendental form. The objective deduction asks: How is the experience of objects possible? The subjective: how is sense-perception possible? In each case it is a given, the experience of *objects*, or the subjective existence of *felt sensations*, which is the starting point; and the grounds of possibility Kant discovers will claim validity precisely for the range of the starting point, and no further. Let us look briefly at the two branches of the argument in turn.[17]

First, then, the objective deduction. Experience comes organized. We have before us and around us a complex and varied network of presentations, which retain in a stable and recognizable way their presented character. What holds this objective 'manifold' together? In the last analysis, simply the fact that all experience is *my* experience. The manifold of phenomena is integrated, synthetized, ultimately, through the fact that the whole complex is present to *one* consciousness. This ultimate unity Kant calls 'the transcendental unity of apperception', that is, of self-consciousness. It is, he argues, a bare fact: *that* I can turn in upon myself and 'see' that all my experience is held together as mine. What this 'I' is in itself, I have, through theoretical reason, no right to ask. This is the farthest point to which my transcendental inquiry can take me. To inquire further would be to cut off the inquiry from its root in experience, in the given manifold–to try to approach, through pure Reason, what is not given us through pure Reason. True, the phenomena are not given to Reason either. They are presented in sensation. But the forms of our sensation, space and time, are the passive contributions to experience of our own minds. Though passive, they are prior to the content of experience, since all experience is contained *in* them. And what Kant is adding now to this passive *a priori* is the organizing activity of mind itself: the fact that it is I who hold my experience together as mine.

But is that all there is to say? What sort of activity is it that is involved here? It is, Kant shows us, *rule-giving* activity. What the mind does to make experience possible is to order the manifold of sense in such a way as to *make* it an integrated, orderly manifold, a manifold of *objects*. And each rule the mind prescribes is a category, a pure concept valid before and for experience, but only for experience, since it is just the making possible of experience in one special respect that constitutes the category in question. So, for example, without the concepts of quantity and quality, we could not perceive objects as having specific dimensions or degrees of particular qualitative characters. Nor, without the concept of cause, could we see objects as connected in such a way as to inquire into their necessary connections with one another. The concept of cause, the principle of necessary connection, are presupposed in the very structure of nature itself. An uncaused object, an object that did not take its place in a regular series of determinate phenomena, would not function as an object within the context of experience. Things as they appear to us fall into place in nature as the things they are through our understanding of the causal relations between them. Similarly, without the concept of substance we could not find in our world stable and permanent entities on whose stability we could reckon as in fact we do. These are not, as Hume thought, concepts instilled in us, irrationally, by association and habit, which we then apply, habitually, but irrationally, to further experience. They are rules which we have always *already* applied. They are the built-in rules which make experience the stable, objective experience, the experience of a real world of objects, which in fact it is. The 'I' of the transcendental unity, itself a bare 'that', cannot indeed be filled in, metaphysically, to make a Cartesian 'thinking substance', but it can be and is articulated and filled in in its application to the manifold of sensuous presentation. It is the ultimate ground of the rules which are in turn the ground of the orderliness and objectivity of things as they appear to the unifying mind whose experience they are. The objects in space and time by which we find ourselves surrounded are *objects* not only as their images flow past in time or as their spatial appearances lie side by side 'out there'; they are objects because the human mind grasps them as such, because as a thinking being I have always already organized all appearances, all possible experience, under the categories, as quantified, qualified, systematically interrelated, and because, in the last analysis, all these aspects are aspects of the experience which is unified through being *mine*. Experience is not atomic but integrated, it is integrated because it is rule-governed, it is rule-governed because it is *constituted* the experience it is by the rules I have made for it. Again, nature does not simply call out to the knower information about her character and contents, but answers the questions he puts. Experience of objects is made possible by the mind acting through the agency of the categories, and the categories are, therefore, valid for all objects of experience, since without them such objects could not be thought.

The experience of objects, we conclude, therefore, has been structured as such by the rule-giving activity of mind. Is it then mind that makes the world? No, Kant emphatically opposes an idealist theory of nature. The appearances integrated through the categories are appearances *of* 'things in themselves', 'things' to which, however, we have no access *as* they are in themselves, but only as they appear to us. Thus, corresponding to the bare fact that all my experience is mine, the Transcendental Unity of Apperception, is the bare fact that there is that other reality, the surface of which the senses present to my consciousness. This other fact Kant calls, in the first edition of the *Critique*, the Transcendental Object = X. He abandoned this term in the second edition, and adopted the concept of 'a possible object of experience'. I do not believe, however, that this represents a fundamental change of view. The pin-point reference to *things*, rendered as 'possible objects of experience', is still the correlate of the bare fact that my experience is *mine*. True, Kant's argument, in the objective deduction, moves from the given presented manifold to the unifying agency of mind, but this point of synthesis refers the intuited manifold at the same time, and at the opposite pole of the structure, to the underlying reality, the Transcendental Object = X. Such an object cannot be *known*, any more than, in Kant's view, mind in itself can be known. But that there is something whose appearances appear is as necessary as it is that all those appearances are appearances to a consciousness whose experience they are. The whole structure can be visualized, as on the opposite page.

The *subjective* deduction concerns one half, the subjective half, of this spindle. Kant starts, this time, not from the *objective* manifold of experience out there, but from the inner flow of experience, from subjective time. Even this most subjective dimension of experience, Kant finds, is possible only through a prior imaginative synthesis, which in turn depends for its unity upon the unity of apperception. Only through the fact that all perceptions can be presented to one consciousness are they perceptions; even the subjective succession in inner sense depends upon this unifying activity, now taken as a unification of images rather than thoughts. Thus corresponding to the rule-giving activity of categorization we have also, and inseparable from it, a transcendental activity of imagination: an ordering of the sequences or concurrences of images, which must also always have preceded and must underlie any given aggregate of sense-impressions. Kant calls such image-ordering patterns 'schemata'. They are the work of the productive imagination, on which he will elaborate in the

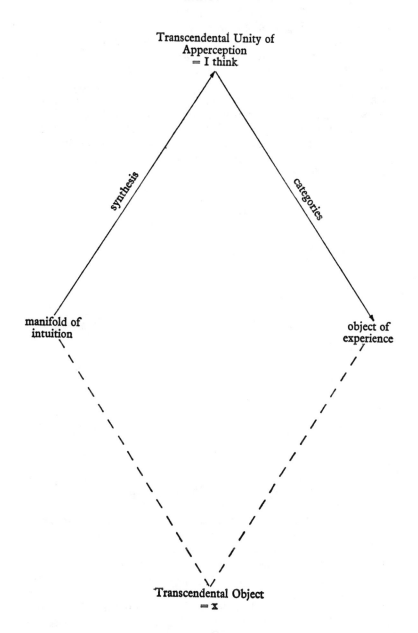

section on the Schematism. Their function is to mediate between the abstract rules of pure thought which are the categories and the purely passive medium of the inner sense. For the productive imagination *transforms subjective time into patterns in the medium of homogeneous time.*[18] (Or rather, in experience as we have it, it has always already done so.) Thus the pure concept cause, for example, operates as a schema of necessary succession; the concept substance, as a schema of permanence. A cause is what necessarily precedes its effect; a substance is what persists through qualitative change. The imagination actualizes these *a priori* concepts through channelling, patterning the flow of time. So we may add, for the subjective deduction, the further model:

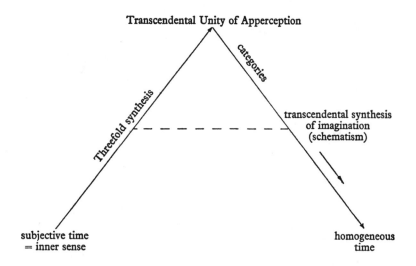

Third, Kant combines the two strands of the argument to show how the inner sense, the subjective flow of precepts in time, is united through the imaginative *and* intellectual syntheses of schemata and categories, held together under the unity of one consciousness. Thus, through the mediation of the schemata, the categories can be applied to objects of possible experience and take their place in principles of pure natural science valid for all possible objects of experience, that is, objects in time and space, in the objective, spatio-temporal world which their presupposition serves to constitute. This culminating stage of the deduction of the categories, combining the objective and subjective phases, completes the transition from time as inner sense, through the schematized patterns of homogeneous time, to space and time; it provides the underlying structure which Kant will amplify in the Principles. The spindle, to use our model again, now looks something like this:

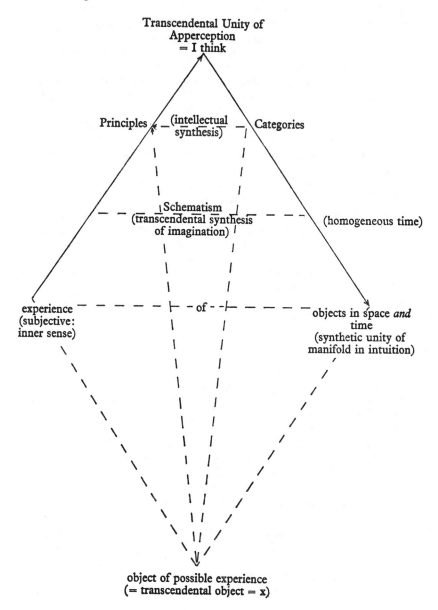

The *principles* are the *synthetic a priori judgments* Kant has been seeking, and the 'object of possible experience' is clearly the 'third' through reference to which they are justified as *a priori* syntheses. We cannot know things in themselves at all, let alone universally and necessarily, by *a priori* reasoning, but we can know, prior to experience, what is necessary, universally, to any possible object of experience as an object of experience. In the combined objective-subjective deduction this concept of any possible object of experience has replaced the transcendental object = X of the First edition objective deduction. But it has the same function. It is the minimal, pin-point reference to external reality which holds the structure together objectively, as the 'I think' holds it together subjectively. Though we cannot know things in themselves, we can and do know that what the mind, through the categories and the schemata, 'constitutes' is *something* given, an object, not literally a creation of our own. It can be presented prior to experience only as whatever can come into experience, a possible experience but nevertheless an *object* of possible experience. Even the inner sense, insofar as it provides awareness of 'self', functions, Kant believes, only in connection with and contrast to outer sense: the presentation of patterns out-there. Subjective and objective synthesis, and the existence of mind and thing which lie beyond them, are both presupposed in the total structure of experience. That is the solid objectivity which Kant's Copernican revolution, the turn inward to mind's activity, has produced. It is minimal, but indispensable.

V

We have now to ask three questions: (1) Has Kant met Hume's sceptical challenge? (2) How adequate, in our situation, do we find Kant's own theory? (3) How, finally, in the light of what our response to Kant's argument has taught us, should we receive Hume's empiricist premises?

First, Kant *vs.* Hume. Kant answers Hume's argument on cause explicitly in the section on the Principles, but the foundation of his answer is laid down in the Transcendental Deduction itself, and it is, on one level, a conclusive answer. In replying to the question, what makes experience possible, Kant has shown irrevocably that mind as agent shapes experience, that the whole empiricist image of experience as purely passive was mistaken. Hume had taken Locke's plain historical method through to its logical conclusion and thereby reduced it to absurdity. Kant has shown us the changed direction necessary for a more adequate analysis of the experience we do in fact have. We must take into account the mind's own activity, and when we do so, we find this activity itself indispensable, not simply for the subjective flow of experience but for its formal structure as experience of objects. There could not be even Hume's gentle associative force working on the items of experience were it not for the rule-giving agency of mind. Hume admitted that he lacked a theory of mind, but wanting this he did not even have, in fact, a theory of experience. Experience is inconceivable without synthesis, and synthesis is something more than an aggregate of isolated or isolable atoms of feeling: it results from the co-operation of sense with *thinking*. But thinking in turn is something minds do, not, as Hume must make it, merely a dimmer facsimile of sense. The deepest root of Hume's scepticism, I have argued, lies in his want of a theory of the person, and similarly, the heart of Kant's answer to him lies, not so much in the specific arguments on cause, as in his demonstration that the existence of mind as agent is presupposed in the very analysis of experience itself.

Kant's primary aim, on the other hand, in the Transcendental Analytic, was to justify the existence of pure natural science in the sense of a body of synthetic *a priori* judgments constitutive of nature as it appears, and must appear, to the human mind. It was through this aspect of the argument and its consequent application, with purgative effect, to metaphysics, that he hoped to steer a middle course between Hume's scepticism and the dogmatism of the ontologists. In this, his explicit purpose, however, he has been less than successful. First, the actual principles he establishes are, we have admitted, historically bound by the eighteenth-century veneration for Newtonian mechanics. Secondly, the ideal of one unified once-for-all body of human knowledge is false. Kant himself has argued in the Antinomies that we can never know the totality even of the world as phenomenal, and if all our knowledge is partial it is always selective and always subject to revision and correction. What Kant has shown is that there are always some *a prioris*, some categorization by mind, at the basis of any experience of or within an organized world. But to have refuted Hume in the way he wished—to have restored the necessity and ultimacy of natural knowledge—he would have had to demonstrate that the system of categories and principles is *the* system characteristic of all human minds everywhere and forever. In this proof we must admit he was unsuccessful, and if it is a question simply of necessity *versus* contingency or certainty *versus* conjecture, then Hume was right and Kant mistaken. Hume was unable, Kant has rightly shown, even to establish a theory of experience, of empirical reasoning; but the completed unique set of synthetic *a prioris* he hoped to have justified against Hume he has not succeeded in vindicating as he thought he had done.

We can see this better if we look once more at Kant's alleged solution of his problem and consider how we should need to revise it. Leaving the reference to Hume, then, let us ask our second question: what lessons shall we say we have learned from Kant's theory of knowledge?

We have learned, first, to recognize in the structure of experience an active together with a passive contribution of our own: we have learned to see experience as the issue of our receptivity and our intelligence working together. We have learned that there is no experience except as shaped by mind's activity. We have learned, secondly, that concepts are rules for the ordering of experience. We must not look for some underlying substrate of our perceptions distinct from them to account for the orderliness and knowability of things, but look rather to the operations of mind on its data as the source of order. We have learned, finally, that the unifying principle of conceptual activity resides in the unity of consciousness, and that this subjective unity is the correlate of the objective unity of appearances themselves. These Kantian lessons are part and parcel of our philosophical heritage. We can neither revert successfully to a naive empiricism nor transcend such an empiricism without paying heed to Kant's argument.

Yet neither can we accept Kant's argument as it stands. We could perhaps abstract from its historical, Newtonian limitations and from its overschematic logicizing framework. But there is still one question we should have to ask, one question, the answer to which demands a fundamental transposition of the Kantian Analytic to another co-ordinate system, or to use Mrs. Langer's metaphor, to a new key.

The crucial question is this: what *is* the 'transcendental unity of apperception', the 'I think' which unifies all phenomena and makes the categories and principles and, through them, experience possible? It is a bare fact of which we can know no more than that, just as we can know of the objects of experience 'in themselves' no more than that they are objects of possible experience. The self as such is unknowable. All we can know in empirical psychology is the contents of inner sense, the succession of items of awareness–the succession of Hume's impressions, in fact. It makes no sense to ask Kant: *who* is knowing? The 'knower' is intelligence as such appearing as the bare fact of a unifying consciousness. It makes no sense to ask Kant, how knowledge is *communicated*. There is for him no problem of communication, no fact of communication. There is simply mind, as active, organizing through categories, mind on its passive side receiving sensations through the media of space and time.

Yet knowledge for Kant is an *activity*. What makes the inner flow of sense impressions and the outer phenomenal world a unity, what makes objects objective is the activity of mind. But human activity, activity of any living thing, if in lesser degree, presupposes an agent. The activity of mind is not like the 'activity' of a strong acid, it is not a bare event, but a *doing*, and it must be done by *someone*. And some one is always some one in particular, born somewhere at some time of some parents, possessing some innate aptitudes, moulded somehow by the setting of his family, society, time. The Kantian agent, however, the I of the transcendental unity, is an agent with no identity, no individuality, no destiny. It is *I* in my concrete historical situation who aspire to know. Apart from the problems that have puzzled *me*, the principles or maxims or ideas through which I interpret their solutions, 'mind's activity' is an empty phrase.

Why did Kant leave the 'I think' so empty? The nearest he came to seeing the task of human knowledge in terms of human destiny, of finitude, Heidegger argues in his book on Kant, was in the passage on the Schematism.[19] Kant describes productive imagination as 'a hidden power deep in the human soul': had he plumbed this depth, Heidegger asserts, he might have come to a fuller grasp of *what* the individual is who makes experience fit his categories, or makes categories to make possible the objectivity of his experience. Caught in the trap of his formal terminology and frightened by the danger of his own insight, says Heidegger, Kant turned back from this 'hidden power' to the elaboration of his over-formal but seemingly safer system. It is true that the Schematism, with its theme of *imagination* organizing *time*, can provide a clue of unique philosophical significance for a twentieth-century philosopher. But Kant himself could not have pursued this double clue in his own philosophical situation, and that for two reasons. First, as Collingwood has pointed out, even the historical conceptions of the Enlightenment were not essentially historical.[20] History was a painted scene on which figures moved, but the conception of man as an essentially historical being was yet to come. We *are* the upsurge of time, and creative imagination, which moulds the present and even the vision of the past out of futurity, out of its projection of what we long to be, of what we believe we ought to be–creative imagination through which we shape the time that we are: this is our most essential gift. Looking back at Kant's argument from where we stand, we can see that this is so, and that, Janus-faced thinker that he is, he *almost* knew it. But he was nevertheless a man of the Enlightenment and could not know it.

Secondly, Kant was still a Cartesian dualist. He was too good a Newtonian not to be so. And only a radical break with Cartesianism can enable us to see the concreteness of life in nature and in mind, and so bring mind and nature together, not only within the closed circle of the Transcendental Deduction, but in historical reality.

Let me exemplify and expand both these points.

VI

With respect to the historicity of knowledge, Kant's own account of the history of science neatly illustrates his error. He distinguishes, as we have seen, between the 'groping' characteristic of the pre-history of a science and the 'sure path' of a science once entered upon. Two points should be noticed about this. First, many, perhaps even most scientists, while recognizing the pre-scientific stage of their history, would abjure the claim to certainty of their theories once the science itself has come into being. They would, in fact they must, admit that scientific theories have, logically, never more than a claim to the status of high probability. This may be equivalent to practical certainty, but it is never either logical or ontological necessity. Secondly, the sure path itself, once embarked on, is by no means so rectilinear as Kant believed. True, many, perhaps even most scientists still wish to retain the model of uniform advance for scientific knowledge once a given field has come to be scientifically investigated. Yet this is itself one of the last illusions of the Newtonians' 'new mechanical philosophy', and that it is so is plain from Kant's own account. If the advance of natural science were as straightforward as Kant believed, the examples he gives of its initiation would have to belong to this area of uniform progress. But do they? On the contrary: one of the three instances he refers to serves for modern historians of science precisely as the arch-example of the ways in which scientific conceptions may *mis*lead and may even lead to new truths *by* misleading. That is, course, the example of the phlogiston theory:

> when Stahl changed metal into calx, and calx back into metal by withdrawing something and then restoring it, a light broke upon all students of nature.[21]

The theory that a combustible material contained in bodies is given off when they burn was, in terms of ordinary experience, a reasonable one, and it led, with Stahl and his successors, to experimentally verifiable results. The theory, well-grounded in experiment, seemed at the time to put chemistry on the sure path of a science, just as Galileo, with his inclined plane, had done for dynamics. The story has been told in detail by Conant in his *Case Studies*; one of the examples that he mentions illustrates well the way the theory 'worked'.[22] Professor Williams of Harvard demonstrated to his classes the existence of phlogiston. He burned a combustible substance in a closed retort until burning stopped. This shows, he said, that the air in the vessel is now saturated with phlogiston. We would say that the oxygen in the vessel was exhausted. But as far as Williams' experiment goes, the 'facts' are explicable on either theory. Just so did Priestley's mice hop about gaily when the bell jar was full of 'dephlogisticated air' or lie down and die when it was full of phlogiston. True, when Lavoisier had established that in combustion the resulting substance weighs more than the original material, supporters of Stahl's theory had to postulate that phlogiston had 'negative weight'. This was not, however, simply 'unscientific' practice; it was the normal procedure of scientists who assimilate anomalous phenomena to an otherwise powerful framework rather than abandon the whole theory when some one phenomenon seems to resist explication on its own grounds. As Thomas Kuhn has shown in his *Nature of Scientific Revolutions*,[23] this is the way, in the practice of 'normal science', that 'paradigms', or conceptual frameworks, always operate. Not only given theories, but the whole 'set' of a particular science in a particular period moulds the way its practitioners see both their problems and the solutions of those problems. But one such set may collapse, as the phlogiston theory did, and a new paradigm arise to take its place. No paradigm, no theory, no network of scientific values can ever be established once for all.

The modern view here is in an important sense still Kantian. It is the case, Kant and others like him would insist, that nature answers only our questions, that the way we see the world enters essentially into the theories in terms of which we interpret it and into the 'factual' statements we make about it. All 'facts' of scientific interest are theory-laden. But no theory in any field is ultimate. Paradigms, though they begin, as Kuhn has shown, in revolution, become the repositories of tradition, and they grow and change and decay as all traditions do. Or, in Kantian terms, synthetic *a prioris* change. In Kant's scientific history there is only one eventful, one really historical period for each science. Human reason is, for him, essentially unhistorical. Once it finds its way, the road, as Kant says, can never more be missed. That is what we must deny. Science is no more exempted from historical development, from historical change–from temporality–than is any other human activity. Scientists as much as the rest of us are 'the upsurge of time'. The Newtonian paradigm itself on which Kant's vision of a unified Reason so firmly rests has given way to relativity on the one hand and quantum-mechanical complementarity on the other. Even mathematics no longer exhibits the Kantian sure path in the simple way in which it formerly seemed to do.

History, in other words, comes first, in a way in which–given the primacy of history–a man of the Enlightenment could not have seen that it does. To this it will be, and has often been, objected that such a view is subjective and irrational, that it puts what blindly happens ahead of logic, substitutes caprice for reason, inner commitment for impersonal truth. This objection must be met, I believe, by an *aye* and *nay*. If I say that there is no grasp of truth apart from the historical situation of the aspirant to truth, I do indeed inject into the cognitive situation a risk of irrationality. I admit that there is no ultimate, unquestionable criterion by which truth can be recognized and labelled and stored away forever apart from human aims and interests. And human aims and interests *can* always go astray, they *can* be 'merely' subjective, 'merely' commitments to what is not. Our cultural heritage comprises, as Polanyi remarks, 'the sum total of everything in which we may be totally mistaken'.[24] That is the risk inherent in being alive, whether as a steeple-chaser, a painter, a parent, or a scientist. But in the search for knowledge, it is nevertheless truth, not subjectivity, that we are after, and if we may be wrong, we may also be right, although we can never know for certain that we are so. In fact, that we are right is precisely what, in every venture, we have gambled on, whether we gamble our money, our time, our loves, or our lives. Granted, the primacy of history puts reason in jeopardy; that is what it is to be 'in situation', and that is where we are. But the primacy of history does not contradict, or abolish, reason. It exhibits the risk of reason, not its non-existence. Logic and situation, the ideal and the factual, reason and history, live as aspects of our lives in tension with one another, in ineradicable ambiguity. They are indissoluble but opposed forces in our fundamental orientation in the world, essential contrarieties, like, in Heraclitus' words, 'the bow or the lyre'.

We have found, in our critique of Descartes, a similar ambiguity in the relation of mind and body. They are not the same ambiguity, but neither are they wholly unrelated. Or at least, the reluctance of philosophers to accept the primacy of history often springs from the (historical) fact that they have not yet wholly overcome, in the grounds of their thinking, the dualism of Descartes, and the concept of wholly explicit knowledge, the concept of the infinite blackboard, that goes with it. Therefore they still seek a pure and independent Reason exempt from the hazards of life.

VII

This brings me to the second reason why Kant could not carry through his insight, in the Schematism, into the historicity of man.

What Cartesianism prevents, in the last analysis, is the mediation between mind and nature through the concept of *life*. True, other living things do not have histories as we do, but neither is human history, or human being as historical, intelligible except on the ground of, in the medium of, an understanding of human being as *alive*. The Cartesian image of thinking mind over against dead nature makes impossible the understanding of man as historical, of human achievement, including the achievement of knowledge. Knowledge as an activity of persons, as something we strive to do, and succeed, or fail, in doing, is beyond the Cartesian's ken. And in the opposition of mind to merely inorganic nature, Kant was still a Cartesian thinker.

True, he was not by any means a simple *bête-machine man*. Living things, for him, eluded the self-sufficient certainty of 'pure science'. They held mysteries which science could not exhaust; there would never be, he said, a 'Newton of a blade of grass'.[25] Such a concession Descartes would not have made. But nevertheless this is a peripheral concession. Kant's conception of natural knowledge remains fundamentally a conception of the exact, mathematicizing knowledge of the inorganic world.

Consider, first, where the references to biological knowledge come in his work. The *Critique of Judgment*, in which organic phenomena are explicitly dealt with, is late. It is in the *Critique of Pure Reason* that Kant deals with the central problem of knowledge: the critical question, what can I know? and here living nature is referred to, except in passing analogies (Reason as an organism and the like) only in one portion of the second part of the main body of the work, in the section of the Dialectic called the 'Transcendental Ideal'. The Dialectic, however, is the part of Kant's argument which deals with the *illusions* of reason, the paths which, admittedly, our minds cannot help pursuing but which never lead to *knowledge*. The study of the constitutive principles of knowledge, the Analytic, concerns the foundations of Newtonian science, the knowledge of inorganic nature, alone. Living things come in for treatment therefore only in connection with the merely regulative ideas of Reason. These, Kant says, are subjective in origin rather than objective. That is, they provide *maxims* which guide the mind in its search for explanations, but they provide no laws, no substantive principles, establishing the nature of the *object* investigated. In other words, we can *know* nothing about organic phenomena as such *except in so far as they are physical and not organic phenomena*. The only objective principles in science are the principles of mathematical physics.

The chief problem Kant is dealing with when he does come to speak of living things in the *Critique of Pure Reason*, secondly, is the problem of classification. Now this is indeed a problem which did deeply concern eighteenth-century naturalists; yet Kant, it seems to me, comes to it here, not as a thinker interested in living nature, but so to speak sideways. His discussion occurs in the section called 'The Transcendental Ideal' where he is attacking the traditional metaphysician's claim to have established a *system* of the universe. It is in this context that the problem of classification claims his attention. Species and genera would be the building bricks of an ideal system of Being, were there such a system. The first examples he mentions, indeed, are kinds of minerals and stones rather than plants and animals. It is system as such, not living nature, that he has primarily in mind. In fact one may say that up to Darwin organic phenomena were in the main an embarrassment to philosophers or to mechanically minded scientists. There is no place in the Cartesian universe for differentiation of kinds except as the diversity of design of machines, which stand ontologically on a single plane. These are either made by a good God with greater lavishness than seemed necessary, and so a Leibnizian pullulating diversity of life distracts us from the simple clarity of a two-substance world; or they must have got themselves there somehow, by some undreamt of mechanical trick. That is what Darwin was to make plausible and so to bring life at one blow into the horizon of the machine view of nature. But this solution was for Kant not yet available.

Meantime, therefore, thirdly, living things assume an ambiguous position in the Kantian universe. The characteristic formula in which Kant describes them both in the *Critique of Judgment* and in the incidental references in the Transcendental Ideal is as complexes of 'reciprocal means and ends'. Every structure in an organism may be analysed *as if* it were both means and end. Again note, we are here not in the range of certain knowledge but of mere 'as if' principles; but further this very conception of the living being is still in effect Cartesian. It is *machines* that are so arranged that each part has its function relative to every other. There are the machines we make and the much more cunning machines contrived by God. Yet at the same time talk about functions of parts is talk about ends or seeming ends, and scientists are not supposed to talk about ends at all. This (pending Darwin's assimilation of function to the mechanistic vision) is disturbing. So organisms are put off to one side for special consideration, in the *Critique of Judgment*, along with the equally puzzling phenomenon of beauty.

In his definitive argument on the nature of scientific knowledge, however, we are thus justified in concluding, Kant is not concerned with living nature at all. The Transcendental Analytic, Kant's most incisive and influential contribution to philosophy, simply does not include the sphere of organic phenomena. He talks about natural

science and *means* the science of non-living nature; he talks about
objects of experience and means objects spread out in space as
distinct from mere internal perceptions: the variety in significance,
character or performance of such objects, whether they are chairs or
children, planets or pigeons, baboons or billiard balls, simply does
not come into the question at all. It has often been objected to Kant's
analysis of knowledge, and rightly so, as I have argued, that he
confined his perspective to Euclidean geometry and Newtonian
physics. But no one so far as I know has objected to the range of
Kant's argument in the Transcendental Analytic on the ground not
simply that it is directed to Newtonian physics, but that it is directed
in any sense to the knowledge of physical objects only. Physics,
Newtonian or otherwise, is not by any means co-terminous with
natural science as a whole. In other words, the nature Kant is dealing
with in the main argument of the *First Critique* is still extended
matter, Cartesian nature reduced to the status of appearance. And
equally the minds we can know, according to Kant, in empirical
psychology, are Cartesian minds similarly reduced. There is nothing
alive in this world except the purely subjective data of inner sense;
and it is plain in the Principles that Kant's chief concern is not even
with these but with the out-thereness of the physical world. He is
asking: what makes experience of objects possible; and the taking-
off place for this inquiry is the subjective sequence of inner impressions: even these would be impossible, he argues, without the imposition of those rules which at the same time make objects possible.
But the objects so constituted, the objects whose knowledge is
secured against Humean scepticism are the bare, inorganic objects
of the Newtonian world. The encounter with plants and animals
which is the first foundation of the biologist's knowledge is missing
altogether from the primary range of experience Kant treats. The two
things which filled Kant with reverence, he confessed, were the starry
heavens above him and the moral law within—not hydra nor homun-
culus nor any of the myriad forms of life revealed to the new micro-
scopes; nor the orang, the mild human-seeming Forest Man in whom
naturalists and voyagers delighted. No, it was the orderliness of dead
nature and the aspirations of human inwardness that moved Kant to
philosophize, and the place of man *in* nature interested him little if at
all.

Let us look once more at the historical context of this fact. The
Cartesian world machine lies at the foundation of Newton's great
synthesis. There is an extended physical universe, and there are minds
fit to know it, and God who made it and nothing else. But how can
we know something so different from ourselves as this great mass
of spread out stuff and the laws it follows? Descartes was confident

enough in the power and goodness of God and veridicity of the mathematical mind to see in this strangely divided world no insuperable gap between known and knower. In fact it was confidence in mathematical method that impelled his whole enterprise. But in Newton, Bacon's inductivist emphasis joins hands with the mathematician's—and theologian's—optimism; and the obvious incompatibility of these two leads ultimately to Hume's scepticism about knowledge. The mind (though who knows what it is?) still somehow mathematizes in itself: internal relations of ideas provide certain if trivial judgments—and the phenomena themselves on the other hand somehow succeed one another so that by custom-grounded guesswork we get into the way of finding our way around them. This is neither Cartesian knowledge nor Newtonian knowledge; it is, for the seeker after certainty, no knowledge at all. Let us, therefore, Kant in effect is saying, renew the Cartesian duality on a safer basis. We cut off both mind and body from their roots in substance and think simply of their modifications as we meet them in experience, inner or outer. What Kant does in his central argument, then, is to start from inner sense, the remainder, for Theoretical Reason, of the Cartesian mental substance, and show that the very same concepts which this minimal inner experience already presupposes are the concepts which must also be presupposed to make possible outer experience: the awareness of objects persisting, ranged alongside one another, causally related to one another, in space as well as time. By reference to *a priori* principles which are in effect the principles of Newtonian physics, experience in here becomes experience out there, and so the two sides of the Cartesian dichotomy, both purged of metaphysical dogmatism, are united to one another in the self-justifying circle of transcendental argument. But it is still within the limits of the Cartesian universe that this whole argument takes place. There are inner experiences which no longer add up to a thinking substance, and outer experiences that no longer add up to extended things in themselves. But these are united by the fact that subjective experience takes on objectivity through the active imposition of categories by the mind. So the unity of knower and known is restored through the mutual reference of categories, which are pure mental concepts, and of objects to one another. And within this circle all is well. The categories and principles are valid for all experience because all experience, inner as well as outer, pre-supposes them.

But, let us ask once more in conclusion, what sort of situation is this? What is known is still mere spreadoutness, the matter studied by Newtonian mechanics and dynamics, not the full range of nature including plants, animals and men, the organisms themselves whose achievement knowledge is. These we cannot know. For what is the 'mind' that knows this limited reality? For Kant, as we have seen, it is one of two things. Either empirically, in inner sense, it is Hume's succession of impressions: a purely subjective temporal stream of consciousness; or, behind this, 'transcendentally'–what? A small point: the bare fact that all my experience is organized as mine, no more. But knowledge is an achievement of living beings, a mode of living: a theory of knowledge which tells us nothing about living things can tell us nothing really about knowledge itself. If knowing is something we, as discourse-endowed animals, do, to know about knowing is to know about a certain kind of living, and every theory of knowledge directed, as both the Cartesian and the Kantian are, to the knowledge of non-life thereby eliminates itself as its own object. Descartes has protected himself on this count through his insistence on the separate, thinking, purely intellectual nature of mind. And Kant has protected himself by the limitation of his inquiry to the structure of appearance. Yet in each case the question arises for *us*: who is it that is knowing? Descartes answers plainly enough: a thinking substance. But what is that? If the 'breath' or 'vapour' of traditional physiology was, as Descartes insisted, an unclear concept, Cartesian thinking substance is for most of us meaningless altogether. For what we know as ourselves and encounter as other persons is plainly body-bound. If there were what Aristotle called separate substances, substances not embodied, they would not be the sort of thing we know ourselves to be: they would be unchanging somethings situated in the Aristotelian emyrean, not learning or erring as our minds clearly and essentially do. No, the act of insight on which Descartes squarely rests his method is the act of a person, and that means a living, historically embodied person.

Thinking substance in its full Cartesian independence Kant has already exorcized. Ourselves as substances he makes it quite plain in the arguments of the Paralogism we cannot know. But, again, knowledge for him is an activity: what makes the inner flow of subjective impressions and the outer phenomenal world a unity, what makes objects objective, is that the mind has imposed rules, forms, order upon experience. Not reference to some hidden unknown substrate but reference in the other direction to the mind's activity accounts for the objectivity of our knowledge. So knowledge for Kant as much as for Descartes, even more emphatically so, is activity; its possibility depends in the last analysis on forms imposed by mind, and what these depend on finally is the I that carries as self-consciousness all the concepts of consciousness. For any given cross section of experience, the intellect has always already shaped the manifold of perception to make it experience, objective experience; and the culminating, unifying point of this rule-making activity is the fact that *I* do it, *I* have done it. But, again, who and what is this I? In the sphere of theoretical knowledge no one can say. The known is tied securely to the knower, but the knower is himself a mere question mark, not an existent puzzled living person–the sort of entity for whom the achievement of knowledge would be a possible goal. All of philosophy, Kant said, deals with one branch or another of the single question: what is man? Yet the likeness and the difference of man from other existences can be discovered, one would think, only if we admit as framework for our inquiry the full range of living things we know of and signal out the peculiarity of man within them. How can we know what man is if we restrict knowledge to non-living nature and so eliminate man himself, knowledge and all, from the object we are concerned to know?

Man as historical person, rooted in man as living organism in a world of living organisms: only this double paradigm can give us a conceptual frame within which the activity of the knowing mind can be adequately understood. The knower is not simply the Transcendental Unity of Apperception, but myself, with my endowments, limitations, hopes, disappointments. It is a full, historical, not a mere logical 'I'. And this transformation given, the object of possible experience, the Transcendental Object = X, becomes itself clearly the *real* reality. It is things in themselves I *aim* at knowing, even though I can never know for sure that it is things in themselves I have, in any given solution of any given problem, come to know. I can never know reality except through my own categorization, my own interpretation. And I can never know it as a whole. Yet in every cognitive situation, it is I as an historical person, trained, well or ill, in this discipline, in this tradition, who am striving to know, and it is some aspect of things as they are which, 'X' though it be, is the goal of my endeavour. Even for Kant, as Lindsay pointed out, the knowledge of nature if complete would be no knowledge.[26] Kant identified knowledge with mathematically expressed knowledge; but fully mathematicized knowledge of events would provide no distinction between events, and so no reality to be known. Thus, Lindsay argues, full knowledge of reality is for Kant necessarily a limiting concept, a *Grenzbegriff*. But the reality to be known, the thing in itself, is for Kant not a limit*ing* concept but a limit-concept, in that it is *outside* the sphere of intelligence altogether. For us, on the other hand, it is a limit to be asymptotically approached, though never fully or certainly attained. The knower is the knowing person, in hazard, gambling on making contact with reality, and the reality he seeks contact with is the real world, though for ever eluding his ultimate, self-sufficient, systematic grasp.

VIII

Finally, in the light of our reflections on the Kantian critique, let us return briefly to Hume and ask how, from a post-Kantian perspective, his principles appear to us.

First, the Genetic Principle. This we must deny. There is no idea which is simply copied from a simple impression. The experiencing organism has always already added something. To make this denial is to reassert Kant's criticism of the empirical method: it is to say, with Kant, that the question of the genesis of ideas is not the same as the question of their validity. There is always involved in the content of the mind, from perception all the way to mathematical knowledge, something more than the items which we could count up if we really went back to the history of our thought as the progressive filling in of a *tabula rasa*. And it is this something more which makes ideas meaningful, which makes experience experience and not just a 'blooming buzz' of sensation.

Of course it is true there are sensations, like intense pain, which carry relatively little intrinsic meaning in them. They are just there; when they have their way they occupy, almost destroy the mind they fill. This is, as a matter of fact, the only sort of mental content Hume's principles really allow. But most of our experience transcends this purely sensuous, structureless character. It is always already in some degree cognitive, carrying meaning in itself and hints of meaning beyond itself.

Further, we may say, still with Kant, that the something more which gives objectivity and validity to experience over and above its simple sensory content can be formulated in the statement that experience is *my* experience. Hume's genetic principle overlooks the validating and organizing contribution of mind to knowledge, *because* it overlooks the personal ground of knowledge. It overlooks the fact that the order which makes experience objective depends, logically, upon the person who both gives the order and submits to it.

This is not to say that the person makes the order, in the sense of making the reality, but that he does play a creative as well as a receptive part: he is responsible for his assertion of order, for his belief in order. Thus as against Hume's genetic principle, which pictures a purely passive mind as acquiring and retaining certain simple contents, we see every act of intelligent apprehension, including even perception, as an achievement which has always already transformed what it has received.

We may find a livelier, if less strictly relevant clue to the conception we are here opposing to Hume if we consider a metaphor which

William James uses in the *Principles of Psychology*: 'The mind . . .', he said,

> works on the data it receives very much as a sculptor works on his block of stone. In a sense the statue stood there from eternity. Yet there were a thousand different ones beside it, and the sculptor alone is to thank for having extricated this one from the rest. Just so the world of each of us, howsoever different our several views of it may be, all lay embedded in the primordial chaos of sensation, which gave the mere *matter* to the thought of all of us indifferently. We may, if we like, by our reasonings unwind things back to that black and jointless continuity of space, and moving clouds of swarming atoms which science calls the only real world. But all the while the world *we* feel and live in will be that which our ancestors and we, by slowly cumulative strokes of choice, have extricated out of this, like sculptors, by simply rejecting certain portions of the given stuff. Other sculptors, other statues from the same stone! Other minds, other worlds from the same monotonous and inexpressive chaos! My world is but one in a million alike embedded, alike real to those who may abstract them.[27]

It is interesting that James should hint here, and elsewhere in the *Principles*, at this very structure of personal knowing the acknowledgment of which forces us to contradict Hume's simple genetic theory – while as a pragmatist he proceeded strictly, and helplessly, within the limits of Hume's thought. If one can say what I have just quoted James as saying, one should be able to go further – not, as Descartes proudly put it, to the overthrow of all one's former opinions, but more modestly to the overthrow of this one: that the mind is an empty room which gets gradually stocked up like the shelves of a grocery store with a lot of nice little tins and polythene packages.

To return to Hume: the denial of the genetic principle by reference to the mind's activity contains, secondly, the ground, if not for the denial, then for the essential modification of Hume's Atomic Principle: namely, the principle that all ideas are separable units (or as Hume calls them, distinct existences). If every mental content is already an achievement, achievement of order, it exhibits in some degree an organized structure. It is, in Kant's words, a *synthetic manifold*. It is at the simplest a perceived form or gestalt, which is a whole in the way in which a human face is a whole: an organic unit which cannot be exhaustively analysed into its particulars or into any finite number of mathematical functions which exhaustively determine it. In a gestalt there *are* inseparable parts: in fact parts *are* parts only of a whole; if they were separated into Humean psychological atoms they would not be parts at all. The whole would disintegrate into other wholes, not the parts of itself.

Now to insist that the elements of experience are formed wholes or gestalten rather than simple atoms of sense is not by itself a solution to the problem of causality or induction as it arises from Hume's atomism. Certainly the conjunction of ideas to form empirical propositions does involve a putting together of units which are not inseparable, either logically or as forming, initially, parts of a whole. No empirical generalization is in either of these senses a necessary unity. Any empirical generalization may turn out, in terms of its particulars, to have been mistaken. In this, as we have seen, Hume remains unanswered. Yet to assert that the elements of experience are gestalten is relevant, not, I should say, to the solution of Hume's problem, but to its reformulation, and in this way: once we acknowledge the part-whole character of the elements of experience, which are the *materials* of induction, we can see that the *result* of induction also has this same part-whole character. What happens when the mind passes from the elements of an empirical generalization to the whole of it: say, from Pasteur's sealed and open tubes to the germ theory of disease, is that an aggregate of elements, themselves structured, become a new whole: take on a new structure. There are no rules for this process, there is no logic of induction; but the end product has the same kind of validity, of intrinsic rationality as the material from which it moved, and which it reinterprets.

The paradigm for this situation is the act of problem-solving, and perhaps we may still take as our paradigm of problem-solving the case of Köhler's chimpanzees. Köhler wrote:

> It is not characteristic of a chimpanzee, when he is brought into an experimental situation, to make any chance movements out of which ... a non-genuine solution could arise. As long as his efforts are directed to the objective all distinguishable stages of his behaviour (as with human beings in similar situations) tend to appear as complete attempts at solution, *none* of which appears as the product of accidentally arrayed parts. This is true, most of all, of the solution which is finally successful. Certainly, it often follows upon a period of perplexity or quiet (often a period of survey) but in real and convincing cases, the solution never appears in a disorder of blind impulses. It is one continuous, smooth action, which can be resolved into its parts only by the imagination of the onlookers; in *reality* they do not appear independently.[28]

The solution, in other words, is not an additive sum, but a reorganizing of the situation into a new gestalt. This insight has been confirmed a thousandfold by later work in learning theory.

The character of problem-solving may also instruct us, finally, in respect to Hume's third principle, the principle of association. A problem is solved, not by the kind of trial and error which could be interpreted as the product of chance or of an associative mechanism which is the next thing to chance. It is solved, as Köhler says, by a 'series of complete attempts at solution',–only all but the last have gone wrong. Problem-solving, in other words, involves not only insight, but risk and if risk, then responsibility. The active person who knows, who discovers order, always, however compelling, however intuitive that order, takes the risk of error, and at the same time the credit for success. For there is always, in the solution of a problem, in the establishment of an induction, the abrupt, logically unaccountable, personal transition from puzzlement to insight: the transition which Kierkegaard called a 'leap'. In other words, to know or to understand is not to follow blindly and mechanically a self-perpetuating chain of habits. It is a personal venture, itself an organic whole, like the wholes it recognizes, in which the responsible participation of the knowing person forms an organic and inseparable part. 'Experience' is not self-supporting, but, even in its most austere and objective guises, the experience of persons.

6 Facts and Values

MY CRITIQUE OF KANT'S CRITIQUE OF HUME HAS EFFECTED A TWO-
fold transformation of Kantian 'experience'. On the one hand, the
pin-point 'I' of the transcendental analytic becomes a fully structured,
fully functioning, historical human person, with all its levels of significance, and its ineluctable contingency. And with this change, on
the other hand, the pin-point of the 'transcendental object = X'
becomes once more the full-bodied reality of the world we are trying
to understand. This revision might be interpreted as producing a
neo-Kantian view of knowledge, since it simply shifts the Kantian
theory into another co-ordinate system, retaining its essential elements. But the matter is not so simple. If we admit the full 'I', my
whole ambiguous, many-dimensional existence, into our account
of knowledge, of our purely theoretical achievements, we have
thrown away the separateness which Kant so strenuously insisted
on, between the questions of knowing, doing and believing.

Nor is it Kant alone who insists on such a separation. Kant was
echoing, in this, one–and one fundamental–consequence of the
Cartesian-Newtonian world view. The dualism of matter and mind
entails a dualism of the external, 'objective', and the internal, 'subjective'. There is the world spread out through space, independent of
my feelings, ideas or volitions; and there are my secret thoughts, the
'modes' of my consciousness. The purity of science, moreover, is
thought to depend on the extrusion of the second from the first. In
Kant this dichotomy is represented, for example, by the distinction
between an outer and an inner sense. In contemporary philosophy,
with its emphasis on language, it becomes the distinction between
statements of fact and statements of value. Again, the purity of science
is held to depend on keeping the former uncontaminated by the latter.

Perhaps the best known formulation of this dichotomy was that
put forward by Ogden and Richards in *The Meaning of Meaning*,
where they distinguished between 'cognitive' and 'emotive' meaning;
and correspondingly, the statements of science, which purvey information, were distinguished from the 'pseudo-statements' of
poetry or religious discourse. Information, it is alleged, is always
*im*personal; where the person, and with him, values, preferences,

emotions, enter, information withdraws. Allied to this kind of categorization is the conception of 'value-free science' which has been held to be the norm not only for the natural sciences, but for the social sciences as well. Here too we are often asked to set against the wholly objective statements of science the impassioned utterances of the arts which are not statements at all.

The assertion that knowing is a form of doing, that it is the full, concrete, historical person who is the essential agent of knowledge, plainly runs counter to this cherished dichotomy. Before I proceed further, therefore, it seems advisable to consider in more detail the alleged distinction between statements of fact and statements of value, and, if I venture to deny it, to give reasons for this denial.

Now I do indeed want to deny the fact-value dichotomy, but in a particular direction. One direction in which I do *not* want to argue should first be eliminated. In recent ethical discussions, the attempt has been made to overcome the duality of facts and values by drawing appraisals out of facts. The argument is roughly as follows. There is no such thing as 'good' in and of itself, there are only 'good' apples, 'good' men, 'good' pop songs, and so on. Now a Pure Food authority can establish objective *criteria* for 'good' apples, the Top Twenty provides objective criteria for 'good' pop songs, and so on, and in each case (including 'good' man), 'goodness', being built into the reality, is just as 'factual' as it. There is therefore no need to consider ethical discourse any less 'rational' than ordinary or scientific language; no need for any one to face, without public and unquestioned criteria to lean on, some inner, inexplicable choice between this 'good' and that.[2] These arguments are reminiscent of Plato's *Republic*, where the *arete* of a pruning knife is compared to that of a man. The 'goodness' of any given kind of entity is just what makes it do its job well; and if you know what kind of thing it is, you know what its job is, for having that job is what makes it that kind of thing. For Plato, however, this is only the beginning of the argument. To establish on rational grounds a criterion for the excellence of human souls is not so easy as it looks. It needs the whole intricate structure of the dialogue to *suggest*, indirectly and metaphorically, what Plato believed to be the true solution–and even for him it was a solution which itself involved vast problems, a solution which he kept modifying and restating as long as he lived. Even for apples and pop songs, let alone for human lives, criteria do not present themselves on the face of the things *for* which they are criteria, but have to be discovered–or decided?–in the light of some standard, to which we voluntarily submit ourselves as to the right standard for judging this kind of thing. I can tell a cat from a mouse by (relatively) objective characteristics, but a good from a bad cat only by whatever criteria I choose to apply in judging feline excellence: number of mice caught per unit time, number of prizes won at cat shows, pedigree, fecundity, or what you will. And for human beings the task of (1) finding, (2) justifying, (3) applying criteria of excellence is vastly more complex and delicate than for cats. The fact that in our everyday behaviour we use such criteria without reflection does not mean that they are automatic, inherent in the situations to be judged. We can make such routine decisions as it were automatically because as mature human beings we are *dwelling* in the whole complex framework of criteria, rules and principles, which from infancy we have taken into ourselves, or into which we have expanded ourselves as we have grown to be human. So much indeed is 'natural' to humankind, but, unlike the posturing of a cat at a mousehole, it is a nature which has had to be acquired, which can be acquired in an indefinite variety of forms, and has to be sustained, in the face of conflict and doubt, by reflective criticism and justification: criticism which is never finished, justification which is never ultimate. What shows us what we are is not the daily routine situation where we live safely within our framework of learned criteria, but the boundary situation: confrontation with frameworks basically different from our own, or confrontation with choices such that one cannot be unambiguously taken as right, the other wrong. Such confrontations exhibit the essential, if ordinarily submerged structure of all judgment. We have to choose not only which apple, but by what standard to judge apples, not only which action, but in the light of what criteria the choice is to be made. Of course we cannot at every moment of decision decide from scratch, as it were, not only what to do, but on what grounds to decide what to do. But as we have taken on humanity that is precisely what we have done. Our humanity *is* the complex of criteria, of evaluative structures, within which we have come to dwell, and are content to dwell. To deny the multiplicity and complexity of such hard-won dwelling places, to deny our 'natural artificiality', is to beg the question of facts and values from the start.

It is not from this direction, therefore, that I want to attack the fact/value dichotomy. I shall argue, on the contrary, that our judgments of fact depend on constitutive judgments of value, not the other way around. Indeed, what was true in the assertion of the duality of facts and values was the insight: that values cannot be elicited from 'bare' facts. The fact that a person called Beethoven on such dates wrote such marks on paper does not by itself account for the existence of the *Eroica* as a musical composition. The fact that millions of Jews and East Europeans died in gas chambers does not in itself make the evil of the Nazi terror. But conversely, the genius of Beethoven made possible the composition of the Eroica, the evil of Nazism made possible the mass annihilations of the gas chambers. Only by an evaluation do we call the Eroica 'music', not noise, and so assimilate the 'fact' of its composition to the history of music rather than to acoustics. Only by an evaluation do we call the story of Ausschwitz or Belsen mass murder and so assimilate it to human history rather than to chemistry or population genetics.

Now these of course are in any case 'facts' which plainly entail value judgments in their ordinary expression. But I should argue, further, that all statements of fact, however free of evaluation they may seem, are possible *only* when some fundamental act of appraisal has already legislated for the manner of their entertainment, formulation and assertion. Instead, therefore, of separating judgments of fact from judgments of value as two mutually exclusive classes, I should want to admit both factual and evaluating aspects in all judgments. Every judgment, I shall argue, either includes *or* presupposes some evaluative component. Some judgments, indeed, are more highly, or intensely evaluative than others; but my point is that even the least evaluative, most 'factual' judgments depend for the possibility of their existence on some prior evaluative act.[3]

I shall present here two general lines of argument for this view: one, to evaluation as the ground of the possibility of all intelligible discourse, and a second from the nature of human action in general.

II

My first argument is: that there can be no *purely* factual statements, i.e., statements which do not even presuppose evaluation, because there can be no intelligible discourse except on the ground of evaluation or appraisal. There are, in other words, no descriptions wholly independent of prescriptions.

Those who separate statements of fact from statements of value often analyse the former in such a way as to distinguish immediate assertions of particular data—protocol statements, in the language of the Vienna Circle, from the abstract, and even conventional, concepts and statements we have erected on this unquestioned base. On this view, all theoretical constructs are supposed to be controlled in relation to the basic protocol statements, or reports of observation, at the foundation of the scientific edifice. Whether this control occurs through verification and falsification or primarily through the latter need not concern us here. This conception of knowledge, and of the speech that imparts it, is, in essence, as old as Epicurus; in one form or another, it recurs in the arguments of Hobbes, Hume, Carnap, Popper, Russell, and many others. We may take as a typical instance

Russell's *Inquiry into Meaning and Truth*.[4] Let us, then, look at one of these protocol sentences, one of the units of presumably purely factual discourse, and see what is involved in it.

The simplest sort of report of observation one could think of would be, for example, 'This is red'. This is in fact one of the 'basic propositions' listed by Russell in the *Inquiry*.[5] In what sense is this a 'statement of fact', which could be contrasted with a 'statement of value'? 'This', or better, 'this is', taken together, comes as close to just pointing as language can come, in fact, so close that, Russell asserts, it can be eliminated from language altogether. Russell is here building up a scientific language on the basis of sentences of 'atomic form'. These have the following structure:

> a sentence is of atomic form if it contains one relation-word (which may be a predicate) and the smallest number of other words required to form a sentence. If R_1 is a predicate, R_2 a dyadic relation, R_3 a triadic relation, etc.
>
> $$R_1(x), R_2(x, y), R_3(x, y, z) \ldots$$
>
> will be sentences of atomic form, provided x, y, z are such words as make the sentence concerned significant.[6]

The variables in such sentences Russell calls *names*. He has here assimilated what are usually called 'proper names' to names in general, and even terms which ordinarily function as predicates, like 'red' and 'coloured', are so assimilated. Thus our sample sentence becomes, not 'this is red', with its implication that 'this' is a Lockian x-somewhat underlying the perceived quality, but 'redness is here', where 'redness' is a name and 'here' a spatial relation.[7] In fact, Russell argues, 'egocentric particulars' such as 'this', 'that', and 'I' can be altogether eliminated from cognitive language. They are neither names, descriptions, nor concepts, but simply expressions of the immediate causal relation of perception to the words expressed. The meaning of 'cat' is the same whether I am saying 'this is a cat' or 'that was a cat'.[8] ' "This" ', he concludes, 'is a word which is not needed for a complete description of the world.'[9] It simply points.

Now it could reasonably be objected to this elimination of 'egocentric particulars', that a 'this is' statement does already entail conceptualization. A 'pointing' statement, like 'this is red' is equivalent to 'this-here-red'. But if a child is able to say 'this', and mean 'this-here', he has already learned to discriminate object from background, and object from object, and so has already acquired in some measure a spatial orientation in his immediate environment. As soon as he can use 'this' in a consistent way, he is no longer simply pointing to particulars, but applying intellectual concepts to particulars distinguishable within his organized world. In this sense 'this' is already implicitly conceptual.

We may overlook this objection here, however, and grant for the moment that the first two words in our sample protocol are purely 'factual'. Even if we do grant this much, what of the third component? 'This' points to something unique, it names just this and nothing else; and this red is perhaps also unique: the pure immediate quality 'sensed' now may never recur again. But to *call* this 'red' puts it into a class of things, a congeries of surfaces assorted in their varying 'rednesses', yet all *red*. Outside my window is a whitewashed wall with a red gutter atop it, and a bit of matching red roof beyond it. Beyond that a tree with reddening fruit, beyond it again red geraniums in a window-box, with one pink one (non-red, off-red?) wilting among its darker neighbours. Even the red geraniums, examined more closely, are not 'the same red': one nearly pink, one purplish red (could they be petunias?), two real 'geranium red', that screaming colour, but even of those one is lighter than the other. And then the two drooping pinks beneath them. Background to all these, finally, is the crumbling ecru plaster of the adjoining house, against which I can see so plainly 'these here red', and again of the nearer roof, 'this here red'. Clearly, I have here available for use a whole scale of colours from plainly non-reds through just off-reds to all the shades I should include in 'red', against which I have already tested 'this here' before I call it 'red'. I do not mean 'before', of course, relatively to this immediate act of observation: I am not moving, in sequence, from this observation to some remembered red thing and saying, by comparison: this is red. But my present percept fits into the range of colours which are part of my organized world: I already *dwell in* a world where 'this' can fall into its place as 'red' or 'just-not-red'–pink (flower) or orange (fruit).

I have referred earlier to W. H. Thorpe's conjecture that even animal perception is comparative, of relations rather than of individuals.[10] A well-known experiment has shown, for example, that chickens fed on the lighter of two grey squares will always peck on the lighter of a pair, even though the shade which was formerly the lighter is now the darker of the new pair.[11] The experimenter, however, can not only distinguish the relative light and dark of each pair, but can see that a constant mid-grey is first lighter and then darker than its mate. He can match a single colour in two cases against a standard. Without such matching, without evaluation, he could not say with confidence, 'this is grey', or 'this is medium grey', or 'this is the same colour'. Far from having first primitive perceptions of particulars, from which we abstract to form, by convention, 'general concepts', relational in import, we perceive, primarily, relations, and to perceive particulars is already to have transcended the relations in which, as perceived, they are imbedded. For to 'see' this particular as red we must know how to isolate the new particular from its context and judge it, instead, *by the general standard of redness*. This is to say, with Kant, that concepts are rules for organising experience, not indeed, formally stateable rules, but norms to which judgment is implicitly referred, by which it is tacitly governed. And where I say 'this here red', I am already applying such a rule–the rule of colour judgment–to this particular instance. Were I not able to exercise such complex evaluations, I should be bound, like the chicken, to the direct impact of a relational context, and unable to isolate it from the particular I wish to report.

Thinking of what I do and of what the chicken does, one is reminded of Hume's case of the missing shade of blue.[12] Confident as he was that every particular item of experience is a precise image which can be retained, more faintly, in memory, he admitted the following possibility, difficult to explain on his theory. If I had experienced a whole range of shades of blue, say intensities 1–8 and 10–12, I should be able, Hume suggests, without ever having seen it, to imagine shade 9. This for Hume would be a contradiction of his genetic principle. What the case indicates, however, is not simply that there are occasional exceptions to the derivation of all particular mental contents from previous particulars; but rather that I could not see any shade as blue at all, nor *a fortiori* assert correctly the sentence 'this here blue' unless I had already built for myself a standard by which blues were to be judged. Have you ever disagreed with some one as to whether a particular coloured object–say a roll of wallpaper–is blue or green? A physicist might settle the dispute by reference to the spectrum–but here again he (or the consensus of physicists) must have decided where to stop saying 'green' and begin saying 'blue'. Far from being atomic, as Hume thought, 'immediate' perception–such as the chicken's–is already relational; the report of a human perception is much more remote again from such direct immediacy. To say 'this here red' I must already have abstracted from my immediate relational perceptions, stood back from them and assessed them, so as to be able to place a new occurrent into the class of like-though-differing particulars into which it fits. Only then can I tag it as 'red'. Not that I have in my memory a series of particular colour images such as Hume suggested; what I have is the power of bringing each new particular to the bar of judgment according to a principle, a standard, by which I judge it. That standard is neither verbally formulable, nor present as visual image, or a series of visual images. The colour pyramid of the psychologist or the physicist's spectroscope may indicate something about the articulation of such a standard as it normally occurs, or about the physical reality to which it has to conform if, in this given universe, it is to work. But I carry about with me neither a picture of the colour pyramid nor an operating spectroscope. The fact is rather that I live in a coloured world, a world which presents sights to me as coloured because, using my eyes and optic nerves and brain and eye muscles, I have acquired the power to subsume my particular experiences, in a particular lighted and superficial aspect, under colour concepts. These concepts, like all concepts, are standards, by which I judge *this* to be such-and-such–in this case, *red*. 'This-here-red' is already a highly structured statement, reflecting a complex achievement of abstraction and appraisal.

There is an interesting historical point to be made here, in connection with the concept of 'protocol sentence' as the Vienna Circle introduced it. Carnap and Schlick and Neurath professed to have been influenced in their new programme by the *Tractatus Logico-Philosophicus* of Wittgenstein, which had appeared in 1922. Wittgenstein had introduced the concept of 'atomic sentences', mirroring 'atomic facts', and had insisted that logic, mirroring the world, must give us in its relations the structural image of the network of atomic facts. Scientific discourse, limited to the precise instruments of logic, in turn, should state 'only what can be said exactly', and of the rest, we were to be silent. This ideal, founded, they believed, on the availability of atomic sentences corresponding to atomic facts, the Vienna Circle proceeded to try to realize, and their protocol sentences were alleged to be identical with the atomic sentences of the *Tractatus*. We start with unquestioned observation reports like 'this-here-red', and build from there. Observation reports, however, are *not* Wittgensteinian atomic sentences, and what they report, such as the this-here-red denoted by 'this-here-red', are not atomic facts. Wittgenstein himself, Miss Anscombe points out in her essay on the *Tractatus*, made statements incompatible with the view that observation reports are atomic sentences.[13] Thus the logical positivist edifice, insofar as it was based on the authority of the *Tractatus*, rested on a misinterpretation.

What, then, are the units with which the fact/value philosopher is to build his safe, impersonal, purely cognitive world? As far as I can see, there are none. The ideal of logical positivism remains an empty ideal, a nightmarish Utopia. That, it seems to me, is the lesson of the *Tractatus*. Logic, and the wholly precise speech of logically governed exact science, would mirror the universe if the universe were composed of atomic facts; but they are nowhere to be found, nor, *a fortiori*, are there any atomic sentences with which to begin such a construction. That is why, in Wittgenstein's oracular phrase, we must throw away at the end of his argument the ladder we have climbed up on. If we can speak only exactly, using an aggregate of wholly precise atomic statements to build our discourse; if, of all not thus exactly articulated, we must silent, then we must be silent altogether. All discourse, even that which has led to this conclusion, becomes absurd. We are left only with what Wittgenstein calls the 'ethical', the 'mystical'; speech is impossible. The *Tractatus*, far from providing, as the Vienna Circle believed it did, a programme for impeccable 'factual' discourse, reduces such discourse to absurdity, and leaves us, beyond it, in speechless wonder. Better to admit, from the start, the 'ethical', the evaluative ground of speech, and let facticity flower, as it does, within and upon that ground. It was this new direction, I suspect, which Wittgenstein's later substitution of the 'game' analogy for the 'picture' analogy, in his reflections on language, was meant to take. Language as a *Lebensform*, a way of doing something, entails from the start, and to the finish, the application of standards to situations, the organization of experience according to implicit rules.[14]

III

Our 'protocol statement', 'this-here-red', we may conclude, then, is not an isolable report of a particular, but already presupposes the application of general concepts, which have already set standards to experience. In this sense at least it presupposes evaluative activity: it is not the bare statement of this bare fact. But, our fact/value segregationist will answer, surely you are not suggesting that 'this-here-red' is a value judgment in the same sense as 'this-here-repulsive' or 'this-here-good'. Suppose I bite into a juicy peach and say, 'delicious' or in effect 'this-here-delicious'. Such a 'statement' is not a statement in the same sense as my report of the colour of the gutter outside the window. Unless of course at a higher level of abstraction my exclamation forms, say, part of a report on the public's taste in fruit, and means 'MG likes peaches', or better, 'MG eats peaches in preference to plums', or the like. But taken in itself it is just another way of exclaiming 'Yum!' The difference between the two kinds of 'statement' is easily specified. If we disagree about our colour judgment, say in the case of the blue-green wallpaper, we can after all appeal once more to the physicist, who will fit our protocol into the framework of optics and tell us which is consistent with it. It is unlikely that we shall want to remake physical theory to fit our errant judgment; we shall learn to improve our protocol reports instead. But on the question whether to a taste I exclaim 'Yum' or 'Ugh', the chemist's analysis of the peach is quite irrelevant. Somebody may have pumped it full of some tasteless poison, it still tastes good. All the way to the most (seemingly) substantive judgments of ethics, on this view, I am *really* only exclaiming 'Yum!' or 'Ugh!' So, Russell remarks, with splendidly consistent absurdity, there is no difference between a liking for oysters and a dislike of merciless cruelty.[15] On the one hand I can *state* facts, or on the other, *express* my positive and negative reactions to facts. But surely I cannot defend the view that it is the same sort of thing I am doing in the two cases.

To answer this objection fully would take us far beyond the scope of this book, let alone this chapter. On the one hand, I am not here dealing with the question of value as applied to moral or aesthetic problems. And on the other, I should not venture to essay single-handed the fundamental reform in metaphysics which alone can remedy the absurdities of the fact/value dichotomy at its most rigorous worst. The direction of this reform, at least, however, I hope that this and subsequent chapters may suggest.

Meantime, I should answer at this point: of course there is a difference in the way in which, and the degree to which, acts of appraisal are involved in the statements reporting perceived qualities and statements reporting personal preferences. That much I have myself insisted on in denying the derivation of 'value judgments' from 'facts' as current neo-Aristotelian moralists propose to derive them. This concession, however, does not entail the thesis that all value judgments are *nothing but* statements of preference. Nor is the difference in question one between simply pointing and simply exclaiming.

Let us start once more not from the protocol sentence 'in itself', but from the perceiving person in his concrete situation. When I look at the scene outside the window, I am absorbed into it, I focus on 'out-there', and what I report I report as out there. On the other hand, when I reported one geranium as '*screaming* red', I was turning back to focus on my own participation in the scene in its enjoyed quality. The original situation is a unity, a gestalt formed by the bearing of sensory and proprioceptive clues on the scene before me: myself-looking-out-the-window-at-the-house-with-the-window-box. This concrete totality, moreover, is auditory, tactile, olfactory, kinaes-thetic, as well as visual. The oddly smooth feel of a Formica desk top under my hand, the roar of cars and buses, the starting car engine in the yard, the ticking of a clock, my posture at the desk, are all part of the scene in which I am engaged. Within this totality I can move in many directions. I can turn inward to savour the jarring harshness of the geranium-red geranium, a withdrawal into pure feeling which carries with it resonances from the past, both distant and recent: my mother's dislike of that red in children's clothing, my surprise when she herself appeared in a black and white suit trimmed with the forbidden colour, my more recent dread of the hideously combined reds and pinks to which the Irish female of all ages is addicted–all these reverberate in the 'screaming' red. All this is part of the present scene turned inward toward its significance for me; and it forms now and forever part of what I am, part of my character, part of my history. This is in itself a trivial instance: if my utterance 'screaming red' is not just equivalent to 'ugh', but a facet of my transcendence, my transcendence, as an individual history, matters little, in itself, to human destiny. But were I a poet, my glimpse of colour might be absorbed, not only into my own transcendence, but into the significance of indefinite transcendences, it might become part of humanity, like Wilfred Owen's

Red lips are not so red
As the stained stones kissed by the English dead.

Suppose, however, instead of letting the clues inherent in this sector of my experience turn inward to enrich the experienced quality of my life–to its firstness, as Peirce would call it–suppose instead I turn to the out-thereness as what absorbs me most. Again, I may do this in a number of contexts, a number of ways. Suppose I want to know why geraniums vary in colour, or want to breed a saleable variety of constant hue, then I must indeed abstract from my own absorption in my present perception, and make not only my transcendence, but the transcendence of my transcendence explicit. I shall still be absorbed by the present, as Mendel was when he looked to see which peas were wrinkled and which smooth, which yellow and which green. But I shall now be using what was focal, the colour with its reverberations and tone and implications, as clue to what I am now focussing on. Thus what Mendel was attending to in reliance on the clues of 'green' and 'yellow' was the relations of segregation and combination which would, when formulated, one day be known as the Mendelian laws of heredity. This is indeed a profound change of focus from the personal or poetic, but far from being a change to the 'purely factual', it is a change deeply imbedded in a series of evaluative acts, of commitment to standards which just as deeply involve and alter the person so committed.

Such evaluative acts, such assessments of experience in accord with standards we have set to it, are presupposed in all 'factual' discourse, from the most 'ordinary' to the most sophisticated and 'scientific'. Suppose I am asked. 'What is that on the sofa?' and answer, 'A cat'. Russell, in the *Inquiry*, would have me revise this, 'A patch of feline colour.'[16] But what do I, or can I, mean by 'feline'? Russell is trying to avoid words that would suggest 'substances' rather than direct and particular percepts. But can any names, such as the general quality words, red, feline, coloured, etc., of which he is trying to build his firmly factual language, work uniquely for *this* percept? Both the words themselves and the things designated are *instances* of *universals*. The *same* word, e.g. 'cat', designates the *same* thing, cat, in the sense that a mark or sound of the same class designates a thing of the same class. But no occasion of 'cat' or cat is identical with any other. It is in each case a *similar* occurrence or object. How do I know it is similar, and similar enough to be subsumed under the same class? By memory, a Humean empiricist would say. But even granting that, meeting cat 2 I recall cat 1, I must *make* the comparison. I must *liken* cat 2 to cat 1 and find them similar by a standard, a standard which *is* the concept cat. 'Cat' designates Carol and Top Cat and Phippeen and any other cat who may come into my ken, say, that excellent tabby Jemima who looms so large in Geach's logic. But 'cat' can designate any cat because it *signifies* cat: because it signifies what-it-is-to-be-a-cat, the standard I apply in order to judge a cat to be a cat. Again, as in our case of colour judgment, I do not mean to suggest that there is an explicit, or even an 'unconscious' inference involved here, every time I recognize a cat as a cat. But as my world is coloured, so too it is cat-inhabited and at the same time structured through language: I dwell in a coherent and mutually interacting framework of word-classes and thing-classes; only within such a frame do individual sounds or written shapes and individual animals become what they are. The power to generalize which speech demands is the power to sort out according to effective norms both utterances and natural events.

This is if you like a suspiciously Platonic argument. Plato argued in the *Cratylus*: were there not something permanent over against flux I could not liken my swiftly flowing percepts sufficiently to name anything. In the *Phaedo* he insisted that I can know (and *a fortiori* say) two lines are equal only by reference to a self-existent standard of equality to which this pair only approximate. Similarly I submit Carol and Top Cat and Jemima to the standard cat and say confidently: they are cats. A child on first seeing a ferret, for example, might ask 'cat?', and looking closely say, 'funny cat' or 'not cat'. Or using too loose a standard a child may call all animals cats, distinguishing only later one kind from another. Now I am not suggesting that to account for the existence of intelligible discourse we need to postulate cat itself or ferret itself, and on to wildcat itself and panther itself and weasel itself, a Platonic world of forms to account for our use of class names. But what was true in the Platonic arguments of the *Cratylus*, the *Phaedo*, and more fundamentally even in the refutation of 'perception is knowledge' in the *Theaetetus*, was this: (1) there is no speech which does not involve the use of class concepts; (2) class concepts demand the recognition of similarity; (3) and that means a comparison, an *act* of comparison, according to a standard, in fact (4) class concepts *are* standards of comparison, norms in the light of which we order future items of experience, at the same time, be it said, on occasion altering the norms themselves in the light of such experience. Plato, seeking for explicitness all along the line, went wrong in transforming these standards themselves into self-existent identities, and so solidifying them. But that we can make sense of experience only through its subsumption under universals, and that such universals act as standards for the evaluation of experience, or rather that we act in submission to these standards as judges of experience: this much in the Platonic account we must admit.

The same fundamental structure of experience organized through the evaluative subsumption under standards characterizes scientific discourse as well. Let us look a little more closely at the case of Mendel sorting green from yellow in his monastery garden, and see what is involved in the 'scientific' observation of a great discoverer. In the first place, what the discoverer does, as we have already noticed and shall see again later, is to alter the normal content of perception and inference so as to see a nexus of relationships, a significant gestalt, where others have not seen it: in this case, what were to be Mendel's laws. Such original vision itself entails evaluation: the discoverer makes sense of experience in a new way. He finds details *interesting* which were not so before and through them glimpses an *order* formerly unseen. Mrs Gasking, in an essay called 'Why was Mendel's Work Ignored?', has contrasted Mendel's interests with those of his predecessors and contemporaries. [17] Scientific experimenters had been concerned with the vexing problem of 'specific essence': if they admitted the intrusion of new species into the genera 'specially created' in the beginning, these should themselves exemplify new 'essences'. In both cases it was the total 'nature' of each species they were concerned with, not scattered characters. Nor were practical breeders, trying for better strength or beauty, attentive to petty variations of detail. Even when, after 1859 and before Mendel's results were published in 1866, the new evolutionary perspective had begun to dominate biological thinking, it was the gradual transition within groups, and so the production of new species, that scientists sought to study. Such gradualism–the continuity in nature demanded by natural selection theory–strongly suggests *blending* heredity: the fusion of variations to produce a slightly different and better, or worse, adapted form for selection to eliminate or leave alone. From both these points of view, both in terms of the concept of 'specific

essence', and of the Darwinian gradualism which replaced it, it is the
whole individual on which the breeder or experimenter's interest is
focussed. Mendel could attend, with ten years' patient labour, to the
detail of particular characters, green and yellow, smooth and
wrinkled, short and tall, because they were for him clues to a new and
beautiful pattern, a pattern of statistical laws quite different from
anything his contemporaries imagined or wanted to imagine. And
that brings us to a second essential point about the scientific use of
perceived detail, or the perception of detail in scientific contexts. The
'observations' accepted by scientists are not simple protocol reports,
standing on their own. To become part of science, they must be relevant to the interests of scientists. They must be attuned to standards
of scientific value, acceptable not only to the individual experimenter,
but to the consensus of scientific opinion whose authority he accepts.
This is just where Mendel's work failed in his own day, and that is
why no one noticed or accepted his results, definitive and brilliant as
we can now see they were. The laws of Segregation and of Independent Assortment were neither interesting nor credible to the scientists
of the time. Mendel sent a copy of his paper to Professor Nägeli of
Munich, a leading systematist and evolutionist. Nägeli was sceptical
of the constancy of Mendel's results, and conjectured that the constant forms if tested further 'would be found to vary once more'. He
urged Mendel to abandon this line of work and to try instead, like
other breeders, to tackle the problem of producing intermediate
forms. On Nägeli's advice, Mendel turned to experiments with the
genus Heiracium, trying to produce hybrid forms. The nature of this
new material, however, was such that he got neither results consistent
with his Pisum experiments, not conclusive results of any other
kind.[18] Only forty years later, at the turn of the century, when advances in cytology had redirected the attention of biologists, did the
work of De Vries, Bateson and others, revolting against the dominance of Darwinism, set the stage for the rediscovery of the laws of
heredity and the rediscovery of their first discoverer. Mrs Gasking
comments:

> Science is organized knowledge, and no piece of work however com-
> plete in itself, is valued until it can be fitted into the general corpus.
> Given the position in biology when Mendel wrote, it was perhaps
> inevitable that his discovery should not have been appreciated. This did
> not make it any the less of a personal tragedy for Mendel, though he
> seems, at least in part, to have recognized the situation and got some
> comfort from it. At any rate, his only recorded comment on the fate of
> his first monograph was to say: 'My time will come.'[19]

Beyond these limited scientific values, moreover, which fluctuate from one generation and even one locality to another, both Mendel and Nägeli, as competent scientists of their day, were devoted to the discovery of truth, and it is this ultimate standard to which all alleged 'statements of fact' and all the theoretical constructs allegedly built atop them–to which all the structures of science must submit. This is the ultimate evaluation on which all facticity depends. What have we said when we have said this? Both much and little. Little, because for scientific existence, the professional life of the scientist, truth is the all-embracing boundary. Attempts to state this are either trivial, if not tautological, or pompous and ranting or flabby and vague. They are so, precisely because the evaluation implicit in the pursuit of truth is comprehensive for the existence of those whose calling it is to seek truth. Such evaluations may be invisible in their everyday functioning, but we can recognize them, again, in the boundary situation, when they are transgressed. Personal ambition, for example, is legitimately a motive working *with* submission to truth in the scientist's professional life. Every research worker wants to be the one to make the discovery that lies ahead in his special field of research. Thus in Canada and the United States Banting and his competitors raced to isolate insulin and Banting won. But supposing that to have the name of discoverer a scientist falsified his results, or the timing of his results. That would be a breach of the ethic on which his calling as scientist rests. Or again, consider the relation of the scientist's loyalty to the ultimate value of truth and his loyalty to the state. Polanyi has analysed in *Personal Knowledge* the radical duality on this question between the Soviet conception, at least in its Stalinist version, and the Western scientific code.[20] Not that Western scientists are holy men of learning who inevitably act solely or primarily out of respect for truth; but in so far as they are good scientists, in West or East, that is what they do, and it is that ultimate standard that makes them good scientists, or even scientists at all. The perpetrator of the Piltdown forgery was *not* a scientist, but a fraud. Only within the area cleared for facticity by the fundamental commitment to seek the truth and declare it can there arise the objectivity, the impersonality, characteristic of statements, concepts, theories that stand the test as science. To follow this road, to submit to the discipline of this commitment, is, as Hippocrates saw, to take a path that is long and hard–and as Socrates warned Hippocrates' namesake, dangerous too. But a non-road, a congeries of utterances uttered by no one and disciplines pursued by no one, it never was and cannot be. To *dis*involve myself, to commit myself to *de*tachment, to attach myself to standards of accuracy and scope transcending my own transcendence, to absorb my destiny into the destiny of a profession, of the world itself which through my commitment to a given discipline I am intent on trying to understand: this is to submit myself to standards so exacting that they demand, as Plato rightly saw, a conversion away from the values of daily life, an intentness on distant goals. The scientist works, indeed, still rooted in his individual situation, working here today in this laboratory with these experimental animals, using X's technique or Y's solution to solve the problem passed on to him by Z, and his whole being is intent on this particular problem with its looming solution or its impenetrable obscurities. But this particular situation expands for him *qua* scientist to his situation in a working community, a continuing tradition, and a community united by the arduous and demanding resolve to follow as best he can the dictates of truth. Every observation report, every theoretical conjecture, every confirmatory deduction, every move in the life of science, is made possible by this fundamental evaluation, this fundamental act of appraisal and allegiance. Where it fails, not only theory fails, but factuality as well.

IV

There is, then, I conclude, no intelligible discourse independently of evaluation. Appraisal underlies all speech, and therefore all knowledge.[21] I shall now try, secondly, to give more body to my claim by considering the nature of any human action as such, and seeing how within this general framework the objectivizing performance of knowledge, including scientific knowledge, can take place. It should be plain from this account where and how evaluations enter essentially into the foundation of all knowledge.

I have already emphasized in my preceding chapter the fact that knowing is something people do, an activity. But what is the structure of an action? What if anything distinguishes the action of a human being from the behaviour of any other animal?

I shall take as the starting point for my reflections, the analysis of the difference between men and animals by the Dutch physiologist and animal psychologist, F. J. J. Buytendijk. Buytendijk draws extensively from the two famous studies of chimpanzees raised in human society, the Hayeses' report on *The Ape in our House*, and the Kelloggs' *The Ape and the Child*, but also from other observations and experiments both on human and animal behaviour.[22] If we look through his account we find that the phenomena which occur uniquely in the human young are all phenomena which express the transformation of the animal 'environment' into a human 'world', that is, into a world which the child freely constitutes as a structure, or complex of structures, to which he takes one or another attitude, and to which he may take, in different ways, more than one attitude:

The essential difference between child and ape is expressed in the growing freedom of the child in his dialogue with the world.[23]

The ape may develop 'islands' of nearly human behaviour, but he always falls back into a specific pattern, tied to particular practical ends. The child, on the other hand, shows growing degrees of freedom, of self-determination, in his handling of situations. Take a few examples, some of which at least bring us close to our question of the activity of knowing.

Take first one which, in itself purely 'affective', yet exhibits the characteristically human : smiling :

> But what the animal, even the most humanized ape, wholly fails to achieve, is the *smile*, the expression of inner, withdrawn cheerfulness, the answer of the human child to its encounter with its mother. In smiling the infant reveals its humanity in the fashion provided for it by its bodily endowment. In their play together Gua and Viki occasionally giggled as the child does, but the child smiles and laughs in many ways, because in its awakening objectification of things it acknowledges new and multifarious, ambivalent meanings in situations as they arise.[24]

This *ambivalence* is characteristic throughout of human as distinct from animal behaviour. We have always the union of 'participation and withdrawal', which creates the breathing space for human freedom and human achievement. It is this, for example, Buytendijk insists, which distinguishes even the most astonishing tool-using by apes from human tool-situations. Of the ape's use of tools he writes :

> The use of instruments in order to reach a goal . . . is not to be confused with the human use of tools. The ape can use a branch as a pole. *This shows that in a new situation an object acquires a new meaning.* If a man should break off a branch, in order to use it as a weapon, as a support, as a lever or for any purpose he has in mind, then he would be understanding the thing *at the same time* in *two* meanings. It would be for him a 'branch turned pole', a thing with several aspects. . . . If the branch is used by the chimpanzee as a pole, it is no longer a branch, and therefore the pole is not, for him, a true tool. Only for man are things equivocal.[25]

And it is this *equivocal* relation to things that underlies our ability to produce full tools—to take things as appropriate for a *possible* use, for one use *or* another. It is the transcendence of the immediate milieu, the immediate need, that characterizes human work as human.

We may take this difference in tool using as our second point. Another aspect of the same essential grasp of ambiguity, of our living in ambiguity, is evident, thirdly, in the fact that, whereas the ape never comes to understand what a picture is, the child soon learns, and delights in this difference.

If we look at the picture of Viki, we see that she puts her ear to the *real* clock and to the *picture* of the clock with the *same seriousness*. Experience teaches us that a child does indeed occasionally put its ear to the picture of a clock, just as it will sometimes kiss the picture of a baby or a puppy, but its behaviour, its mimicry and the whole course of the proceeding demonstrate that the child is 'only joking'. The child acts 'as if' he were listening, he is teasing the adult, and especially so if he puts on a serious expression. *Here we see the difference between the highest animal and man.* The animal, even the 'humanized' chimpanzee, does not regard a picture in the human way as the presentation of a non-present reality.[26]

Animals too of course delight in play, but not in the same manner in pretending, in taking a role. Once inducted, moreover, by human society and its own gifts, into the delight of make-believe, the child can also, fourthly, hold itself at a distance from the impact of its environment, and *question* it:

The first role which the child takes upon itself is that of the questioner. Man is 'a questioning being'. If the child starts by asking *inauthentically*, rather like Viki, by way of expressing his needs, he soon starts asking for the sake of asking. The need to ask develops, along with objective perception, into the need for knowledge, which is indicated by the *authentically* child-like question, '*What is that?*'[27]

This is of course the beginning of human language:

Then the child speaks. The word is no longer 'only' a signal or 'only' an expression of meaning in the particular situation, but it has like all speech the function of constituting a situation. Speech is achievement.[28]

And speech, of course, is the most conspicuous human achievement: speech, that is, as a structure of symbols, which again can be developed, manipulated, interpreted and re-interpreted in an infinity of directions–unlike the code of the bees, which, however marvellously complex and effective, functions as a system of fixed signals. Human language, by contrast, becomes itself a growing world of meanings within meanings, which we not only use for practical ends but dwell in as the very fabric of our being, while at the same time changing it by our participation in it, enacting the history of our language in our history.

Before we go further, let us consider the epistemological implications of this suggestion that *asking* is the beginning of true human speech. Origin-theories usually contend either that language was originally meant to express emotion, or to communicate information, or to get something done. It seems to me significant to recall how characteristic of the early speech of the human individual is the questioning use. It is his withdrawal from immersion in the environment, his questioning of particular impressions, of the events that come to meet him, that marks the emergence of the child's humanity, the emergence of the richer intangible world in which he will come to dwell. It is truly a layer of nothingness, a fold in being, as Merleau-Ponty calls it, that makes us human. And this otherness between self and world, this power of questioning, of criticism, marks, as we have already emphasized, the venture of knowing from beginning to end. No matter how triumphant the forward march of science, no matter how precise, how far-reaching our formulations, they are founded on a question mark.

We need not go so far even as the achievement of language, to find this ambivalence in the human being's relation to the world. Even before he learns to speak, in the achievement of upright posture, the child has won for himself that equivocal relation to his world so pervasive of, and essential to, his human history. This mark of our uniqueness may well be added to our list. Dr Erwin Straus in a series of essays has studied its significance, not as an anatomical accident, but as the bodily vehicle, and expression, of the structure of our being-in-the-world. In achieving upright posture, he points out, man is opposing the force of gravity, yet never wholly overcoming this opposition: 'upright posture always maintains its character of counteraction. It calls for our activity and attention.'[29] Through *standing* we achieve distance from the earth, but in a tension demanding to be relaxed in its abandonment; distance from things, overcome in the use of tools; independence of our fellow men, overcome through 'inclination'. Even the extension of ourselves into the world we dwell in is embodied, as Straus points out, in the varied, space-stretching uses of hand and arm.

It is, in every sense, this *lifting* of ourselves out of our environment to make of it a world, further, that makes possible, what we have already noticed in our comparison of the chicken and the experimenter: *objective* perception. The human child, as it were, places the object over against itself, as *Gegen-stand*, takes it as there for this or that purpose, as object in the world. Such *objective* perception, according to Buytendijk's analysis, always includes two aspects: *sensing* and *noticing*[30], and in *noticing* we have already a normative procedure, a bringing of aspects of experience under a system of values. Thus:

> man does not exist, like the animal, simply sensing and acting, but also knowing and achieving.[31]

That is to say, again, that man, rather than flowing, relatively passively, into and from a species-specific niche in nature, sets appearances over against himself, makes them objects, gives them their being in a world, in his world:

> this world for the human being is gift and task (Gabe und Aufgabe),[32] which he understands and responds to out of his own initiative. His response is not just reaction, but a reaching out to grasp, it is shaping, creative achievement under the guidance of reason and of the normative system of values which the child had found there in the world as already constituted and which it had accepted, appropriated, and renewed.[33]

The child 'responds to the world on its own initiative': it shapes its world under the guidance of a 'system of values' which it has accepted and made its own, on its own. Buytendijk mentions the difference in method of play between Donald and Gua when each was given a toy cart to pull along. Gua simply pulled the toy; Donald stopped to set it up 'right' whenever it toppled over. The objectification of the world and the acceptance of standards, the assumption of a value system, are inseparable aspects of a single process. To see this grey as this colour now in one background and now in another is to withdraw from my natural perception of the relation between two parts of a single gestalt on more than one occasion, and to appraise them in the context *I* choose: this time of colours. Objectification, evaluation and freedom are inseparable. Through submitting to certain rules of judgment, and imposing them on what confronts him, the human person makes himself with a part of himself into an impartial observer. But *he* makes himself so by imposing on himself the standard of impartiality, the value of truth. He takes on the role of detached spectator, and accepts the responsibility for living his part. He legislates into existence the *value* of *de*tachment. Far from preventing impartiality, the 'intrusion' of 'judgments of value' is essential to its existence. Only as the child comes to, or better takes it upon himself to, live in a value-governed world, does he learn the discipline of objective perception, and beyond that the more sophisticated objectivities of scientific discourse.

All the factors I have been mentioning are aspects of what I have already referred to in Plessner's phrase as the 'natural artificiality of man', part of the disparity and union, the transcendence and immanence, the confrontation and indwelling, which together characterize the human being's relation to his world. The same ambivalence characterizes the ontogenesis of the human being as a member of society. For here too, and here most fundamentally, the child takes upon himself fundamental values which he both assimilates to himself and yet can partly criticize and revise. This situation is in fact already well developed when the child begins to question, and so to speak. He must ask *someone*; he must confront others before he can inquire. Here again, also, in social life, the likeness to other animals is far-reaching, yet, Buytendijk argues, superficial. Human society is unique:

> Only men *form* a community, a society and a state. In these social units there is division of roles. Only man can assume a role. Even if this takes place with apparent compulsion, 'instinctively', this is nevertheless always historically conditioned and realized though decisions or acts of assent. The social life of animals is founded on the categorical meanings of their physical endowment and environment and adapted to special situations through habit formation. Human society is constituted through normative obligations. The contrast between inter-individual relations in animals and human personal relations is the contrast between nature and culture, environment and world, development and history, custom and tradition. Even the aspect of social life most deeply anchored in the bodily endowment of man, that of man and woman and of mother and child, is different from that of animals, because it is *always* bound to definite *norms* and follows a rule in every society.[34]

Thus in all human societies, for example, there is some kind of prohibition of incest; such rules are wholly lacking in all the animal kingdom.[35] With man, in short, a wholly new principle of social life emerges: the taking on of roles which constitutes culture:

> This new principle, which makes possible verbal language, creative achievement, objective perception, and the freedom of normative obligations, determines all phases of the child's life. Even though the efficacy of this principle is not apparent in the infant in his first months, the new born child is nevertheless a being different from an animal. The child is a developing human being. As he awakens he finds his humanity already in the image of his mother, which is not merely sensed, but known as being and as being-such-and-such. This knowledge is supported by the nature of the body, but this nature is from the start a human nature in two ways. First, the child *discovers* his own body as situation *and* as object. Secondly, he *discovers* the other person, in the first instance his mother, as the 'complement' of himself, that is, as an 'alter ego'.[36]

Buytendijk proceeds to contrast the life of mother and child in man with that of other species. They have, of course, a great deal in common, in biological situation and emotional contact: 'animal mother and young are given to one another as situation. And with man too this is the case'.[37] But the difference is fundamental:

> Let us observe exactly how an infant even at a few months looks at his mother. It is evident that his way of looking is radically different from that of a young animal, even from the way in which a dog, for example,

looks his master in the eye. In particular the human child shows in his regard a certain 'reserve', he constructs, in looking, a certain distance, which he at the same time bridges. We understand this peculiarity at once, and understand it as human. The child's look expresses familiarity, knowledge, but also identification *and* objectification. This manner of looking at some one is in principle the same in the infant as in two-year old children looking in play at a doll: in this case too the look shows participation *and* withdrawal.[38]

It is, again, this reciprocal 'participation *and* withdrawal' which characterizes the human situation, and which underlies the free submission to standards constitutive of human society:

> The life of mother and child has from the beginning a style of its own, which is not determined by genetic endowment and habit, but takes its stamp from directedness towards the assignment of roles, toward rules, which are maintained because the participating individuals *pledge themselves* to maintain them. Mother and child soon constitute a human society. Every society is founded on identification with the *alter ego*, which is nevertheless an *other* I precisely because every individual distinguishes himself from his fellow man. This distinction does not have to be accompanied by clear self-consciousness. It is rather the basic motif of behaviour. In this way human social life becomes an unreflective, routine assumption of a changing assignment of roles, and of the binding rules which have validity because each individual pledges himself to respect them.[39]

We see here, then, even in the behaviour of the months old infant, characteristic human attitudes. What Buytendijk calls the taking on of obligations is sometimes described by philosophers as 'rule-bound behaviour', but it is important to remember, as Buytendijk also stresses in the above passage, that the unspoken acceptance of standards by the awakening infant will underlie, all his life long, all articulable rules. This is still the case at all levels of maturity and sophistication. I dwell in the fundamental evaluations which I have learned in and since infancy. Some aspects of that fundamental structure I may withdraw from sufficiently to formulate and criticize, or assent to them at a new level of reflection. So Socrates, for example, presents to Crito the general principles of promise-keeping and the implicitly contractual relation of the Athenian citizen to his state, principles and relations which Crito unwillingly admits, but which in his routine concern with everyday interests he would not have noticed. Yet it is always the tacit but nevertheless responsible and free forming of oneself in the image of one's own culture that carries all one's articulate rules and preferences.

Again, this structure shows up dramatically in boundary situations. That is the philosophical lesson of Primo Levi's *If This is a Man*.[40]

The destructiveness of the murder camps lay not only in the brute fact that so many died, but in the annihilation of the victims' humanity. What the Nazis showed there was that humanity is made and can be unmade; what they 'created' was life 'more bestial than any beast's' on a scale and of a ghastliness such as neither Goethe nor the devil himself could have imagined. Levi reports, as others too have done of other such situations, how it was madmen and criminals, those who lived already at the fringe of or beyond the borders of normal human worlds, who best 'survived' these unthinkable ordeals. He describes the destruction of personality implicit in the very organization of the camps: the loss of one's own clothing, profession, name and entity. He makes plain too that to the Nazi and even the ordinary German participants in the Buna plant ostensibly 'using' the camp's labour, the inmates *were* non-human, revolting worse-than-animals in their grotesque approximation to human shape and speech. This is the issue too that confronts today every non-coloured American. It is not only that we have relegated a great sector of our society to second-class *citizenship*; by assigning to them other rules than ours within our community we have made them second-class *men*. That is what, through politics, through the conventions of social organization, no man has any right to do to any other. The submission to the death camps, the revolt against racialism: both bring us to the edge of the human situation and reflect, from the boundary, its nature in its more routine and unimperilled functioning.

VII

What has all this to do with knowledge? We may say, first, in general, that if all knowing is essentially a kind of doing, and human doing is always value-bound, then knowledge is so as well. But more particularly, three aspects of Buytendijk's description bear directly on the problem of knowledge. First, as we have already noticed, the *objectivity* of human perception which underlies all scientific accuracy and all canons of evidence, whether in scientific or historical disciplines, is an *objectification*, the result of a commitment to withdrawal, a fashioning of the world as a dwelling place in which I can move, in communion with others who have oriented themselves in a world that communicates with mine. The recent studies in orientation by I. Kohler, as well as other psychological experiments, e.g., by the transactional school of Ames, Cantril and others, stress the same fundamental fact.[41]

Again, what is involved here is the 'projection of a world', not simply the habituation to a changed environment.[42] And the development of scientific theories, each of which both relies on and modifies its predecessors, consists in the multiplication of mutually harmonious projections of this same essential kind. To become a competent specialist in any one branch of science is to participate with one's whole intellectual being in such a projection, to come to dwell in it and move about in it as one dwells in the familiar spatio-temporal framework which all normal human beings have in infancy and childhood built up for themselves. The fundamental values, implicit principles and explicit rules which enclose the structure are necessary conditions of our unimpeded and orderly manipulation of objective concepts and of our constatation of impartially ascertainable facts.

I have already called attention, secondly, to the epistemological significance of the *question* as the child's characteristic form of speech. If problem-solving is the paradigm case for the process of knowing, which is itself essentially an elaboration of the learning situation, it is again the characteristic equivocity of questioning that lies at the basis of all the conceptual structures which we come to inhabit. Animals in so far as they achieve knowledge of their environment, may also make mistakes; but if they do, they simply go wrong. We have, further, the great if tragic power of *calling* in question, of holding one aspect or another of our world over against ourselves and calling it in doubt. In this respect Popper is right in identifying rationality with the power of criticism.

The critique of certainty in Part One has sufficiently emphasized this aspect of the cognitive process. Two points have been added here: its rootedness in the achievement of objective perception, its emergence together with and inseparably from the positing of social institutions. Mother and child, as Buytendijk says, already form a society. The child's discovery, and construction, of the world already takes place with and through others, through question and answer, through social play, through the older child's or the adult's interpretation of pictures, the teaching of language and writing–all the way to the research student's training in the school of a master. All the way we are shaping ourselves on the model of or in criticism of others, and of the standards embodied in the lives of others. All knowledge, even the most abstract, exists only within the fundamental evaluations, first of the total community which permits and respects such knowledge, and second, within this totality, of the special community whose consensus makes possible the existence of this particular discipline. The social rootedness of science is often associated with the utility of applied science; this is an error and a dangerous error. But precisely the *detachment* of the theoretical scientist is rooted in the institutions of his society and in the evaluative choices which underlie those institutions. He can focus his whole attention, bringing every relevant clue to bear, on a problem wholly without appetitive or utilitarian implications, he can put his whole heart and mind into the search for understanding for the sake of understanding alone. How can he do this? First, because he himself has been nourished and disciplined by traditions cultivated within his society which have produced this kind of devoted attention to impersonal goals. And secondly, because the society itself, in its deepest foundations, respects those independently self-sustaining traditions of scientist or scholar. No discipline, however 'factual', however 'detached', can come into being or remain in existence except insofar as the fundamental evaluative acts of the individuals belonging to a given culture have legislated into existence and maintain in existence the area of free inquiry and of mutual confirmation or falsification which such free inquiry demands.

We can perhaps see more plainly what this situation amounts to by returning to formulate once more in a different way the relation between assertions of fact, affective attachments or preferences, and acts of evaluation. A fundamental error of the fact/value dichotomy, it seems to me, was to see these three aspects of the human situation as two only, and so to miss the unique phenomenon which both unites the other two and holds them apart: the phenomenon of responsible acceptance of standards, the *Verpflichtung* which Buytendijk describes as so constant an ingredient in the infant's incipient history. 'Values', in fact, as the fact/value dichotomist sees them, are not fully values at all, but degenerate values, merely subjective likes or dislikes. So, it is alleged, I either assert *this* or ejaculate 'ouch' or 'yum' as the case may be. Indeed, this conception of language and of human experience represents in fact the last stand of Cartesianism, where the world has shrunk to Humean atoms of sensation and the self to secret, equally atomic inner states. But Cartesianism was a falsification of experience from the start, much less in this last, residual form. The trouble is that in this tradition from start to finish it is purely the *explicit* poles of experience that are noticed: on the one hand, the presented, objectified surfaces of things, and on the other the self-enjoyed quality of my 'inner sense'. As Kant already saw, both poles of experience, inner as well as outer, are held together, and made the experience they are, on the ground of my *constitution* of them, through my legislation for their order, through my *Sinngebung*. An act, however, can not be stated, only enacted, and as long as we seek wholly the stateable this constitutive element eludes us. Neither the 'ghost' nor the machine nor both together can provide an adequate concept of our minds and their power to know.

Professor Pumphrey in a lecture on the origin of language has pointed out that the 'intelligence' conveyed by a message is only part of the whole information carried by speech, whether animal or human.[43] He puts this aspect of the situation well when he describes intelligence as coming in an *envelope* of emotion, an envelope which human objectification has greatly enlarged and if you like stretched thin, but by no means annihilated. This metaphor of the emotional envelope of intelligence already helps to correct the error of setting fact and value over against one another as two mutually exclusive, antagonistic components of our discourse. It helps also to remind us of the continuity between the speech of animals and men. But to mark the difference, and to delimit properly the scope and power of human knowing, we need to include as well reference to the third and legislative component: the act of standard-setting which enables intelligence to come free of individual appetite and create a public, knowable world. If the human infant, and the human adult, can move *between* immersion in sense with its pervasive quality and confrontation with objects to be assessed and reassessed as other than oneself or one's own feelings: this distance, this envelope-stretching, is made possible by the acts of standard-setting in which I have both created and controlled my world and submitted to it as the reality which has created and controls my being.

Part Three
The Complexity of Things

7 The Faith of Darwinism

WHATEVER I SUCCEED IN KNOWING, IT IS *I* WHO ACHIEVE KNOW-ledge: I in my contingent, personal existence, I-in-situation. Such an 'I' is alive. 'Minding', as Ryle calls it, is one form of living, and can be understood only as a species within that genus. But living, in turn, is one kind of natural being. The sort of conceptual reform I have been urging, therefore, must be grounded, in turn, in a revised ontology, an ontology which allows to life its due place in the natural world. The kind of distinction I have been describing, for example, between men and other animals needs to be related to an account of reality in general such that it makes sense to talk about living things at all.

This is a more difficult aspect of the conceptual reform with which we are here concerned. We are so used to thinking, or thinking that we think, of the *real* as the physico-chemically real, we are so used to apologizing for life, and assuring ourselves that Nobel prizewinners are just on the verge of explaining it away. We are so used, like O'Casey's Young Covey, to identifying enlightenment with the reduction of all else to 'molecewels and atoms', that to admit, *au fond*, the reality of living nature seems a betrayal of science itself. What is real is by definition the *non*-living. That is the fundamental untruth we have still to overcome.

But, it will be objected, what of evolution? Did not the brilliant development of biology under Darwin's influence put life, its nature and history, squarely onto the centre of the intellectual stage? On the contrary: what was so triumphantly successful in Darwin's theory was precisely its reduction of life to the play of chance and necessity, its elimination of organic categories from the interpretation even of living things. True, modern Darwinians are attempting, in a confused and confusing way, to deny, or to rectify, this reductive tendency; but the fact remains that Darwinism as a comprehensive theory is reductive, and still essentially Cartesian, in its interpretation of the organic world. Not, indeed, nature in the eighteenth-century sense, not nature as *a* machine, but nature as a mechanically interacting aggregate of machines: that is the Darwinian vision. It is the extension of the machine image to life itself. It appeared to its first adherents, for this very reason, as the last great liberating agency *against* bigotry and superstition, liberator *for* the spirit of science and the heroic pursuit of truth.

To justify this allegation, let us look a little more closely at Darwinism past and present. When we have seen why we cannot trust it to do the job for us, we can move on to adumbrate, more positively, the kind of concepts and principles that will be needed if the job is nevertheless to be done.

II

The eighteen sixties and seventies saw the triumph of Darwinism over religion, but also the rise of Darwinism *as* religion: as a religion of humanity, inspired by the inhumanity of literal Christian belief. Darwin, though himself only partly a Darwinian, yet set the tone for this aspect of the Darwinian cult in his autobiography–in a passage suppressed by his widow and included in the complete edition:

> I can indeed hardly see how anyone ought to wish Christianity to be true; for, if so, the plain language of the text seems to show that the men who do not believe, and this would include my Father, Brother and almost all my best friends, will be everlastingly punished. And this is a damnable doctrine.[1]

This 'damnable doctrine' of Christianity has been the target of evolutionary ethics from the early T. H. Huxley to Julian Huxley, George Gaylord Simpson, or Theodosius Dobzhansky in the present generation. Sin, punishment, the last vestige of the jealous Hebrew god, such thinkers feel, have been vanquished under the benevolent banner of purely naturalistic nature, unplanned and therefore unresentful. So we have, for instance, Julian Huxley's 'morality of evolutionary direction':

> Anything which permits or promotes open development is right, anything which restricts or frustrates development is wrong.[2]

Some Darwinians, it is true, deny this ethical implication of Darwinism. T. H. Huxley, in his later years, denied it; so does the naturalist David Lack in a book called *Evolutionary Theory and Christian Belief: The Unresolved Conflict*.[3] For such thinkers, Darwinian nature, which scientific conscience compels them to accept, is the blind ongoing of fact indifferent to value and incapable of generating value. Morality must maintain itself, on this view, not within, but against the evolutionary stream. But this is, on the whole, an exceptional view; the humanitarian *Leitmotif* has been a genuine force in the origin and spread of Darwinism.

Yet this is only half the story, and the lesser half. It is as a *religion of science* that Darwinism chiefly held, and holds, men's minds. The derivation of life, of man, of man's deepest hopes and highest achievements, from the external and indirect determination of small chance errors, appears as the very keystone of the naturalistic universe. And the defence of natural selection appears, therefore, as the defence of the integrity, the independence, the dignity of science itself. In this spirit T. H. Huxley first rose to its defence:

> ... I have said that the man of science is the sworn interpreter of nature in the high court of reason. But of what avail is his honest speech, if ignorance is the assessor of the judge, and prejudice the foreman of the jury? ... To those whose life is spent, to use Newton's noble words, in picking up here a pebble and there a pebble on the shores of the great ocean of truth–who watch, day by day, the slow but sure advance of that mighty tide, bearing on its bosom the thousand treasures wherewith man ennobles and beautifies his life–it would be laughable, if it were not so sad, to see the little Canutes of the hour enthroned in solemn state, bidding that great wave to stay, and threatening to check its beneficent progress. ... Surely, it is the duty of the public to discourage anything of this kind, to discredit these foolish meddlers who think they do the Almighty a service by preventing a thorough study of His works.[4]

Thus, a century ago, Darwinism against Christian orthodoxy.

Today the tables are turned. The modified, but still characteristically Darwinian theory has itself become an orthodoxy, preached by its adherents with religious fervour, and doubted, they feel, only by a few muddlers imperfect in scientific faith. Sir Gavin de Beer's great classic *Embryos and Ancestors*, for example, presents in brilliant array a host of embryological data bearing on evolution, but with no apparent relevance to the process of natural selection. Yet he concludes the third edition:

> It is now recognized that evolution is the result of selection acting on heritable variation in the form of mutation and recombination of Mendelian genes. *These processes must have been at work in all the evolutionary changes considered in this book.* The morphological modes describe aspects of the course which the changes took, *but it was variation and selection which caused them.*[5]

And accordingly, in his centennial essay in *Endeavour*, Sir Gavin assures us that

> ... with the same confidence as it accepts Copernicus's demonstrations of the movement of the Earth round the sun and Newton's formulation of the laws of this movement, science can now celebrate the centenary of the first general principle to be discovered applicable to the entire realm of living beings.[6]

Biology, thanks to Darwin (with assistance, indeed, from the rediscoverers of Mendel), has at last matured into a proper science, 'Lamarck nonsense' is disinherited, old metaphysical follies re-echo only distantly in the ears of a few foolish mystics. Branches of biology once disparate–palaeontology, embryology, ecology, taxonomy, genetics–converge on the new, great synthesis. Matter becoming life (and mind) through natural selection of small chance mutations; life spreading in ever new directions through opportunistic exploitation of the unexpected: of new niches in nature happening to fit a slightly new departure in the arrangement of established genotypes, or slightly new genotypes happening to tumble into hitherto unexploited environments–this is the vision which experiment and mathematics, field observation and its statistical analysis combine to support.

There was a time, about the turn of the century, when the concept of mutation–i.e. of a sudden change in the structure of the germ plasm–appeared to contradict Darwin's view of a slow and gradual process in which slightly less fit variations were eliminated in favour of the slightly better adapted. But beginning with Sir Ronald Fisher's *Genetical Theory of Natural Selection* in 1930 there has arisen a most imposing synthesis of these two conceptions.[7] Darwin did not know whether inheritance was blending or particulate–whether variations once occurring were or were not assimilated in some unknown way into the material of inheritance. Mendel, whose work lay buried till the early twentieth century, had, in fact, in Darwin's lifetime, proved the particulate basis.[8] This seemed at first to mean that variations, for the use of evolution, are sudden and large, and not minute and gradual as Darwin imagined. What Fisher saw, however, was (1) that particulate inheritance retains variations for selection to work on, as blending inheritance would not, and (2) that it is not the changes in individuals that matter, for the purposes of evolution, but the changes in populations–and these are gradual. For if you have an active interbreeding population, say, of a thousand flies, and you get a changed gene, say, for eyeless, in one chromosome in one of them, the proportion will now be 999 normal flies to one containing the mutation (and the corresponding change in the genes will be to 1,999 of the normal *allele* and one of the mutated form); in the next generation you may have 998 to two (or 1,998 normal genes to two mutated ones) and so on. This kind of change in a population is usually, and can be, very gradual; and it is measurable by statistical methods. In fact this measurement is said to *be* the measure of selective intensity–the change in Mendelian proportions in a population *is* natural selection, or genetical selection, as it is more properly called, and Darwinism is vindicated.

Yet surely, one may protest, Darwin's theory had to do with the 'preservation of favoured races', the survival of the fittest and all that. On the face of it, these changing Mendelian ratios seem to have no connection with increasing adaptation, or the elimination of the unfit, or anything of the sort. Yet here, too, the modern theory is more Darwinian than Darwin himself. 'Evolution', Fisher says, 'is progressive adaptation and consists in nothing else.'[9] And life itself is evolution: populations evolving, fitting in here and there, weeding themselves out here and there, as changing opportunities appear and disappear. That is what selective intensity measures; for what else could it conceivably be measuring? Darwin excepted some characters from this rule, seeing no reason to consider them advantageous or otherwise. But modern ecological methods have greatly amplified and codified the relevant data, and have proved even some of Darwin's exceptions–notably, for instance, colour polymorphism in the common land snail–to be in fact confirmations of his view. For modern Darwinians only trivial variations can be indifferent to selection pressure. Whatever characters are stable must have a reason, and the reason must be adaptive, otherwise natural selection could not control it.

The compelling power of the selection theory–that is, the view that all major trends in evolution are adaptive, and that the genesis of adaptations is explained by the gradual and external control of chance variations through selection pressure–is well illustrated, for example, by de Beer's reasoning in the centennial essay quoted above. Attacking those who invoke against the selection theory its 'mathematical improbability', he argues that they

> ... can be refuted out of their own mouths. Muller has estimated that on the existing knowledge of the percentage of mutations that are beneficial, and a reasoned estimate of the number of mutations that would be necessary to convert an amoeba into a horse, based on the average magnitude of the effects of mutations, the number of mutations required on the basis of chance alone, if there were no natural selection, would be of the order of one thousand raised to the power of one million. *This impossible and meaningless figure serves to illustrate the power of natural selection in collecting favourable mutations and minimizing waste of variation, for horses do exist and they have evolved.*[10]

In other words, if horses have evolved–and few are those who would like to deny it–and if an explanation of this transformation through random mutations alone is excessively unlikely–as indeed it seems to be, since the great majority of mutations so far observed are adverse or even lethal–then it *must* be the automatic selection, in each generation, of very slightly advantageous variants that has built up the otherwise astonishing result. But how, one may ask, do we know this? If mutation alone cannot explain the evolutionary process –the origin of life, of sentient life, of intelligent life–why is natural selection, that is, the elimination of the worst mutations, a negative and external agency, the only conceivable alternative?

And what does this selective process really consist in? Selection selects by definition the better adapted alternatives; yet adaptation often leads not to survival, let alone to the evolution of new forms, but to extinction. In de Beer's centennial argument, however, this fact appears as evidence against a belief in teleology or providence, not against selection. So he argues, on the very same page as the passage just quoted:

> It can be shown that the more detailed the adaptation, the more 'improbable' it may appear as a product of 'chance', the more likely its possessor is to be doomed to extinction through inability to become adapted to changed conditions. Structures may be developed which at first benefit individuals in their competition to survive; but by continued selection such structures may become exaggerated and lead to extinction of the species. This seems to have been what happened to the Huia-bird, where mated pairs constantly remained in company together, and the beaks of the male and female reached an extraordinary disparity of size in adaptation to their very special feeding, but failed to enable the birds to obtain ordinary food when their special diet was unavailable. Excess, even of adaptation, is harmful, and the fossil record shows that the vast majority of lines of evolution have led to extinction, which is a grim comment on the alleged powers of providential guidance and purpose.[11]

So it is; and surely, thanks largely to Darwin's influence, few educated people believe literally any more in 'providential guidance and purpose' in nature. But is it not also a 'grim comment' on natural selection? Yet convinced neo-Darwinians apparently see no such implication in the Huia-bird's fate.

In short, three concepts, *evolution*, in the minimal sense of 'descent with modification' (no 'emergence', no 'higher and lower' allowed), *variation*, in the sense of Mendelian micromutation, tiny fortuitous changes in the structure or arrangement of the genes, the ultimate material of heredity (no sweeping or sudden alterations allowed), and *natural selection*, the decrease in frequency of those variants that happen in each successive generation to be less well adapted than others to their particular environment: these three form a tight circle within which, in happy self-confirmation, neo-Darwinian thinking moves. The basic explanatory concepts here are *chance* and *necessity*. Mutations are chance failures of the duplicating mechanism; selection is the agent of external compulsion, eliminating less well adapted variants through environmental pressure. These two, chance and necessity, have been, indeed, since ancient times, from Democritus through Hobbes to modern physicalism, the sole permitted instruments of reductivist explanation. To those who believe in such explanation, these concepts form an ample intellectual dwelling place, roomy enough, in the case of Darwinism, to house all the immense achievements of modern biological research. To those not so convinced, however, the circle they constitute seems a strangely constricted one. They may even agree with Sir James Gray that 'no amount of argument, or clever epigram, can disguise the inherent improbability of orthodox (Darwinian) theory'.[12] And although, as we are constantly reminded, a poll of such non-believers would still exclude 'the majority of biologists', the heretics are nevertheless neither so few nor so feeble as neo-Darwinian writers sometimes suggest.

III

How, then, does this tight trio of concepts take so firm a hold upon so many and such able minds?

First, it is one of the major paradoxes of the history of science, that the Darwinian theory, speculative as it must be by the nature of its subject-matter, has been held up as a model of simple Baconian induction through the patient accumulation of facts. In this misconception, Darwin himself led the way. As he wrote in a famous passage in the *Autobiography*:

> I worked on true Baconian principles, and without any theory collected facts on a wholesale scale, more especially with respect to domesticated productions, by printed enquiries, by conversation with skilful breeders and gardeners, and by extensive reading.[13]

Now no one denies that Darwin did patiently accumulate facts— but the facts he accumulated during the voyage of the *Beagle* did not at the time lead him to his species theory, and moreover, for many of the years during which the species theory was maturing in his mind, he was in fact accumulating facts, not directly about evolution, but for his extended work on barnacles. No, the species theory, like most great forward steps in science, was a triumph of scientific *imagination* rather than of fact collecting. There were in fact two major leaps of imagination through which Darwin's theory took shape: first in the sketch of 1837, where he speaks of *adaptation* perpetuated through *generation*, and secondly in the notes of 1842 and 1844, which follow his reading of Malthus on population, the text which by his own account suggested to him the concepts of struggle for existence and survival of the fittest, the essential agents of *natural selection*. These steps once made, the new conceptual scheme took over, and the task of the *Origin* was to amplify the evidence in its support–evidence gleaned everyhow and everywhere–with the passion of genius, but not by unusually accurate or systematic collection of data–and to assimilate within its all-enclosing scope whatever evidence might appear at first sight to conflict with it. The method is one of imagination, of extrapolation from a few facts to many more inferred realities seen in terms of the imagined scheme, and proof of these realities by the exclusion of other possibilities. Much the same method, as Dr Gertrude Himmelfarb has pointed out in her book *Darwin and the Darwinian Revolution*, was employed by Darwin in his work on the origin of coral reefs.[14] The *subsidence* theory, he held, must be true of all such formations because as a conceptual scheme it was so clearly superior to the current alternative, the volcanic-crater theory. And the other alternative being excluded, this one is proved: 'If, then,' he writes, 'the foundations of the many atolls were not uplifted into the required position, they must of necessity have subsided into it; and this at once solves every difficulty.'[15] This style of argument occurs again and again in the *Origin* also–and it is also very like Sir Gavin's argument about mutation, selection, and the horse.

This is not to suggest that Darwin or Darwinians, past or present, are 'speculative' rather than 'scientific' in their reasoning. Darwin himself certainly was not of a philosophical turn of mind; and he certainly believed sincerely, as his followers have done and do, that, as against such day-dreaming evolutionists as his grandfather or such systematizing evolutionists as Herbert Spencer, he was patiently and empirically and critically pursuing facts and rejecting hypotheses not confirmed by facts. Yet what the genius of Darwin achieved, surely, was not to discover a host of new facts unknown to his predecessors that somehow added up to the further fact of evolution through natural selection; what he did was to see the facts in a new context–an imaginative context, the context of an idea, but an idea which seemed and seems to many modern minds peculiarly factual, an idea so convincing, so congenial, so satisfying that it feels like fact.

Moreover, the circular structure which seems so oddly illogical to the outsider is just what, seen from the inside, most firmly supports the theory. 'The genius–and the folly–of such a theory,' Dr Himmelfarb says of the *subsidence* theory, 'is that it can explain anything and everything', and she shows how this applies to the argument of the *Origin* as well.[16] This, again, it seems to me, is an important point if one wants to understand the modern as well as the nineteenth-century evolutionary literature. Difficulties such as the want of intermediaries in the fossil record or the problem of explaining on a chance-plus-elimination basis the slow cumulative evolution of organs like the eye, Darwin overcame sometimes by adding further hypotheses to support his original hypothesis, sometimes by urging us not to let our reason give in to a mere difficulty of imagination; and his very frankness in facing these difficulties *as* difficulties seemed to turn them from difficulties of the theory into parts of its proof. How could this be? Dr Himmelfarb suggests that Darwin moves between two senses of explanation: to explain and to explain away. That may be what happens in effect, but the root of the matter, I suspect, lies deeper. It was the idea of natural selection that convinced the Victorians that evolution happened: so much so that for many people the idea of evolution *means* natural selection still. Now the chief direct evidence for evolution is the fossil record, but this, with its gaps, its explosive periods, its development of structures past any apparent adaptive end, is not in the main evidence for the very gradual, adaptation-controlled process envisaged by Darwin. Yet if it is evidence for evolution, and evolution *means* natural selection, then natural selection, by its convincing power, assimilates to itself the very evidence which would seem at first glance to tell against it. Thus Darwin's argument on the one hand *proves* that evolution happened by natural selection, and on the other hand, *conceiving* evolution as the result of natural selection, identifies all evidence for evolution with evidence for selection. It is not evolution as such but evolution by selection that defines the circle. *Difficulties* of selection theory, if they are proofs of evolution, must be in fact *proofs* of selection–since that is what, essentially, evolution is.

Modern arguments work in much the same way. Thus for example the work of H. B. D. Kettlewell on industrial melanism has certainly confirmed the hypothesis that natural selection takes place in nature.[17] This is the story of the black mutant of the common peppered moth which, as Kettlewell has shown with beautiful precision, increases in numbers in the vicinity of industrial centres and decreases, being more easily exposed to predators, in rural areas. Here, say the neo-Darwinians, is natural selection, that is, evolution, actually going on. But to this we may answer: selection, yes; the colour of moths or snails or mice is clearly controlled by visibility to predators; but 'evolution'? Do these observations explain how in the first place there came to be any moths or snails or mice at all? By what right are we to extrapolate the pattern by which colour or other such superficial characters are governed to the origin of species, let alone of orders, classes, phyla of living organisms? But, say the neo-Darwinians again, natural selection is the only mechanism we observe in present-day nature. But again, if this were so, we should still have no right to say that the only mechanism we see at work now is the only one that has been at work in all the long past of the living world. Nor, for that matter, is it the only 'mechanism'. What of the mechanisms of development? Why not look at phylogeny as an ontogeny writ large, at the history of groups as expressing a fundamental rhythm still, in its intimacy, unknown to us, but analogous to the rhythm of individual development? Because the chance-variation/natural-selection schema, which through Darwin's work first convinced the world that evolution did in fact happen, still holds the mind entranced, absorbs into itself *all* evolutionary data, and at the same time rejects all data not so absorbable.

To say that neo-Darwinian thinking moves within a circle of concepts is not, in itself, however, to challenge its validity. For all comprehensive theories, all fundamental theories that the mind really dwells in–the corpuscular theory of the Newtonians, the relativity theory of twentieth-century physicists–are similarly circular, since they rest in the last analysis on the self-satisfying character of their own premises. But in the case of neo-Darwinism the circle seems too narrow, and the detours taken to maintain it in the teeth of the evidence too circuitous and so many. Some years ago, for example, Professor C. H. Waddington described some experiments which at the time seemed to some people to shed some doubt on some aspects of the current theory; now his findings appear to have been happily assimilated and their puzzling aspect forgotten.[18] He produced a character called 'crossveinless' in fruit flies by subjection to high temperature for a short period of time. Breeding crossveinless flies, he got a higher proportion of flies which reacted in this way to the heat treatment; but after a time he got a race of flies that were crossveinless even *without* subjection to heat. This looked like a cousin, at least, of the geneticists' old enemy, inheritance of acquired characters. But no, genes and selection explain it all with ease. So P. M. Sheppard writes in *Natural Selection and Heredity*:

> In other words, selection had resulted in a character, usually only produced under exceptional environmental conditions, being produced under normal conditions. Selections for those individuals that produced the character only with heat-shock would give a phenotypically flexible stock, whereas selection for those that produced it under both conditions would give a phenotypically fixed one.
> This result explains how some plants or animals can develop a gene-complex which produces a particular form fitted to a particular environment under most environmental conditions; that is to say, they are not phenotypically flexible, whereas in others the form is only produced under the appropriate environmental conditions (i.e. it is phenotypically flexible).[19]

In short, the gene-complex, together with the theory of polygenic inheritance, can do anything. For each character is controlled, not, as used to be thought, by one gene, but by many genes, all balancing and buffering one another; and every change in the environment is balanced against the resulting balance. Thus in stable environments natural selection is conservative, preserving advantageous arrangements against disruption; but let the environment begin changing ever so slightly, natural selection causes—or rather *is*, by definition—the slight preponderance of a genotype slightly more favourable to the new conditions. Whatever might at first sight appear as evidence against the theory is assimilated by redefinition into the theory.

Finally, if evolution is axiomatically evolution by natural selection, it is at the same time evolution as progressive adaptation, since it is adaptive relationships that natural selection controls. This identity—the dependence of Darwinian and neo-Darwinian thought on the axiom that organic phenomena are explicable primarily in terms of adaptation, of the usefulness of particular structures and functions in particular niches in nature—is also emphasized, in its nineteenth-century background, in Dr Himmelfarb's book mentioned above. Firstly, as she points out, the sketch of 1837 argues plainly *from* adaptation as its basic datum. Secondly, 'adaptation' is a matter of means and ends; and the reception of the *Origin* as Dr Himmelfarb describes it shows how essential such means-end relations are to its argument. From the first the *Origin*, dispensing with a planner and with fixed ends for the processes of nature, seemed to many critics materialistic and mechanistic in its inspiration, but, saturated as it is with the conception of utility, fitness and the like, appealed to others as the triumphant vindication of teleological thinking. For the in-between teleology of utilitarian thought is indeed the proper habitat, the natural niche, of Darwinism. Darwin, Shaw said, threw Paley's famous watch, the paradigm for the argument from design, into the ocean. It was not really, however, the watch he threw away, but the watchmaker. Darwinism is teleology decapitated; everything in nature is explained in terms of its purpose, but an unplanned purpose in which the organism is tool, tool-user, and beneficiary all in one. And the artefact analogy is as basic to Darwinism, both old and new, as it is to natural theology: not only is the concept of natural selection grounded on the analogy with the work of the great livestock breeders, but organisms themselves are conceived in Paleyan terms as contrivances, aggregates of characters and functions good for—what? For survival, that is, for going on being good for, going on being good for—and so on *ad infinitum*. For the *summum bonum*, like the maker, is dispensed with; yet the means-end relation, the notion of 'this as useful for that', is fundamental still.

Moreover, despite the attempt of some of the leading neo-Darwinians to prove a selection theorem independently of the fact of adaptation, in purely mathematical terms, all this, again, is equally true of neo-Darwinism. For again and again in the course of their arguments the bare mathematics has to be swelled out to its full adaptive context in order to make of it a theory of evolution–though it may be drawn in again to statistical and mathematical form as scientific respectability demands. From this point of view by far the most honest and consistent statement of Darwinism in recent years is that of John Maynard Smith.[20] He starts, for example, with an account of Dice's experiments proving that owls take more mice against a contrasting than a similar background. This is to begin fairly and squarely with the old Darwinian idea of adaptation for survival, and from here he argues ingeniously but openly to fit a wide variety of evidence into a frankly utilitarian context. He uses, and cites others who use, modern statistical methods in the service of selection theory, but he does not pretend to *deduce* the equation of evolution with adaptive relationships from a mathematical base. Both the strength and the limitations of the theory appear with much less ambiguity in this form.

IV

It is precisely the insistence on the equation of life with adaptation that defines the limits of Darwinism, and it is doubt of the all-inclusiveness of adaptation as a concept definitive of life that motivates the most effective objections to the Darwinian synthesis. As between the Lamarckian and neo-Darwinian views of the origin of adaptations Darwinism appears to have won out; and though many critics of Darwinism still challenge it on the grounds that the infinitely complex harmonies of mutual adaptations could not have been produced simply by a set of curious chances, the most fundamental opposition comes from a more sweeping challenge. One may indeed ask whether all adaptations have arisen by Darwinian-Mendelian means; but one may also ask, as some eminent biologists do, whether evolution, on a large as well as on a small scale, is essentially a matter of adaptation at all. To such biologists–such as A. M. Dalcq of Brussels, O. Schindewolf of Tübingen, or A. Vandel of Toulouse–there appear in fact to be two divergent directions in the evolutionary story.[21] There are, indeed, all the minute specialized divergences like those of the Galapagos finches which so fascinated Darwin; it is their story that is told in the *Origin* and elaborated by the selectionists today. But these are dead ends, last minutiæ of development; it is not from them that the great massive novelties of evolution could have sprung.

For this, such dissenters feel, is the major evolutionary theme: great new inventions, new ideas of living, which arise with startling suddenness, proliferate in a variety of directions, yet persist with fundamental constancy–as in Darwinian terms they would have no reason in the world to do. Neither the origin and persistence of great new modes of life–photosynthesis, breathing, thinking–nor all the intricate and co-ordinated changes needed to support them, are explained or even made conceivable on the Darwinian view. And if one returns to read the *Origin* with these criticisms in mind, one finds, indeed, that for all the brilliance of its hypotheses piled on hypotheses, for all the splendid simplicity of the 'mechanism' by which it 'explains' so many and so varied phenomena, it simply is not about the origin of species, let alone of the great orders and classes and phyla, at all. Its argument moves in a different direction altogether, in the direction of minute specialized adaptations, which lead, unless to extinction, nowhere. And the same is true of the whole immense and infinitely ingenious mountain of work by present-day Darwinians: *c'est magnifique, mais ce n'est pas la guerre!* That the colour of moths or snails or the bloom on the castor bean stem are 'explained' by mutation and natural selection is very likely; but how from single-celled (and for that matter from inanimate) ancestors there came to be castor beans and moths and snails, and how from these there emerged llamas and hedgehogs and lions and apes–and men–that is a question which neo-Darwinian theory simply leaves unasked. With infinite ingenuity it elaborates the microscopic conditions for such macroscopic occurrences; but it provides no conceptual framework in terms of which they can be admitted to exist, let alone an 'explanation' of their descent from 'lower' forms. In short, reflections on some of the problems of macroevolution may well lead to remarks like that of Professor Waddington, tucked away in the folds of his ingenious and 'orthodox' argument on *The Strategy of the Genes*:

> . . . the unprejudiced student is likely to derive the impression that the failure of present theory to provide any plausible explanation for such occurrences has played a not unimportant part in weighting the scales against an acceptance of their real existence. It would certainly seem that in this field . . . the adequacy of modern theory may be doubted.[22]

Moreover, evolutionists sceptical of the neo-Darwinian synthesis have themselves empirical evidence to support their doubts. For despite the neo-Darwinians' claims, two great biological disciplines, palaeontology and embryology, appear to lend their chief weight against the selectionist dogma.

Palaeontology, once more, furnishes both the most direct evidence *for* the fact of evolution and the most imposing evidence *against* the conception of evolution as a continuous, gradual progression of adaptive relationships. 'Gaps in the fossil record' were a serious stumbling block in Darwin's time, and despite the discovery of many missing links—for example the striking completion of horse family history, or the discovery of the bird ancestor Archaeopteryx, with its reptilian features—they still persist. Moreover, they persist systematically: over and over, with suddenness termed 'explosive', a bewildering variety of new types appear: this is true, notably, for example, of the origin of the major mammalian types. Thus, as G. G. Simpson's calculations of rates of evolution show, the bat's wing, if evolved by Mendelian mutation and selective pressure at the same rate at which it has altered since its origin, would have had to begin developing well before the origin of the earth![23] Once new types appear, moreover, they frequently continue, so some palaeontologists at least believe, in directions bearing no systematic relation to adaptive needs; in fact, they often exceed the demands of utility so grossly as to lead their species and genera and families to the common fate of life: that is, to death. Again, of course, if one is convinced in advance that all extinction *must* result, not from any general 'evolutionary trend', but from environmental change, one can interpret these cases too in accordance with selectionist principles: as T. S. Westoll has done, for instance, with the oyster ancestor Gryphaea, which looks as if it had secreted so much limestone that it left itself no room to live in its own shell. These over-specialized creatures, Westoll argues, were probably aged individuals of no evolutionary interest and their particular form of senility may have been associated with an actual reproductive advantage earlier in their individual lives: so that selection kept them going because of this advantage, which happened to carry with it what looks to us like a disadvantage; and in fact it may have been not this 'disadvantage' but an environmental change (for which however we have no evidence) that carried them off. Thus we must infer both an unknown advantage and an unknown environmental change in order to avoid making the much more obvious inference that this kind of animal—this pattern of living—simply played itself out.[24]

But if the major rhythms of the history of life in the past seem to some students to resist compression into the Darwinian-Mendelian mould, these stubborn palaeontological data agree, on the other hand, in the opinion of a number of biologists, with the evidence provided by our knowledge of development, that is, of the history of the living individual. There has been interesting speculation during the past thirty or forty years, and even earlier—speculation based on increasing knowledge of comparative embryology—on the role of 'heterochrony', or change in the temporal rhythms of development, in effecting evolutionary change.[25] Instead of being tacked on, as evolutionists used to think, to the adult stage of early forms, it looks as if new developments may occur at any stage in the life cycle–the earlier, the more basic: and, in terms of the fossil record, the more sudden. Sometimes such early changes appear, indeed, to have consisted in a kind of inspired infantilism: the retention of a larval stage into adult life, permitting, as it were, rejuvenation of the race. This would explain the poverty of the fossil record at transitional stages and the relatively sudden bursts of evolutionary energy that so frequently occur. The late Professor Garstang of Leeds, one of the great originators of this kind of evolutionary thinking, first published in 1894 his theory that the chordates may have developed from something like an echinoderm (starfish or sea urchin) larva; a free-swimming form which, being dorsally exposed to light, might be stimulated to develop the dorsal nervous system characteristic of vertebrates. Or again, it has been pointed out that a human adult holds his head like an embryo dog: presumably, the failure to grow up in this respect enabled our ancestors to adopt an upright posture, and to achieve binocular vision. A host of arguments of this kind are substantiated and systematized in de Beer's book, to which I have already referred. To biologists like Vandel or Schindewolf, however, the view of evolution they suggest does not, as de Beer thinks, complement selection theory, but runs directly counter to it. Along with the growing evidence from experimental embryology (stressed, for example, by Dalcq or by the late R. S. Lillie of Chicago), conceptions like these suggest, not that life's history is a function of two variables, variation and selection, but that it hides a much richer complexity, a spontaneity, an inventiveness, an orderliness which eludes explanation in terms of such simple conceptions, however masterly the statistical edifice on which they are enthroned. Once more, if one *must* reduce the macroscopic to the microscopic, one can indeed say, there *must* have been 'rate genes' to bring these changing rhythms about; but this is, once more, to postulate an unknown to explain away an uncomfortable aspect of the known.

Yet, if all this is so, why is the neo-Darwinian theory so confidently affirmed? Because neo-Darwinism is not only a scientific theory, and a comprehensive, seemingly self-confirming theory, but a theory deeply embedded in a metaphysical faith: in the faith that science can and must explain all the phenomena of nature in terms of one hypothesis, and that an hypothesis of maximum simplicity, of maximum impersonality and objectivity. Relatively speaking, neo-Darwinism is logically simple: there are just two things happening, chance variations, and the elimination of the worst ones among them; and both these happenings are just plain facts, things that *do* or *don't* happen, *yes* or *no*. Nature is like a vast computing machine set up in binary digits; no mystery there. And—what man has not yet achieved —the machine is self-programmed: it began by chance, it continues automatically, its master plan itself creeping up on itself, so to speak, by means of its own automatism. Again, no mystery there; man seems at home in a simply rational world.

As against this simplistic and reductive explanation, however, this cosmic behaviourism, the objections I have mentioned, such as the need to recognize the harmony of adaptations or the persistent structures and rhythms in phylogenetic development, are complicating and hence mystifying matters. They introduce a need for a more complex logic, permitting levels of emergence, for example; they introduce a need for frank retrospective assessment of the evolutionary story, and hence for personal appraisal of our own situation in evolution, as the outcome of evolution. Thus Professor Dalcq has warned us, for example, that, even should life be synthesized in the laboratory, it would be we ourselves, thinking and continuing products of life's long history, who had achieved this synthesis: and this fact would make an essential, logical, even a metaphysical difference to the import of the achievement.[26]

From another perspective, David Lack, loyal Darwinian though he is, gives the game away. In the book I have already mentioned, he refers to Darwin's question: 'Can the mind of man, descended, as I believe, from the lowest animal, be trusted when it draws such grand conclusions?'[27] and he comments:

Darwin's 'horrid doubt' as to whether the convictions of man's evolved mind could be trusted applies as much to abstract truth as to ethics; and 'evolutionary truth' is at least as suspect as evolutionary ethics. At this point, therefore, it would seem that the armies of science are in danger of destroying their own base. For the scientist must be able to trust the conclusions of his reasoning. Hence he cannot accept the theory that man's mind was evolved wholly by natural selection if this means, as it would appear to do, that the conclusions of the mind depend ultimately on their survival value and not their truth, thus making all scientific theories, including that of natural selection, untrustworthy.[28]

Lack concludes from this that the old opposition of science and religion is still, and must remain, an 'unresolved conflict'. But I think one may conclude, on the contrary, that it is the conventional logic of science, and the view of mind implied in it, that needs revision. For, as Plato argued long ago about Protagoras' 'man the measure', there is surely something wrong in a theory which, at its very root, invalidates itself.

Darwinism, then, we conclude, represents a last and self-destroying model of the Cartesian world-machine. It is persuasive partly because of what it opposed and partly through the ambiguity of its own central concepts. But it does not offer the mediation we are seeking between knower and known; it evades the problem rather than solving it. Where then are we to look for help? It may take a new Darwin to give us a comprehensive theory equal in explanatory power to the persuasiveness of the present orthodoxy. But we can take some steps on the way by looking at the actual practice rather than the theory of biologists, to discover what concepts they do in fact use in describing and explaining organic phenomena. Over and above the concepts of chance (variation) and necessity (the external compulsion of selection), which are supposed, classically, to suffice for Darwinian explanation, what more is involved in the knowledge of living things? The two concepts which present themselves, over and over, as resisting reduction to Darwinian categories are those of structure or *form*, and goal-directed process, or *end*.[29] Biologists acknowledge, in the world of living things, many and diverse shapes. And they acknowledge also temporal patterns, life-histories ordered through time. In other words, however impassioned their denial of 'teleology', they do acknowledge the existence in living nature of ordered processes and therefore of ends. A glance at such acknowledgments, both in biology and outside it, may help us to overcome our Cartesian bias and to open the way for a richer metaphysical vision.

8 The Multiplicity of Forms

IT HAS BEEN, AND IS, THE DREAM, NOT ONLY OF PHILOSOPHERS AND physicists, but of biologists as well, that some day all biology will be reduced to physics and chemistry. Science, it is held, is, ideally, applied mathematics, and as the more 'backward' sciences advance they move inexorably closer to this single model. It is this model which, as we have already noticed, Darwinism essentially serves: the model of a one-level world, where there are bits of matter moved by 'mechanical' laws, and nothing else. Wholes are explicable by analysis into their parts, and events by their precedent events, which are their 'causes'. Yet, I have suggested, the practice of biology, as well as of our ordinary, everyday handling of living things, continues to resist conformity to this simplistic archetype. Let us look a little more closely at the types of performances involved in this resistance, and see what we can infer from them about the natures with which they have to do. So far I have been talking chiefly about knowledge as the achievement of knowers, and I shall continue to do so. What we want to look for now, however, in our survey of certain aspects of the activity of knowing, is something about the *objects* of that activity.

As far as the problem of knowledge is concerned, we can put the framework of our inquiry as follows. Only *persons* can succeed in knowing anything. Therefore there can be no knowledge unless there are persons. Polanyi has developed this argument on a massive scale in *Personal Knowledge*: even in the exact sciences, he argues, knowledge entails the *personal commitment* of the scientist. From this it follows that even the knowledge of Newtonian 'hard, impenetrable particles', even the knowledge of a Laplacean universe, would be impossible if the universe were in fact Laplacean. As we have seen in the case of Darwinism, a one-level universe leaves no room for the knowledge even of that universe. E. Straus, in his book *Vom Sinn der Sinne*,[1] has stated the same argument under the slogan: 'Physics refutes physicalism'. He writes:

> The physicist's observations begin and end within the field of human action. In it and from it he develops the mathematical and physical conception of space. The personal relation of the observer to his environment differs in principle from the spatio-temporal relations of

things observed. If the observer's original relations to space and time corresponded to those in which the observed objects and their ultimate hypostatizations, such as atoms and electrons, are conceived, defined, and measured, he could never devise a science of physics.[2]

The existence of knowledge, then, has ontological implications. There is something other than bits of matter, there is at least knowing mind. We have already found ample reason to doubt, however, whether mind is, as Descartes would have it, a self-existent intellect at the opposite side of a neatly bisected universe from a self-existent matter. Let us try, therefore, to evade altogether the confinement of the Cartesian alternatives and see from the practice of knowing agents what sorts of real things they do in fact acknowledge to exist. We may thus come round to finding where knowing itself stands as one reality among others, and where the objects of knowledge stand in relation to the knower.

Our enterprise will succeed, however, only if we recall, what we acknowledged as early as Chapter One, in our reflections on the *Meno*, the fact that knowledge is not, and cannot be, wholly explicit. It is not a variety of formalisms we are looking for, but assent to a variety of existences, a variety which need not be exhausted by the multiplicity of formulae devised for the analysis of these existences. It is precisely the over-emphasis on formalism which has allowed philosophers to neglect the complexity of the world and to insist that because formulae can be written all on one line, beings too must be all of one sort and on one level. We shall start, contrariwise, not from formalisms, but from what Polanyi calls the *unspecifiable* component of science, or from what Professor C. F. A. Pantin, in a paper on 'The Recognition of Species', calls its *aesthetic* element.[3]

Professor Pantin contrasts the yes-no matching of specimens against characters by museum taxonomists with the informal 'aesthetic' recognition of species in the field. He is chiefly comparing a deductive process: All such-and-suches and only such-and-suches have characters 1, 2, 3, 4; specimen n has characters 1, 2, 3, 4, therefore specimen n is a such-and-such, with the intuitive recognition of an individual as belonging to a certain kind: as when he tells his students to bring in 'all the worms that sneer at you', or when he finds a specimen of a new species and exclaims, 'Why it's a rhynchodemus, but it's not bilineatus, it's an entirely new species!' But he concludes his essay with the suggestion that inductive as well as deductive inference has traditionally been treated as if it were of the same yes-no character, and he tells us that we ought to consider whether 'aesthetic' elements may also be implicated in the inductive as well as the deductive processes not only of biology, but of science as a whole.

Now what I want to do here is to look at these aesthetic or un-specifiable constituents both outside and inside biology and see how biology both differs from and resembles the exact sciences in its reliance on such constituents. By unspecifiable constituents, it should be noticed, are not meant propositions that are probable rather than true or false, nor arguments that yield probability rather than truth or falsity. The probabilities which induction is supposed to yield, as we have just noted, are usually intended to be just as yes-no as are the certainties of mathematics. I shall return to this problem briefly later on. The point here is threefold: (i) There are constituents of knowledge which, though not only psychologically but epistemologically indispensable to it, are not stateable in the form of propositions or arguments. That is what is meant by calling them *unspecifiable*. (ii) Such constituents of knowledge are unspecifiable because they are *personal*. They exist because knowing always expresses a personal commitment, and a commitment can never be wholly reduced to, or exhaustively stated in, non-committal form. (iii) Knowing always expresses a personal commitment, because it entails the apprehension of a whole in terms of its parts, or of an aim in terms of the means to it. It entails, in Polanyi's language, both *focal* and *subsidiary* aware-ness. Again, I have stressed this distinction earlier, but it is worth repeating it here, for it is the failure to recognize this structure in all knowledge which makes knowledge both *of* living things and *by* living things, in terms of traditional philosophizing, so mysteriously *un*real.

Accepting then, the general conception of unspecifiable con-stituents in scientific knowledge, I shall try to distinguish four types— or better, four levels, at which they occur, for they seem to form a hierarchy, in so far as each entails all the previous members of the quartet. Adopting my nomenclature from Professor Pantin's sug-gestion about 'aesthetic recognition', I shall call the first type the recognition of pattern, the second, the recognition of individuals, third, recognition of persons, and fourth, recognition of responsible persons.

The first is common to the biological and the physical sciences—or for that matter to any knowledge at all. What I am referring to here is often called an awareness of gestalt—and a familiar example in the history of science is Kekulé's reported day-dream of snakes chasing their tails which is supposed to have led him to the discovery of the benzine ring.[4] All discovery relies in the last analysis on such intuitive perceptions of form. The achievement of the scientist in successful pursuit of a new theory is to glimpse a gestalt as yet unseen by his predecessors or contemporaries. Maxwell's equations are a paradig-matic example of this. As Max Born says in his *Theory and Experiment in Physics,* 'Maxwell's addition of the missing term is just such a smoothing out of a roughness of a shape.' And of such processes in general he says: 'A synthetic prediction is based on the hypothetical statement that the real shape of a partly known phenomenon differs from what it appears to be.'[5] And the testing of a theory, then, is the endeavour to find out by accepted procedures, mathematical or experimental, whether the gestalt thus envisaged is 'really' there. Nor are these testing procedures necessarily yes-no; they may be themselves unspecifiable or aesthetic. The theory of relativity, Professor Dirac has said, was accepted for two reasons, its agreement with experiment and the fact that 'there is a beautiful mathematical theory underlying it, which gives it a strong emotional appeal', and of these the latter reason, in his opinion, was the more important. 'With all the violent changes to which physical theory is subjected in modern times', Dirac writes,

> there is just one rock which weathers every storm, to which one can always hold fast—the assumption that the fundamental laws of nature correspond to a beautiful mathematical theory. This means a theory based on simple mathematical concepts that fit together in an elegant way, so that one has pleasure in working with it.[6]

What is often misleadingly referred to as the 'simplicity' of theories is an aspect of this aesthetic component: a theory *feels* simple when the mind rests happily in the pattern it offers. This is not of course by any means always a pattern in the visual sense of Kekulé's snakes; it may be an intellectual pattern—a mathematically elegant formulation, a formulation which, as Dirac says, mathematical physicists like working with, or, in biology, statistical generalizations like those of population genetics which geneticists like to work with. Or it may be a model from a familiar aspect of our experience applied analogically to the unfamiliar, as in Darwin's application of the experience of stockbreeders and pigeon fanciers to the origin of species. (There is, of course, more to Darwin's argument than that—that is not my subject; but Darwin's theory does have an astonishing way of bringing the remote past into the area of the familiar and making us feel that we know how it was because it *was* the way it still is.)

I have suggested that we call this first kind of unspecifiable factor in knowledge the recognition of pattern. Perhaps we might describe it even more weakly and inclusively as a sense of relevance; and its necessary presence in this minimal form becomes evident if we look, as we may do here briefly, at one of the many recent attempts to analyse the structure of scientific knowledge without admitting such a factor. Consider for example Sir Harold Jeffrey's *Scientific Inference.*[7] Jeffreys is, in effect, describing scientific inference as the reiterated application of Bayes's theorem of inverse probability. But Bayes's theorem starts from an initial probability. How do we obtain this? What his theory amounts to, Jeffreys says, is that he has turned the traditional principle of causality upside down: we start, he says, with *random* correlations and work in the direction of necessary connections as our objective.[8] Yet, as Bayes's theorem indicates, random events are precisely what we do *not* start with, for they would be random only if they did not entail any prior probability, or conversely, if they were random we could not establish any initial probability and so could never begin. Only the acceptance of a rational context, the choice of one set of data as more relevant than another, will get us started at all. Bayes's theorem formalizes a procedure applicable within an accepted context, but not the discovery of context, the recognition (if we may platonically call it so) of *novel* pattern, and with it scientific advance, inference that is heuristic rather than routine. In other words, it is the recognition of pattern that supports the logical gap between evidence and theory.

Incidentally, I might bring similar objections against Professor Braithwaite's rules of rejection in his *Scientific Explanation*: for, as I have argued earlier, one must choose such a rule, and one's reason for choosing depends upon a sense of relevance, or of irrelevance.[9]

II

The recognition of pattern, then, is essential to all scientific discovery, and at one remove, therefore, to the mastery of any scientific discipline by the student–which is a process of discovery for him though not for humanity as a whole. This much is true of biology and of the exact sciences equally. But in addition to this common situation there is also a difference. Once recognized, an explicative context in the exact sciences can be left far behind in its routine application. In biological practice, on the other hand, in the field recognition of which Professor Pantin is speaking, or equally, for example, in medical diagnosis, the awareness of pattern continues all along to play a prominent part. Nor is this because biology is a 'younger' science or a less 'developed' science, but simply because it is *biological* science.

This is a tautology, but it is a heretical one. As I have already acknowledged, it is an article of faith with many, if not most, biologists, that their science is really not biological at all but is only physics and chemistry writ large. And when they get the writing small and precise enough, they say, it *will* be physics and chemistry. So, to take one example of many, say Fraenkel and Gunn in their classic work on *The Orientation of Animals*.[10] And yet the kind of skill described by Professor Pantin as aesthetic recognition persists in biology. Is this then a remnant to be superseded when mathematical biophysics takes over? I think not; for the practice of biology entails a recognition of pattern in a more pervasive sense than do physics and chemistry. Over and above the recognition of abstract patterns characteristic of the sciences of inanimate matter, the practice of biology demands the recognition of individual living things, and analysis in biology is always analysis *within* the context set by the existence of such individual living things. Thus a second kind of aesthetic recognition, the recognition of individuals, adds to the subject matter of biology a logical level missing in the exact sciences, and at the same time limits the range of analysis to the bounds set by the acknowledgement that individual living things exist. I do *not* mean that at some mysterious point analysis will have to stop, but that an analysis of an organism which analysed the organism *away* would contradict itself by destroying its own subject matter. Nor do I mean that when we recognize an individual we are adding some mysterious vital something that comes from I know not where, but that we *are* affirming the existence of something which is more than a brute fact, in the sense that we acknowledge it as an achievement: as an entity that succeeds or fails relatively to standards which we set for it. It is a good or a bad specimen of *Cepaea nemoralis* or *Spiraea vanhoutiens*. We recognize it as an individual in respect to its trueness to type,[11] and no matter how far analysis may proceed, this recognition will always be essential. Otherwise we should not know what we were analysing.

Again, I have to lay this down here as a flat pronouncement against the authority of the biological profession itself, or a large and authoritative part of it; but let me try to support my assertion by reference to one of the branches of biology which considers itself well on the way to the ideal of withering away into biochemistry. As everyone knows, genetics since the revival of Mendel's work at the beginning of this century, and since the work of Johannsen, Morgan, and many others, has been founded on atomistic principles. Its guiding maxim seems to be: if we could specify all the genes we could specify the organism. And the brilliant work of recent years on the chemistry of the cell nucleus and on reproduction in viruses and bacteria phage has given this maxim new and apparently overwhelming support. Thus a leading geneticist summarizing this work at a conference for teachers of biology just before Crick's final 'code-cracking', spoke of the DNA, RNA and protein composing the nucleus and set as the theme of the experiments he was reporting the question: 'Which of these is the genetic material which chiefly causes the effects that we see?'[12]

This question expresses for biology the same kind of hope that Henry Oldenburg, the first secretary of the Royal Society (as he was to be) expressed for natural philosophy as a whole when he wrote to Spinoza:

> In our Philosophical Society we indulge, as far as our powers allow, in diligently making experiments and observations, and we spend much time in preparing a History of the Mechanical Arts, feeling certain that the forms and qualities of things can best be explained by the principles of Mechanics, and that all the effects of Nature are produced by motion, figure, texture, and the varying combinations of these.[13]

Divide and conquer! Specify the parts and you have the whole. The parts of an organism are chemical molecules; specify these and you need worry about 'life' no longer.

But parts by definition are *of* a whole; and as genetical research proceeds, along with specification, the nature of the whole, too, makes itself felt. The parts are the *conditions* for the whole, which certainly could not exist suspended in some heaven of essences without them; but it is the whole that *explains* the parts, not the parts the whole. The whole is the system (the organism) that makes the parts the parts that they are, even though the parts are the conditions (in traditional language, the material causes) for the existence of the whole.

So far this is only to say that all explanation is systematic, and this we have admitted already in different words in saying that all discovery entails awareness of form or gestalt. Biological explanation, however–and that is my point in reference to genetics–entails the recognition not only of systematic connections–between *such* genes and *such* phenotypes–but of individually existent systems: organisms existing as unitary four-dimensional wholes, as individuals with a life history in a particular portion of space-time. This ought to be clear from the breakdown of one-gene-one-character genetics, but the physico-chemical, atomistic habit of thought is so strong among biologists that few of them recognize the re-orientation which this change implies. It is admitted explicitly, however, in a very strong statement by that eminent elder statesman of genetics, R. B. Goldschmidt, in his *Theoretical Genetics* (and Goldschmidt is certainly no 'holist' or anything of the sort, but an old-fashioned materialist who has the honesty and courage to admit what confronts him). This is what he says at the beginning of his account of the action of the genetic material:

> Here, at the start of our discussion of genic action, one point should be made clear. It is one of the general tenets of genetics that a mutant locus

of the gene, assumed to be the normal allele, does not control a character but is only a differential: the visible character depends upon a large number of genes, if not on all of them. This idea is frequently illustrated by the fact that many loci are known to influence the same character if mutated. Thus the numerous eye-color mutants in *Drosophila*, scattered over all chromosomes, would indicate that there are at least that many genes for eye colour. The work on biochemical genetics of eye colors as well as nutritional requirements in *Neurospora* shows that a number of mutant loci individually interfere with different steps of organic synthesis from the lowest raw material; for example, in eye-color synthesis, from tryptophane to kynurenine, then to 3-hydroxykynurenine and further steps not yet well known. A corollary is that for each of these steps a number of mutant loci are known, which interfere with it specifically. If we wish to express this factual situation by saying that a phenotypic trait is the product of action of many or all genes, we must realize that this *façon à parler is nothing but a circumscription, in terms of the atomistic theory of the gene, of the unity and integration of the organism.*[14]

Now notice that the atomism is here supplied by the theory and it is the unity that is the fact: that is the important point. In scientific discovery as common to biological and physical science, the unity is the new context, the theory. The facts may be all over the place – as are the fossils, the embryological structures, the pigeons, the clover, field mice or old maids relevant to the Darwinian theory of evolution; or as are the scattered populations of Neurospora, Drosophila, castor beans or cattle relevant to the atomistic theory of genetics. But in biology, over and above this unifying relation of all theories to their data, there is the unity of the individual living thing underlying the abstractions of the theory, the unity that *is* the fact on which all the abstractions, atomizing or otherwise, bear.

But surely, it will be objected, theories explain facts. If the theories specify parts, as in genetics (or original conditions as in evolutionary theory), then is it not, after all, the parts that 'explain' the whole? Here the ambiguity of 'explanation' and the prestige of physical theory combine to confuse matters. Ideally, or (what is considered the same thing) in the exact sciences, an explanation provides some sort of formulation, whether a model or a mathematical formulation, from which statements about a certain range of phenomena can be deduced. From theory T we can deduce statements of fact a, b, c, d. . . . For even though evidence never entails the theory that explains it, the theory once envisaged entails the evidence. What Goldschmidt's statement tells us, however, is that genetical explanation is never wholly of this sort, since we must supplement our theory by reference to a fact which we can indeed circumscribe in the language of the theory but could never have predicted from it: the fact of the existence of the organism O, not as an aggregate of any number of genes, but as an integrated whole. From his breeding experiments the geneticist can indeed predict an impressive range of mutations a, b, c, d . . . n, but no specification of DNA's, tryptophanes, or what you will *entails* a, b, c, d . . . n, *except in the context of O*. The recognition of O puts the *facts* of biology in a different and more complex relation to its theories than is the case for the exact sciences. The geneticist's recognition of a fruit fly stands in a different logical or epistemological relation to the theories of genetics from the relation, say, of the reading of the temperature or pressure of a gas to the kinetic theory of gases. For over and above the recognition of pattern implicit in the grasp of data relevant to theories, biology demands the recognition of *individuals*, to which as its *raison d'être* it has continually to return.

I suspect that there is a relation here to the role of causal explanation in the biological as against the exact sciences. Explanation in genetics, as in all the most 'advanced' branches of biology, aims at being 'scientific' by being causal. Yet the exact sciences, we are often told, are not for the most part interested in causes at all.[15] Thus the kinetic theory of gases explains the behaviour of gases under changes of pressure and temperature in the sense that the phenomena follow logically (not temporally) from the theory. But there is no question of before and after and so of cause and effect. The theory supplies logical reasons, not historical causes. But the sum total of genes times environmental influences is supposed to *cause* the organism. DNA experimenters are seeking for the genetic material which '*causes*' the effects that we see; the story of template reduplication is a *causal* story. What does all this add up to? To the fact that certain aspects of the organism are controlled by certain conditions, so long as there exists an organism to be affected by such conditions–somewhat as a machine which operates according to a certain principle can be made to work faster or slower, with more or less efficiency, by a number of contributory causes. Like explanations in engineering, explanations in biology depend on the pre-existence and continued existence of a particular whole or a set of particular wholes, machines or organisms respectively, of a particular character. The machine is a whole existing for some end beyond itself, but the organism–though in an evolutionary context existing as a means to the existence of future organisms–is as an individual organism an end in itself: it *is* the system on which causal explanations are based and to which they have to return. In both cases–machines and organisms–the causes specified are relevant to the reasons or principles in virtue of which the wholes in question exist: in one case the operational principle of the machine, in the other the 'unity and integration of the organism'. And in both cases, the causal analysis is possible precisely because the whole–the system being analysed–is a historically existent whole, a four-dimensional entity, and not merely an abstraction from which statements about phenomena are deducible *sub specie eternitatis*. Thus the conspicuous use of causal explanation in biology appears to be a sign that biology is 'scientific' not in the same way as, but in a different way from physics and chemistry: that instead of deducing particulars from abstract systems it specifies causal connections bearing on concrete, existent systems, on individuals.[16]

To many biologists, however, such statements as I have just been making are either nonsensical or false; they 'smack of teleology' or of 'vitalism'. For if we insist that in explaining organic phenomena scientists are doing something different from what they do in explaining the phenomena of the inorganic world, we are supporting in effect W. D. Elsasser's thesis that there are 'biotonic laws', regularities inexplicable by the laws of physics and chemistry,[17] and so we are re-introducing into the natural order the very discontinuity which Darwin and his heirs had so brilliantly banished. For the fundamental law of biology for a hundred years now has been the principle of *uniformity* which Lyell had applied in 1830 to the rocks alone and which Darwin took to its logical conclusion in its application to the history of life as well. If, as we must surely admit, there was a time when there was no life on this planet, and life has its own laws, then the laws of nature are not constant and uniform. And if in understanding and explaining organic phenomena we are proceeding in a fashion different from the way in which we proceed when explaining physical phenomena, this suggests also that *what* we are explaining is in fact existentially and historically different.

Yet to insist on epistemological and even ontological discontinuity is not to deny historical continuity, for conditions which are continuous can give rise to, or trigger, systems which once in existence are self-sustaining and hence not explicable entirely in terms of the conditions which produced them. As it is when we strike a match and produce a flame, so was it when the open systems which are organisms were produced from the conditions prevailing on the earth's surface at the first emergence of life. This by no means implies that anyone was there to strike the match, only that the principles sustaining an open system are different from and additional to the conditions necessary to initiate it. This is the point Leibniz was making when he used the analogy with algebra to show how the principle of continuity could apply throughout nature–for if you moved one focus of an ellipse continuously, at infinity you would get a parabola, and so you have a second figure which differs discontinuously from the first yet is produced from it by a continuous process.[18] For the epistemology of biological knowledge, this is an extremely important analogy. The discontinuity of emergence is not a denial of continuity but its product under certain conditions.

III

Once we have admitted the principle just stated, we may grant a unique epistemological status to the recognition of individuals without violating our underlying belief in the continuity of nature. Moreover, I need this principle here also to establish the third kind of aesthetic recognition I want to talk about. Let me return for a moment to Professor Pantin's worms that sneer at you. All recognition of individuals is of an aesthetic character whether the individual in question belongs to the species *Rhynchodemus bilineatus* or *Ranunculus bulbosus* or *Felis domestica* or *Homo sapiens*. Is there any difference in all these cases? Jennings, the great Protozoologist, insisted that if paramecia were the size of dogs we should know them personally as we do our domestic animals.[19] They are not so and most of us do not know them in this personal way. But still there is a difference between recognizing a buttercup and recognizing an animal that we do know personally. Somewhere along the evolutionary sequence we find animals whom we do recognize as persons rather than simply as individuals of a species. Here we seem to have a second discontinuity in the continuous series of advancing forms of life. Polanyi identifies this division with the distinction between our morphological judgments of trueness to type, as in taxonomy, and our judgments of a more active form of achievement of success or failure according to rules of rightness, as in the analysis of animal behaviour. He mentions the case of a rat who drinks saccharine solution, 'mistaking' it for 'food'. Such a rat has made what he calls a 'reasonable error'.[20] But buttercups do not seem to make mistakes, nor to succeed.[21] Not that rats 'think' in these terms— that is not the point; but we do, and we judge the rat's behaviour according to the standards we set for it, according to what seems reasonable for a rat. This is to think of the rat as a centre of appetites and interests which may be satisfied or not, not as an individual simply, but as a sentient individual, that is in some sense as a person. Again, such recognition of incipient personhood establishes a new level over and above the others we have been talking of: to recognize a person means to recognize a coherent form, an individual living thing, *and* a centre of appetites and interests, capable of error and therefore in some degree of rational performance (and if this seems absurd, consider that rats can go mad).

Once more, however, such statements seem to contradict the most cherished maxims of biology. The very existence of the science of ethology, for example, is said to depend on the resolute renunciation of any ascription to animals of 'sentience', feelings, or the like. And indeed the scientific study of animal behaviour could not have got far through accounts like those of Romanes in the eighties. In comparing a bird's flying into a window with insects flying into a flame he says:

> Here there can be no question about a possible mistaking of a flame for white flowers, etc., and therefore the habit must be set down to mere curiosity or desire to examine a new object; and that the same explanation may be given in the case of insects seems not improbable, seeing that it must certainly be resorted to in the case of fish, which are likewise attracted by the light of a lantern.[22]

This does indeed seem a strange misinterpretation of instinctive behaviour, and by contrast one might reasonably suppose that only a strictly 'objective' account of what the animal in fact does and an objective analysis of the factors 'eliciting' its responses could produce a science of ethology. So, for example, argues Dr Tinbergen in opposition to an animal psychologist like Bierens de Haan.[23] But again it seems to me that (though no one could wish to reinstate Romanes's indiscriminate subjectivism) the magnificent analytical achievements of modern behaviour studies do in fact take place within the context of the recognition of persons. Again, let me take one example to illustrate this: Tinbergen's popular but nevertheless detailed and systematically 'objectivist' *Herring Gull's World*.[24]

That instinctive behaviour lends itself in large measure to objective analysis is plain. Take the case of egg retrieving.[25] The gull doesn't 'think' of putting out its wing and sweeping the egg back in to the nest, but executes what looks to the bird-watcher like a succession of clumsy and ineffective movements. Clearly its behaviour is determined by a series of rigid and precise instinctive mechanisms. It would be quite irrelevant to try to imagine what the gull was 'thinking' about in such cases. The whole apparatus of Internal Release Mechanisms, for instance, in the intricate series constituting nesting behaviour,[26] works so much more rigidly than our so-called intelligent appetitive behaviour that analogies with human activities are more often than not misleading; so the maxim of objectivity is methodologically and factually correct up to a point.

At the same time the ideal of objectivity repeatedly breaks down in Tinbergen's account. For one thing, there are his references to the 'meaning' of behaviour; e.g. the upright threat posture is 'full of meaning' for all herring gulls,[27] or, more subjectively, the choking situation is 'really loaded with hostility'.[28] Sometimes 'meaning' clearly refers to functional significance such as could be explained by natural selection–for example when Tinbergen reports, 'The bird makes some curious motions with the bill without making any sound. . . . I do not know what these motions mean.'[29] Here to find the meaning might be to find the function in terms of the evolutionary conception of the bird as a machine for the survival of its descendants. But the references to threat posture or choking are not of this type.[30] In general, moreover, such analyses suggest at the least that behaviour patterns are not being simply described, nor yet reduced to physico-chemical terms, but referred to in terms of an understanding of the whole life of the organism or the community of organisms. For instance, Tinbergen describes as follows a piece of behaviour difficult to interpret:

> One bird walks round the other, uttering a peculiar call not unlike the begging call of a half-grown Herring Gull chick. It tosses its head up and down and even touches the other bird's bill. The latter seems to try to get away, but the first one keeps bothering it. Finally, the harassed bird stands still, twists and turns its neck, a huge swelling appears in its neck, moves upward, and suddenly the bird bends its head down, opens the bill widely, and regurgitates an enormous fish. The begging bird begins to eat gluttonously before the food even reaches the ground. The other joins it, and together they finish the meal. It is easy to understand that this behaviour was feeding. *But who was feeding whom, and why?*[31]

This is far from the description in terms of muscle contractions which Tinbergen had earlier set up as the ethologist's ideal.

In this case, moreover, we have a clear instance not only of the degree of personhood implicit in appetitive behaviour in the individual, but of interpersonal relations also. And elsewhere Tinbergen speaks more generally of 'genuine personal ties',[32] and says that 'personal likings and dislikings play a prominent part' in gull life.[33] Elsewhere also he points out that gulls know the difference between the alarm calls of 'nervous, panicky' gulls as against more placid individuals, since they fail to react to the cries of the former.[37]

Further, not only the gulls, but Tinbergen himself came to know the gulls apart: 'It is quite a thrill', he writes,

> to discover that the birds you are studying are not simply specimens of the species *Larus argentatus* but that they are personal acquaintances. . . . Somehow, you feel, you are at home, you are taking part in their lives, and their adventures become part of your life. It is difficult to explain this more fully but I think everybody who has studied animal communities will understand how we felt.[35]

This is surely a striking admission by a leading programmatic objectivist of the recognition of persons – and *a fortiori* of an unspeci-fiable constituent of his science, 'which is difficult to explain but which everyone who has studied animal communities will under-stand'.

And finally, although the interpretation of gull behaviour in terms of human subjectivity is rejected, the interpretation of *human* behaviour in terms of *gull* behaviour is not. 'Much of what little understanding I have of human nature,' Tinbergen confesses,

> has been derived not only from man-watching, but from bird-watching and fish-watching as well. It is as if the animals are continuously holding a mirror in front of the observer, and it must be said that the reflection, if properly understood, is often rather embarrassing.[36]

In short, Tinbergen, for all his objectivistic faith, gives overwhel-mingly the impression of a man who knows not so much the physics of muscle contractions or the chemistry of nuclear proteins, as *sea-gulls*, and that in a personal way that is different from knowing physical or chemical phenomena or even from knowing buttercups and worms.

IV

What, in conclusion, about my last type, or level, of aesthetic recognition? This takes us beyond biology, but in a direction sug-gested by the road we have been travelling so far, and yet takes us back also to our starting point: to the knower engaged in the activity of knowing. In the last passage I have quoted from Tinbergen, the ethologist puts himself in a sense on the same level, or even on an inferior plane, to the herring gulls; but in general his comparisons, for instance between gulls and crows or between gulls and men, suggest not only the recognition of persons, but a hierarchy of persons according to the relative predominance of intelligence over instinct, a hierarchy continuing the series of kinds of individuals, from butter-cups to worms to sea-gulls, along which we have already marked off one division. And now if we consider the ethologist himself observing his subject, whether gulls, fishes, or his fellow men, we find we have once more, without admitting any discontinuity, and granting the mirror held by gulls and sticklebacks to human nature, yet taken a new step. Tinbergen, in justifying his interest in bird watching, tries to explain it as fulfilling a kind of hunter's instinct. Doubtless it does so, but this explanation seems halting and incomplete: for it omits the thrill of personal acquaintance which he had talked of earlier, the contemplative aspect which has a share in all knowledge, but more conspicuously in disciplines concerned with the immediate know-ledge of living things as living. Watching a bird-watcher watching, we are acknowledging the existence of a person in the fullest sense we know of, a person motivated not by appetite but by an intellectual passion, a passion for the understanding of other living things. Similarly, if we could watch a theoretical physicist at work we should be watching a person motivated by an intellectual passion, a passion for working with beautiful mathematical theories in the confidence that the world is as these theories dictate—that, as Norman Campbell put it, 'pure thought aiming only at the satisfaction of intellectual desires' can lead us to knowledge of the external world.[37] As the sea-gull, the stickleback or the man are driven by their individual appetites, the man who happens to be a scientist is driven also by a drive continuous with instinct yet emergent as something profoundly different from it: not an appetite consuming that which it is nourished by, but a passion which seeks intellectual satisfaction not only as what satisfies itself but with universal intent. As Polanyi states the distinction:

> The social lore which satisfies our intellectual passions is not merely desired as a source of gratification; it is listened to as a voice which commands respect.[38]

He continues:

> Yielding to our intellectual passions, we desire to become more satisfying to ourselves, and accept an obligation to educate ourselves by the standards which our passions have set to ourselves. In this sense these passions are public, not private: they delight in cherishing something external to us, for its own sake.[39]

This is in fact the basic difference between appetites and mental interests:

> we must admit that both are sustained by passions and must ultimately rely on standards which we set to ourselves. For even though intellectual standards are acquired by education, while our appetitive tastes are predominantly innate, both may deviate from current custom; and even when they conform to it, they must both ultimately be accredited by ourselves. But while appetites are guided by standards of private satisfaction, a passion for mental excellence believes itself to be fulfilling universal obligations.[40]

Here, in short, we meet full, responsible personhood. We meet responsible persons also, of course, in all our dealings with other human beings who share with us aspirations transcending the limits of individual appetite, aspirations which may be moral as well as intellectual, practical as well as theoretical. What I have been doing here is to acknowledge that knowing is *one* of the things which we recognize responsible persons are doing, whether they happen to be knowing matter, life or other persons, electrons, rhynchodemuses, sea-gulls or themselves, as doers or knowers. And to acknowledge this is to acknowledge, further, that there *are* electrons, rhynchodemuses, sea-gulls and scientists: that the world is full of a number of things. Still further, our brief journey has shown us, in proceeding from the recognition of matter to life to persons to responsible persons, we are proceeding up a scale of complexities, each of which entails the earlier levels. Responsible persons are persons, persons are individuals, individuals are physical structures, yet each kind we recognize as also more, and other, than the preceding, or underlying, level.

V

I have outlined here a very simple and summary sketch of a series of 'levels of reality'. Polanyi, in *Personal Knowledge*, has painted a broader picture, and my argument here may in fact be taken as an attempt to illustrate and elucidate Part Four of that work. Polanyi has shown, in Parts One to Three, that all knowledge entails the personal commitment of the knower to the reality with which he believes himself in contact. The knower, so committed, is limited by his bodily endowments, and he is also rooted in the traditions of his society; but as knower he stands, so far, alone. Knowing is a theme in *his* life-history. But in knowing he is doing one of the kinds of things that other living beings also perform. Thus the structure of intellectual commitment can be confirmed and expanded by its extension to the rest of the living world:

> The ontology of commitment . . . can be expanded by acknowledging the achievements of other living beings. This is biology. It is a participation of the biologist in various levels of commitment of other organisms, usually lower than himself. At these levels he acknowledges trueness to type, equipotentiality, operational principles, drives, perception, and animal intelligence, according to standards accepted by him for the organisms in question. . . . These achievements are personal facts which are dissolved by any attempt to specify them in impersonal (or not sufficiently personal) terms.[41]

It is such a series of 'personal facts' that I have been tracing in this chapter. There are several comments still to be made about them in our present context.

First, over against the tradition which insists that only one kind of reality is real at all, we are clearly hoping to reinstate, in some form, a conception of *grades* of reality. But even from the few lines from *Personal Knowledge* just quoted, it is evident that such hierarchical distinctions can be made on more or less complex, more or less generalized lines. Polanyi's list, 'trueness to type, equipotentiality, operational principles, drives, perception and animal intelligence', stresses types of *achievement* rather than, if you will, types of *existent*. Most philosophers who make such distinctions of level do mark out, in some way or other, matter, life, and mind as main stages of 'ascent', but beyond this very general division there are a variety of perspectives from which such a survey may fruitfully be made. If, indeed, as I have repeatedly insisted, our situation as knowers is ineradicably ambiguous, if we are questioning beings, if the very fact of speech springs from a question mark, we may well find the degrees of being whose reality we risk asserting, to be themselves equivocal. What is most important here, I believe, is not that there are precisely such and such kinds or grades of being in the world, so many and no more, but *that there are beings of more kinds than one*. There are many ways of being, as many, Aristotle said, as there are kinds of unity.

It is worth looking at the world from the point of view of that Aristotelian maxim. Wherever we acknowledge that a set of events or characters form in some–any–stable and interesting way a unity, we acknowledge the existence of some being. But such constitutive unities may be of very different sorts: as in the range of biological examples we have been dealing with, the unity of a cell, the unity of a dragon-fly, the unity, say, of the dragon-fly's mating behaviour, the unity of the entomologist's performance in studying the dragon-fly, and so on. Such unified structures do indeed always unite, as wholes, a multiplicity of parts. They always exhibit what Professor R. Kapp calls 'double determinateness', the whole depending on the parts as conditions of its existence, but the parts existing as parts only as so constituted by the unifying principle of the whole.[42] Thus in themselves, at least in living nature, all entities exist on at least two levels at once. The insistence that organisms are machines only serves to confirm this thesis, since it can easily be shown that machines themselves are essentially two-level existences: they function in accordance with the laws of physics and chemistry as specified, not *by* those laws–which in themselves leave open a wide range of possible blue-prints–but by the operational principles according to which they perform their functions as machines. Further, such organic wholes are sometimes related to one another, in turn, as higher to lower, both in terms of existential dependence and of relative complexity of organization. But sometimes they are *just different one from another*. The tendency of modern naturalism has been to reduce all existence both to one level *and* to one sort; both these reductions must be overcome. For the world is much richer in its ways of being than Boyle or Newton were willing to admit. There are indeed some things that are more highly organized, more 'real' than others, and there are also things that are simply different from others, different not only in number but in their way of being. To break the stranglehold of reductivism, we must acknowledge once more *the multiplicity of forms of being.* That liberating acknowledgment achieved, we can then recognize as well the stratification of some of these many forms relatively to one another. True, such multiplicity can be recognized only in terms of double determinateness, therefore a one-*level* ontology and a one-*type* ontology, and, *a fortiori,* their negations, are logically related. But we should nevertheless keep separate three aspects of the situation : (1) the double determinateness of comprehensive entities, including living things and the achievements of living things. (2) the multiplicity of kinds of such doubly determinate entities, (3) the question of their stratification relative to one another.

Secondly, for the variety of entities whose existence we acknowledge, we need to ask what we mean by their being, or their reality. Is there no more to be said than the bare and metaphysical assertion : that there are kinds of things, some more real than others? Does such an assertion mean anything at all? Or are we perhaps once more smuggling in existence as a predicate as Kant has classically forbidden us to do? One thing can be harder or hotter or older than another, but *more real*? In the Duke lectures of 1964 Polanyi has developed further a criterion of reality, or of comparative reality, already implicit in the argument of *Personal Knowledge.*[43] One entity is more real than another, he suggests, when it carries the possibility of a greater range of interesting and unexpected consequences. He has been showing how the same structure of tacit knowing holds good in a number of different kinds of cases. Thus we rely on clues in order to attend to entities as diverse as a scientific problem, another person, or an inanimate object like a cobblestone. He continues :

The structural kinship between knowing a person and discovering a problem, and the alignment of both with our knowing of a cobblestone, call attention to the greater depth of a person and a problem, as compared with the lesser profundity of a cobblestone. Persons and problems are felt to be more profound, because we expect them yet to reveal themselves in unexpected ways in the future, while cobblestones evoke no such expectation. This capacity of a thing to reveal itself in unexpected ways in the future, I attribute to the fact that the thing observed is an aspect of a reality, possessing a significance that is not exhausted by our conception of any single aspect of it. To trust that a thing we know is real is, in this sense, to feel that it has the independence and power for manifesting itself in yet unthought of ways in the future. I shall say, accordingly, that minds and problems possess a *deeper* reality than cobblestones, although cobblestones are admittedly more real in the sense of being *more tangible*. And since I regard the significance of a thing as more important than its tangibility, I shall say that minds and problems are more real than cobblestones. This is to class our knowledge of reality with the kind of foreknowledge which guides scientists to discovery.[44]

This statement on the one hand suggests views so orthodox as to be almost trivial and on the other consequences so revolutionary as to make it seem to many almost absurd. Let us consider its implications in both directions.

On the one hand, the reference to future consequences is reminiscent of reductivist theories like pragmatism or positivism. Thinkers who wished to evade the problem of truth have often insisted that theories are acceptable not for their conformity to some elusive and mysterious reality but simply for their fruitfulness: for the empirically observable consequences which may follow from them. Polanyi attacked this theory in *Personal Knowledge*, and it may seem odd that he should himself now use a formulation superficially so similar to it. But let us look at the situation a little more closely. It seems reasonable to suppose that Copernicus believed his theory to be, not simply a device for 'saving the phenomena', but a statement of the truth about the heavens. He *could* not himself accept it *because* of its fruitfulness, since he could not himself know, in the explicit sense of 'know', how fruitful it was to prove. He accepted it because he believed it to be true, and he would have hoped that it would prove fruitful *because* of being true, because in formulating it he had come into contact with reality. If truth is in some sense a congruence of thoughts and things, it follows that a true theory may have unforeseen consequences because things themselves may unfold themselves in unforeseen ways, while a false theory will display no such fruitfulness because it is not founded on the real. Fruitfulness works ultimately, therefore, as a criterion of the truth of theories because it is a criterion of *reality*. Discoverers assert their theories because they believe them to be true, not because they are (now) fruitful (which they must prove themselves to be hereafter). But if they are true, they *will* be fruitful; if false, empty of consequences. There is the same sort of confusion here in the positivist theory that there is both in positivism and pragmatism about the relation between *meaning* and *truth*. Fruitfulness is a *test* of truth; positivists make it not a test, but the essential nature, not of truth only, but of meaning as well. A theory is supposed to be *nothing but* a device for drawing out further observations. This, as we have seen, is absurd, since no one can equate a theory stated now with its non-existent future results. What its discoverer judges it by, however, is the confidence he feels in its truth, that is, his confidence that he has made contact with a significant aspect of reality, and that therefore out of his explanation many unforeseen consequences may flow.

As against the positivist view, moreover, that a theory is simply a device for prediction, Polanyi's concept of fruitfulness stresses *un*foreseen consequences. What marks off important theories is that they prove so much *more* fruitful than their discoverers could possibly have foreseen. It is not predictability, but *un*predictability that distinguishes the more powerful and most interesting discoveries, because it is unforeseen consequences that distinguish the real from the unreal.

But, it may be objected, is it not its very predictability that distinguishes the real world, for example, from that of dreams? If I dreamt I had won the sweep nothing would follow from my dream; if I had really won, I should be rich, and a solid and coherent set of consequences would follow from this fact. Dreams are unreliable, realities reliable–not, as Polanyi's definition seems to suggest, the other way around. True, reality is also full of predictable consequences; but the point is that as against the unsubstantial, the artificial or the false, these consequences are *inexhaustible* and therefore unpredictable. They are systematic and therefore up to a point predictable, but real systems are also richer than our predictions and so capable of *indefinite* consequences as well. Our dreams, on the other hand, being relatively arbitrary figments, are soon exhausted. That is why, again, great discoveries often prove to have more, and more kinds of, consequences than their discoverers know or could have known. All this fits in well enough with ordinary concepts of 'real' and 'unreal'.

The really surprising aspect of Polanyi's criterion, however, emerges from its *comparative* use. An entity is the *more* real, the more unforeseen consequences could flow from it. But *ideas*, like the Copernican theory, often contain more unforeseen consequences than do ordinary external things, like the cobblestone. Can anything mind-dependent be *more* real than what is out-there, measurable in space and time? Plato's major thesis, for example, in his refutation of atheism in *Laws X*, seems to go perversely against common sense:

> thought and attention and mind and art and law will be prior to that which is hard and soft and heavy and light; and the great and primitive works and actions will be works of art; they will be the first, and after them will come nature and works of nature . . . these will follow, and will be under the government of art and mind.[45]

And in particular it goes against what we believe to be scientific common sense. Dr John Beloff, a psychologist himself opposed to behaviourism and so sympathetic with Polanyi's attempt to renew the philosophy of mind, nevertheless professes himself shocked by the case of the problem and the paving stone. What makes the cobblestone real, he says, is just that it is *independent* of any mind's perceiving it, while the problem has not this independence.[46] What about this objection? If to be real is by definition to be independent of mind, then whatever is mind is non-real. Or if psychology is not wholly to deny the existence of its own subject-matter, it must add to the external real the ghostly reality of an inner mind, and take refuge once more in Cartesian dualism. But this refuge of despair is unnecessary if we apply Polanyi's criterion. Human minds turn out to be not a mysterious addendum to the inventory of more obviously real things, but one of the more real of the many kinds of things there are. And so do the mind's achievements, theories, works of art, inventions, laws. The paradigm of the problem and the paving stone may hold for any skilful performance or for its product.

Surely, however, it will be objected, the basic distinction to be made here is that between the natural and the artificial: all human achievements are cultural, that is, at bottom, the products of convention. Are we not making *fictions* more real than *facts*? In answer, let us take a case literally from fiction and see how Polanyi's criterion might apply to it. Jane Austen is dead, and no further unforeseen consequences can flow from her character. Even if some new discovery were made about her, say, that she was secretly married, that would be an unforeseen consequence for us, not for her. Emma, though a fiction, is alive; she is the kind of live character who continues to develop between the lines of the novel the more one is acquainted with her. Being, as E. M. Forster remarked of Jane Austen's creatures, a *round* character, almost the round character *par excellence*, she shows just the kind of living richness exhibited by our friends, at least the more interesting among them. But Emma's creator did exist and Emma never did. Are we to call such a fiction more real than its inventor? Yes and no. We may, and should, distinguish, as I have already suggested, between different ways, different dimensions of being. What Polanyi's criterion applies to we might call *intensity*, or, as he calls it, *depth* of being. Existence and non-existence, the sheer *that* of being or non-being, corresponds to what Sartre calls *facticité* or Heidegger *Geworfenheit*. It is an *extensive*, linear dimension. In making a judgment of reality we count it as one factor against others, and also we count it in a different way. When we say Jane Austen is dead, we are referring to the historical non-existence of an individual; when we say Emma is alive, we are speaking of the depth of being of a non-historical individual. No direct comparison between them is possible or intended.

Yet, in general, Polanyi's criterion does enable us, I believe, to handle conceptually the difficult problem of the *reality* of works of art. Berenson in a famous essay has described how Giotto's treatment of bodies makes us *feel* more intensely than we otherwise do the three-dimensionality, the sheer solidity of objects around us. This is not just a pointer *from* the painting to the observer and his perception of bodies. The solidity is in the painting. In the heavy kneeling or slightly turning figure, the solidity of bodies *is* more intensively than in the ordinary objects of the ordinary world, even though, even because, we 'know' it is 'only' painted, only 'represented' on a two-dimensional surface before us. This would be true if the Arena Chapel were to vanish tomorrow, if the human race were to vanish tomorrow. This is a dimension of being as unrelated to contingent fact or non-fact as are the relations expressed in mathematical formulae.

Of course it will not do, on the other hand, to absorb, as Hegel seems to do, extension into intension, contingency into depth of being. That is why it seems to me also important to insist that it is not one fixed, universal hierarchy which the recognition of degrees and dimensions of being seeks to restore. It is by no means true that all that is real is rational, and that, conversely, all that is irrational is unreal. There is no one whole System of Being which, happily, all the sufferings of countless individuals are intended to realize, of which they are instruments. Such a conception is as false as it is unfeeling. But neither is the non-significant, neither is sheer givenness, the only way things are. The achievements of all living things, the achievements of human minds, are more than tiny superscripts on a single monotonous succession of mere facts. They are enrichments of being itself.

Only such an acknowledgment, thirdly, will enable us to see knowledge itself as a real achievement of real beings. The recognition of scientists at work, we have seen, is an instance of the recognition of responsible persons, a performance of the same general kind as the recognition of patterns, individuals, or persons at lower levels of existence. Now if we interpret this situation in the light of Polanyi's criterion, we can see how and why our scale of forms turns out to be a spiral, in which we return at a new level to the point from which we set out. We found the recognition of pattern common to all acts of knowing. In such an act the knower is relying on a variety of clues, grasped only subsidiarily, in order to attend to the focal object of his knowledge. This is everywhere the structure of *comprehension*. But when the knower is engaged in the business of knowing living things, further, the object of his knowledge itself is, in Polanyi's language, a *comprehensive entity*. Not only the process of knowing, but the thing known consists of an organic whole whose parts have their meaning, and their existence as parts, through their bearing on the whole. From simpler comprehensive entities, or individuals, then, we have proceeded to persons and to responsible persons, including the knower himself whose activities we have been all along inspecting. Thus we find the task of knowing knowers smoothly assimilated to the task of knowing life. To know life is to comprehend comprehensive entities; to know knowing is to comprehend those particular achievements of living things which consist in their acts of comprehension. Mind is once more a natural reality, and nature once more both the medium and the object of mind's activity.

I am not suggesting, of course, that this is a wholly novel thesis. Even since Descartes, even ever since Democritus, men have tried to rectify the alienation of the intellect and to make our thoughts once more at home in the world. In this century, the most profound and comprehensive effort of this sort has been the philosophy of Whitehead. Indeed, the ontology that issues from Polanyi's or from Merleau-Ponty's arguments about knowledge is in many points close to that of Whitehead. It is of interest in this connection that Merleau-Ponty himself, shortly before his death, had been stimulated by a remark of Whitehead's to investigate the concept of nature.[47] For Whitehead, too, knowing is a form of life, and for him too, the things we call living are more real than other things. But, as I suggested at the start of this book, it is a renewal of epistemology that is needed if we are genuinely to overthrow our Cartesian inheritance. Some few thinkers have seen Whitehead's importance, but in general he seems to philosophers only one more odd systematist, an anachronistic renewer of idealism. Only, I believe, when a deep-lying conceptual reform in our view of knowledge has been assimilated, when we have overcome within ourselves our Cartesian fear of the category of life, and our Newtonian simplemindedness about the nature of the nature we strive to know, only then will we be able to open our minds to a new and richer ontology. Such an ontology, to be adequate to the facts of our cognitive experience, will have to include the recognition of the multiplicity of forms as an aspect of the multidimensionality of being.[48]

One last point, out of historical piety. To recognize a multiplicity of forms, all or most of them exhibiting a doubly determinate structure, is in a sense to revive the Aristotelian concept of form as the correlate of an appropriate matter. But only in a sense. The relation on a series of levels between form and matter does indeed parallel closely the relation between higher and lower levels of organization characteristic of such objects of aesthetic recognition as I have referred to here. And for any one trying to think in terms of degrees of being,

Aristotle's carefully contextual application of his correlative concepts furnishes an important precedent. But Aristotle's form-matter analysis succeeds, as I have argued elsewhere, only in a finite and eternal world. Once we have seen, or tried to see, what happens to Aristotle's other basic pair of concepts, act and potency, in a world that is fundamentally in process, we may be able to see more clearly our basic difference from Aristotle on the question of form as well. To do this, however, is to turn to the other member of the pair of concepts referred to at the close of the last chapter, the concept of goal-directed processes or ends.

9 Time and Teleology

I

IN HIS LECTURES ON 'THE IDEA OF NATURE', COLLINGWOOD LISTED among the characteristics of the *modern* as distinct from the Renaissance concept of nature, the *reintroduction of teleology*. Renaissance thinkers, he said, saw nature as a machine; final causes belonged outside it, in its origin or in its use, not within it. Modern thinkers, on the other hand, he believed, were beginning to lean on a new analogy, not between nature and machines, but between nature and historical process. 'The historical conception of scientifically knowable change or process', he says, 'was applied, under the name of evolution, to the natural world.'[1] And this application entailed, among other consequences, a return to teleological thinking about natural events. Such thinking seems to echo Aristotle, who laid down, in Book Two of the *Physics*, the principle that 'the things that are by nature are precisely those which move continuously from some principle in themselves to some goal'.[2] The new teleology, however, is by no means identical with Aristotle's: the key to it, Collingwood rightly insists, lies in the word 'evolution', and the beliefs which that word suggest are contradicted by Aristotle in the very same sentence I have just quoted. In each species, Aristotle is confident, the principle in question is always directed 'to the same goal, if nothing interferes'.[3] And by such interference he means the sort of circumstance that would produce abnormalities within a species, not what Goldschmidt has called 'hopeful monsters', mutants on the way to some new species.[4] Aristotelian species are eternal. In other words, Aristotle's world was not radically in process, as the modern 'nature' must be seen to be. It is not my purpose here to elaborate on this difference; suffice it to mention among Collingwood's list of consequences of the 'modern' conception of nature the substitution of *function* for *substance*: a substitution which if allowed destroys Aristotle's cosmos with one blow. Yet in some sort of transposition Aristotle's recognition of goals in nature, Collingwood argues, is to be, and has been, reinstated. Discussing Aristotle himself, he writes:

> It is widely recognized that a process of becoming is conceivable only if that which is yet unrealized is affecting the process as a goal towards which it is directed, and that mutations in species arise not through

the gradual working of the laws of chance but by steps which are some-how directed towards a higher form – that is, a more efficient and vividly alive form – of life. In this respect, if modern physics is coming closer to Plato as the great mathematician-philosopher of antiquity, modern biology is coming closer to its great biologist-philosopher Aristotle.[5]

Against the purely quantifiable, dead nature of Galileo and Newton, Collingwood is confident that this reorientation toward organic phenomena has brought about a significant reform in our whole view of the natural world. Apart from professional biologists' disputes, 'On the ground of philosophy', he says,

> I think it fair to say that the conception of vital process as distinct from mechanical or chemical change has come to stay, and has revolutionized our conception of nature.[6]

Collingwood wrote these words some time in the thirties: after '33–4, the year in which the course of lectures on which *The Idea of Nature* is based were first given, and in which, also, Whitehead delivered the four lectures *Nature and Life* on which Collingwood seems to be relying heavily – and justly so, for *Nature and Life* ought, together with *Process and Reality*, to have constituted as marked a turning point in Western philosophy as that initiated by the Cartesian *Meditations*.[7]

But conceptual reform comes hard. It is startling to read, in 1966, that something like Aristotelian teleology 'is widely recognized' or that 'the conception of vital process as distinct from mechanical or chemical change has come to stay'. True, Collingwood warned us, we should not be surprised if 'many eminent biologists have not yet accepted' the revolution he describes. 'In the same way', he continues,

> the anti-Aristotelian physics which I have described as the new and fertile element in sixteenth-century cosmology was rejected by many distinguished scientists of that age; not only by futile pedants, but by men who were making important contributions to the advancement of knowledge.[8]

Scientific discoverers may indeed be, and sometimes are, philosophical reactionaries. Many biologists, in particular, are still held in the grip of what was called three centuries ago 'the new mechanical philosophy'. But philosophers too have failed by and large to accept Collingwood's 'modern' concept. By now a good handful at least of 'eminent biologists' are groping for concepts that will not, as strict mechanism demands, eliminate 'bios' from their subject, yet philosophers stand aloof from this effort: the effort to implement from the side of science the philosophical revolution which Collingwood believed already accepted a generation ago. So, for example, P. F. Strawson remarks quite by the way, in *Individuals*, that 'the category of process-things is one we neither have nor need'.[9] But in terms of Collingwood's revolution, as we may call it, of course there are process-things, and if we do not have such a category, we do nevertheless need it, for we are ourselves among such things, as is every living species, as is the universe. Only the ghost of Newton's dead nature, cunningly masked as common sense, prevents us from admitting it.

To put finally to rest our Newtonian delusions, to renew our conception of nature as *living*, and so to see ourselves once more as living beings in a world of living beings, still constitutes the major task of philosophy in the twentieth century. It is far from accomplished; the rise of a new 'new mechanical philosophy', founded on biochemistry and cybernetics, makes the task not only more difficult, but more urgent. As, again, Strawson's failure to notice the problem indicates, only a radically revisionist metaphysics and, even more fundamentally, a radically revisionist epistemology can fully effect the conceptual revolution that is needed. In the hope of helping to lay the groundwork for such a reform, let us ask, for end or living function, as we did for form, or living structure, some questions which may at least indicate the direction from which the necessary change may come.

II

As a first step towards 'Collingwood's revolution', then, let us ask: how teleological concepts enter into biological explanation. I want to put this question, however, in a restricted context only. Two sorts of teleology in particular I am not talking about here. First, I want to exclude purpose entirely from my inquiry. Neither in Collingwood's nature nor in Aristotle's does *telos* or goal mean primarily, much less exclusively, conscious purpose. In fact, one of the great obstacles in the path of a renewed teleology has been the idea that natural events are *either* planned *or* wholly undirected: an idea implicit in the Cartesian bifurcation of extended matter and cogitating, or planning, mind. As Hume recognized in the *Dialogues*, plans, or conscious schemes of action, are not the only principles of order. Admittedly, the existence of human purposes, or human aspirations, the hope of reinstating man *in* nature, may be prime motives behind the effort of many thinkers to renew our vision of 'nature' in a direction permitting the reality of goals, of trends, and ultimately of thought. But the larger metaphysical task which, in agreement with Collingwood, I believe to be necessary, may be assisted by an inspection of the sorts of goal-directed patterns that appear in nature outside the range of conscious purposes.

Nor, secondly, shall I be speaking here of the vast cosmological teleology which seems to some people inherent in the concept of evolution. Evolution is an achievement, but whose achievement? Here again, I believe, whatever our alleged modernity, we are still Cartesian enough to find the concept of an achievement by populations, by 'life' itself, extremely odd; and we need to prepare ourselves for such a notion by attending to some more limited fields in which teleological concepts force themselves somewhat less paradoxically upon us.

Setting aside, then, both purposive behaviour in men and other higher animals, and the main sweep of macro-evolution, let us ask (1) what phenomena seem to demand some sort of teleological language when we try to speak about them, (2) what characterizes these phenomena as distinct from others not demanding this type of description, and (3) what sort of philosophical account can we give of the whole situation: the phenomena and the way we talk–or think–about them. I am using 'phenomena' here in what seems to me the Kantian sense–not meaning sense-data; I shall refer to the phenomena in question, using Sir Julian Huxley's term, as *telic*, reserving 'teleological' for the words or concepts through which we characterize such phenomena.

First, then, what kind or kinds of phenomena, apart from conscious purposes, seem to demand teleological language when we speak about them? Or as Aristotle would put it, where in nature do we find occurrences needing to be explained as 'for the sake of something'? We may distinguish at first glance three general types: part-whole relations or structures, for example in morphology, means-end relations or functions as in physiology, and directed processes of the sort most obviously exemplified in individual development. In the first of these three cases, if not in all of them, I am admittedly assimilating to 'end', phenomena already counted as examples of organic form. I am saying, in effect, that wherever there is double determinateness, there is not only form, but end. This is true. Development and evolution are among the most plainly telic of organic phenomena, but all organic phenomena, looked at one way, are *achievements*, and display double determinateness through change. What we are discussing here, therefore, is the same range of phenomena looked at from a different point of view. This should become plainer as we proceed.

We may take as a thread for looking at all three types of telic phenomena the question put by Darwin:

What can be more curious than that the hand of man, formed for grasping, that of a mole for digging, the leg of a horse, the paddle of the porpoise, and the wing of the bat, should all be constructed on the same pattern?[10]

What does it mean, first, to be 'constructed on a pattern'? Take any one of Darwin's examples, the human hand, for instance. The bones, 27 of them, are so arranged as to take each its place in the pattern of the whole. A bony character like Mr Venus if he found them scattered about a graveyard could put them together again into the outline of the familiar human appendage. Vertebrate palaeontology, of course, depends largely on such reconstruction, and from only some of the particulars. A famous case was Owen's reconstruction of the extinct Moa from a single fragment of a thigh bone.[11] Organic fragments to be organic must fit into structured wholes; unless we knew by experience or guessed by imagination what these wholes were like, an inventory of the pieces on its own, let alone one piece, would never tell us what they were. The pieces become significant only as parts of the whole; they exist, as natural entities, 'for the sake of' the whole.

This subordination of many details to one whole is strikingly apparent in evolutionary *convergence*, where quite different sets of materials have developed into strikingly similar structures. Another of the cases listed by Darwin in the sentence I have quoted: the paddle of the porpoise, is in shape similar to a fish's fin. The fish, however, never had land-dwelling ancestors; the porpoise has redeveloped an aquatic limb which begins to look again like a fin although its particulars are distinctly different. So in general with the porpoise's streamlined body in comparison with the more ancient streamlining of the fish. Even more striking is the parallel structure, for example, of the eye of the cuttle-fish and the mammalian eye: here you have two very distinct and unrelated kinds of animal developing out of quite unrelated materials two strikingly similar organs. In other words, you have two different sets of particulars each composing essentially the same pattern. Another case of the subordination of detail to pattern is the fact that a single structure may be kept in being by a variety of loci, that is, by a number of alternative genes each independent of the other but producing the same structure as their effect. One could take Waddington's experiments on genetic assimilation as an example of this.[12]

Our first general type of telic phenomenon, then, consists in the relation of particulars to a pattern. Structure is here our guiding concept and mechanical or biochemical details are interpreted in subordination to structure. But Darwin's list gives us another kind of telic relationship as well. Hand, foreleg, paddle, wing, and so on: these are all limbs, organs, instruments, which are of use for some function which they help to perform. In fact we have here the classic example of the subordination of structure to function, the case of *adaptive radiation*, where the same array of particulars, forming the same structure (constructed on the same pattern), is deployed for different uses: grasping, digging, running, swimming or flying. In convergence, too, of course, structure is in fact subordinate to function: the porpoise's paddle has come to resemble a fin because, like a fin, it is adapted *for swimming*. But perhaps the subordination of structure to function comes out most clearly where we find two very different structures with the same function: the compound insect eye and the simple mammalian eye are made, on very different principles, *for seeing*. What kind of 'for' is this? In the case of the particular-pattern relation, we find many details bearing on one structure. So here we find one or more complex structures, i.e. at least one whole of many particulars already organized, bearing on one (or at least one) use. It is not necessary, on the face of it, that we think of this sort of phenomenon in terms of a temporal sequence. A bat's wing is of use for flying while the bat is hovering; and when by day the bat is sleeping its wing will still be described in functional terms. The concept of function seems to involve a stable potentiality rather than a moving one. I am labouring a very obvious point here, but I think it is worthwhile to separate out temporal series from means-end relations as such: partly because teleologically minded philosophers jump too hastily to the identification of telic phenomena with temporal sequences and partly because physiologists, analysing the functions of organisms—many of which are directed to keeping a system in equilibrium—like to think their science non-teleological because it is not *prima facie* historical. But wherever there are means-end relations, there is something for the sake of something else even if the one is not taken in time, in the sense of an objective sequence, before the other. This is not to deny the essential relation, to which we shall return, between time and teleology; but both realities may be misunderstood when they are too hastily equated with one another.

Thirdly and finally, directive *processes*, which *are* temporal, are clearly the most complete cases of natural goal-directedness. Indeed, the bat's wing would not function for flying nor the porpoise's paddle for swimming if in each case the embryo of bat or porpoise had not developed in such a way as to grow limbs adapted, the one to aerial, the other to aquatic life. In the context of Darwin's list, of course, we also infer that the species referred to by the names 'bat', 'porpoise', 'horse', 'man', etc., have all, themselves, developed, over time, in the direction of these adaptations. For our present purpose, however, we may ignore phylogeny, and consider simply the fact of individual development. It was ontogenesis even more than human purposive action, I believe, which led Aristotle to formulate his doctrine of causes for the sake of something; and it is still development which most strikingly produces 'the appearance of end' in living nature. Many embryologists, indeed, hope some day to obtain an exhaustive chemico-physical analysis of ontogenesis, but others hold that the peculiar plasticity of the phenomena will make this impossible. For the issue of development is clearly more determinate than the path to it, and in this sense the end seems to control the steps to its achievement. As Aristotle put it, 'nature as genesis is the path to nature as goal'.[13] Some of the earliest researches in modern experimental embryology confirmed this. If for example the lens of the new triton is removed it regenerates from the tissue of the iris. Normally, however, the lens is formed from ectoderm, while the iris originates from the mesoderm. Thus when the normal source is not available the need for a lens seems to be able to evoke from neighbouring tissues a contribution it would not otherwise make to the functioning of the whole. Since the 1890's when this experiment was first performed there has been a very great deal of further experimentation on regeneration. It occurs in this general form only in the lower animals, but it constitutes nevertheless a pervasive characteristic of living tissue, represented in higher forms in wound healing or in the ability of some areas of the brain to take over functions normally carried on by other areas.[14] All this dramatically confirms Aristotle's insight that in organic processes the end though last in time is in some sense prior to or causative of the steps that lead to it.

III

Looking at these three general types of telic phenomena then: part-whole relations, means-end relations and directive processes, how can we describe the peculiar nature of all of them, as distinct, say, from the phenomena described by inorganic chemists? The most pervasive characteristic of the whole group seems to be the fact that they exhibit *many–one relations on more than one level*. Thus we have the bearing of many particulars on one pattern, the subordination of complex mechanisms to the function they perform, and the predetermination of a series of steps through their direction to a definite goal. This is, so far, a generalization of the whole-part relations we were considering in the previous chapter. In each case the one: whole, activity, or adult organism is on a higher level than the many we have referred to it: parts, organs or steps in development. This 'higher' may consist, as it is often said to do, in a greater complexity of organization or integration. Admittedly, it may not look, at first glance, as if flying, for example, is more complex than a wing, although it is obvious that in the other two cases the whole or the end point of development is more complex than the parts or the starting point of the developmental process. Yet if one considers flying as the whole activity it is, involving a great many physiological conditions, in the circulatory, nervous, muscular systems, and so on, as well as just the existence of a wing, then it does indeed appear a much more highly organized set of events than the organ which is used in its performance. And it is the *end* of flight that all the co-operating mechanisms subserve. Let us say then that in general the higher level is more highly organized than the lower.

Being more highly organized, however, it is, in the light of Polanyi's criterion, also more real. In the wing of Archaeopteryx lay hidden the then untold future of all the fowls of the air. Or better, it was the first *flight* of Archaeopteryx in which that future lay: what made the class Aves a major group was not its possession of wings as such but its use of them, which conquered a new element, a vast new range of ecological niches for life to grow into.

Taking, in each case, the higher and lower level together, moreover, we can see that, in general, what the higher level of organization does is in some sense to *control* the lower. Parts become the parts they are in relation to the whole, organs are organs *as* their function dictates, embryos develop toward their specific norm. Between each pair of levels, in other words, there is a relation, not of complementarity, simply, as has often been insisted, but of *ordinal complementarity*, as distinct from the cardinal complementarity of waves and particles in quantum mechanics. True, organic life cannot exist without both levels: wholes without their parts, functions without the mechanisms needed to perform them, or living individuals without the whole development from fertilized egg which produced them. But in some sense the higher level provides a principle which orders or determines the lower. In every case the lower level specifies conditions, while the higher gives us principles of organization, ends or reasons. The conditions are indeed necessary, but while it is possible to understand the principles without reference to the detailed conditions, it is *not* possible to understand the conditions *except* as conditions of the whole, the activity, or the endpoint of development on which they bear. In other words, it is possible to think about and observe natural phenomena purely in teleological terms – even though biologists may think this a primitive way to treat their subject; but it is not possible to analyse them into their conditions without any reference at all to their overall shapes, principles of operation, or directions of development, however 'scientific' biologists may think they would be if they *could* do this.

In each case, moreover, the higher or controlling level sets some sort of *norm* for the lower. I have argued earlier that evaluation enters into all our knowledge, even of 'facts'; when we look, without objectivist prejudice, at telic phenomena, we see that in this part of our experience at least norms, standards of value, form an integral part of the facts themselves. As it is in our conceptualization, which is one kind of living activity, so in all the phenomena of the living world. In the second and third cases, further, the norm in question amounts to an attribution of success or failure. Mechanisms are more or less effective in fulfilling their functions; embryos develop normally or abnormally; flying, swimming, or walking are achievements; so is being born or growing up. In each case, the higher level furnishes the standard by which the goal in question can be said to be successfully achieved or no. The possibility, and the fact, of success and failure characterize uniquely the phenomena of the living world. Finally, in our third case at least, a relation of temporal sequence is essential. To the question of the underlying relation of time, life and *telos* we shall return by and by.

IV

So much, then, for our sketch of the kinds of telic phenomena there are around us and the general characteristics they display, or that our discourse about them displays. What are we to say about them when as philosophers we reflect on the nature of our knowledge and on the nature of things insofar as they are knowable? The central question is this: what, in each case, is the higher level doing with respect to the material it controls? How does a higher principle of organization operate on a lower? Or, more practically, what are we doing when we relate patterns to particulars, functions to the mechanisms subserving them, or the *telos* of development to the complex steps towards its achievement? I shall suggest a series of answers to this question, each of which leads on the next, and the last of which brings us to the threshold of the philosophical revolution in which, if we are not, we ought to be engaged.

The teleological reference in biological discourse may be characterized as (1) reflective, (2) regulative, (3) descriptive, (4) operational, (5) explanatory, or (6) ontological.

First, it is sometimes argued, that while teleological concepts are in fact wholly inappropriate to scientific thinking, they enter into the philosopher's *reflection* on the data of science. On this view, therefore, any reference to patterns, functions or goals in living nature must be extruded from the biologist's vocabulary. It is metascientific and must not enter into the speech, or the thinking, of scientists themselves. The theoretical framework of the biologist's training is centred–implicitly and indirectly if not explicitly and directly–in the theory of evolution by Mendelian micromutations and natural selection. In terms of ultimate beliefs, this means the view that the present population of the earth's surface is derived by a repetition of a few simple mechanisms (internally, a template mechanism or something of the sort; externally, selection and other environmental pressures) from unicellular and ultimately from non-living particles of matter. This picture is associated also with an aggregative conception of the organism itself. 'Ultimately', one believes, an organism such as a mouse or a frog or a man will be identifiable in terms of material particles and their spatio-temporal relationships. 'In a sense', writes Dobzhansky, 'the development of the organism is a by-product of the processes of self-reproduction of the genes.'[15] Recent biochemical research has given a new impetus to this atomistic conception, just as research on natural selection, against the background of the telephone-exchange theory of the behaviour of higher organisms, has given new support to the mechanistic view of causation which is associated with it. The trained biologist, in other words, works under the aegis of a guiding principle that organisms are aggregates of material particles moved by mechanical physico-chemical laws. His thinking, his research, are motivated by the search for (in Professor 'Espinasse's eloquent phrase) 'little causal thingummies'.[16] Scientific discourse, accordingly, *qua* scientific, must be wholly non- and anti-teleological, and any speech tainted with teleology must remain wholly extraneous to science. It can be, at best, reflection about and upon it.

This ideal, however, is, to say the least, impracticable. For teleological concepts have at least a *regulative* function within the practice of biology. This was well argued by Frank Baker in a paper read to the Royal College of Science in 1934. Imagine, he says, an observer looking in the field of a microscope at the filaments of a fungus. 'He witnesses', says Baker,

> that at the tips of the filaments are disposed a number of radiating branches more frequently segmented than those of the stalk to which they are attached; which adjointed elliptical segments are easily set free by pressure in the surrounding medium. But, supposing that he decides to investigate these segments, what kind of ideas are going to control his choice of further observations; how will he proceed, loosely speaking, to discover 'the nature' of these structures; and, in brief, in such a context, what does his notion of 'investigation' already imply?[17]

An old-fashioned chemist, Baker suggests, might throw these segments (which, unknown to him, we may call spores) into concentrated H_2SO_4. He would learn something; but would this 'lay an effective basis to the study of mycology?'[18] And why are these not as good facts to start with as any other? But suppose our investigator places the segments on jam (where he first found them) or sugar, and in the warmth, and watches what happens. He may then discover 'their relation to the life cycle of the fungus'.[19] Actually, Baker remarks, it would take a whole series of investigators 'animated by a single scientific impulse or tradition' to lay the foundation which would so much as show him where to start.[20] When he gets this far he can then, but not before, undertake his chemical analysis. Only, in other words, when the concept of germination is understood and its designatum assumed to exist, do the details 'fall into order and acquire a significance', such that detailed analysis of some parts of the process of germination can be undertaken.[21] Both the interrelation of parts with reference to the whole and the orderly development of the organism under investigation must have been assumed, Baker concludes, before the right 'facts' could be selected for further investigation and analysis. Teleological concepts, therefore, at least *regulate* the biologist's choice of data and of problems. They are not merely meta-scientific.

But is that all? Can the biologist proceed to describe what it is that he is analysing without referring to structures, uses, or achievements? I think not. In other words, teleological discourse has not only a regulative, but at the least a *descriptive* function within biological research. For example, the statement that a particular spot on the petal of the cotton flower or the wing of a butterfly or the character *cv* on the wing of a fruit fly may be determined by alternative genetic loci–that is, in 'Espinasse's terms, that different little causal thingummies are causing the same effect–are assertions inferred from breeding experiments which show that the same phenotypic result is produced through breeding different strains of plant or animal. Nobody (so far) has inspected these loci directly. They are inferred from the shapes and functionings of the organisms which are held to possess them. If the scientist could not see and describe the structures, functions and developmental processes of the cotton bloom or fruit flies involved in each case, he would, like Baker's misguided chemist, be unable to begin, continue or conclude any genetical investigation whatsoever. As Professor Paul Weiss puts it (for the case of experimental embryology), 'we cannot address biophysical or biochemical questions to words', but only 'to clearly *described* phenomena'.[22]

It may be thought, of course, that this *descriptive* function is only the starting point, and that the subsequent scientific *analysis* of organic phenomena is wholly non-teleological in character. That is perhaps the most common view of the matter. The biologist may have to use two-level, teleological language to get the object of his investigation so to speak into focus, but then go on searching wholly in terms of small parts arranging themselves in causal sequences in 'mechanical' fashion. If scientists can only put their biochemical and biophysical questions to well described phenomena, the questions themselves seem to be analytical and mechanical, not teleological. Against this contention, however, we may observe that the *operations* performed by many biologists seem to entail reiterated or even continuous teleological reference. As to part-whole relations, for example, not only does classical taxonomy depend for its operations on the recognition of structures; but it has recently been argued that the new quantitative and statistical operations of numerical taxonomy also depend on the recognition of 'types'.[23] Or again, if we consider the typical occupation of geneticists, a good deal of their time is spent, one gathers, in counting the fruitflies of wild type or of a given mutant type that result from breeding experiments: here the recognition of certain characters—cv, redeye, bithorax, or what you will—are essential to the actual experimental procedures; the underlying mechanical details, again, are inferred from these results. A similar situation holds in ethological experiment: where tinkering with the size and shapes of eggs or substituting red patches for actual sticklebacks, and so on, are devices meant to elicit certain behaviour sequences from the subject: the behaviour patterns which display their own internal lines of organizations are still what the ethologist is working with from start to finish. Similarly in embryology: as Professor Jane Oppenheimer puts it, the experimenter can succeed only if he puts questions 'the embryo can comprehend'.[24] The answers, in the last analysis, always come from 'the embryo alive', and the embryo answers, she says, 'at the supra-cellular level'.[25] So, in a good deal of biological work at least, teleological concepts and principles are more than descriptive: they are *operational*. They control not only the way the phenomena are described but the way experimentation with them and therefore the subsequent scientific analysis of them proceed. We have teleological discourse, then, firmly within the *procedures* of biological science not only at the outset, whether in the guise of philosophical reflections, regulative principle or orienting descriptions, but as essential to the *operations* of the experimental biologist.

It may still be asserted, however, by the die-hard anti-teleologist, that however finalistic his techniques, his *explanations* are nevertheless wholly mechanistic, wholly in terms of 'little causal thingummies'. Certainly this has seemed to be the case with classical Mendelian genetics and with its modern heir, population genetics—for statistically treated aggregates of little causal thingummies are still particulate in nature and anti-teleological in their explanatory import. And of course many biological theories are of this sort. But is this true, or can it be true, of all biological explanation? The application of information theory to biology suggests a negative answer. Professor C. P. Raven of Utrecht, in a paper on 'The Formalization of Finality', finds that, in his research, not only the problems, but their solutions are *finalistic*.[26] *Causal* explanations of the same phenomena would be complementary to these, but could not replace them. Thus about the transmission of the DNA code he says:

> we can consider this from two points of view: first as transmission of order, as a problem in information theory. It is a problem of the translation of one system of order into another. But it is not a causal explanation. The causal explanation would involve knowing how it can happen that these three groups of nucleotides attract this amino acid, what are the effective forces of attraction among the atomic groupings. The two explanations complement each other, but are not mutually exclusive. We must distinguish clearly between the formalization of finality, that is, the process of making it susceptible to mathematical treatment and axiomatization, and its transformation into causality, which would be quite another matter.[27]

Here the explanation itself is teleological, in the Aristotle-Collingwood sense. It is a two-level explanation, concerned with the particulars comprising a message, in which, as in the telic phenomena it explains, the upper level controls and sets a norm for the lower. Again, as we saw to be true of telic phenomena, so here, a relation of ordinal complementarity obtains between two levels. For the relation between a message and its particulars is *asymmetric* and *normative*. A message may be analysed into its particular constituents, but it cannot be reduced to them, let alone explained by them. The particulars, on the other hand, though physically *caused*, are *explained* by their role in the message. A given message can be transmitted through a variety of particulars, but in terms of its particulars alone it cannot be apprehended as a message, it cannot be distinguished from mere noise. In interpreting developmental events in cybernetical terms, therefore, the scientist is explaining a lower level (the actual particulars) through reference to a higher (the message conveyed and 'understood'). Further, such finalistic explanation is distinct in structure and explanatory power from the causal explanation which, again, is complementary to it. In this manner, the application of information theory to biology provides not only a 'formalization' of finality but a clear exhibition of its occurrence as an integral part of biological explanation.

There are other instances of such new teleological techniques, for example, the application of von Neumann's theory of games to the theory of evolution.[28] Or one might mention also the application of engineering principles to a problem in plant physiology by Professor

W. T. Williams of Southampton. But any one instance is sufficient to demonstrate that there are some inescapably teleological explanations of organic phenomena.

I have now dealt with five of my six successive functions of teleological language: reflective, regulative, descriptive, operational and explanatory. This brings me back, finally, to Aristotle and Collingwood and the *ontological* import of teleology. There are teleological explanations. But any explanation that succeeds in explaining anything does so in virtue of our impression that we have achieved an understanding of something in the real world which we had previously found puzzling. If, therefore, teleological explanation is a genuine part of the knowledge of living things, it is so because living things are not only apparently but genuinely telic. 'Nature', in some sense of the word, is in fact to be ranked among the causes that act for the sake of something.

But, again, this is more easily said than believed. The conclusion that there are telic phenomena is inescapable, but also so incredible to most scientists and to a public nourished in the mythology of purely one-level, purely 'mechanistic' science, that it is suppressed as a piece of lingering superstition or wilful obscurantism. In this century alone, Bergson, Whitehead, Alexander, Collingwood, Husserl, Merleau-Ponty, Polanyi among philosophers; E. S. Russell, J. S. Haldane, Cuenot, Vandel, Spemann, R. S. Lillie, Portmann, Buytendijk, Straus, Goldstein–and a number of others–among biologists have presented irrefutable refutations of a dogmatic mechanism. Yet, over and over, every doubt of current dogma is swept aside as dogmatism. To be sceptical of teleology is 'scientific', even if this means denying what is as plain as the nose on one's face. To be sceptical of such dogmatic denial, on the other hand, we are constantly told, is to deny altogether the cogency of 'scientific method'. What can lend credit to a truth so implausible in the eyes of most authorities?

The trouble is that the denial of teleology fits smoothly into the metaphysical 'paradigm' (in Kuhn's sense) of the world machine, while its assertion either hangs, a bare statement, unframed by an adequate cosmology, or, worse still, seems to the proponents of objectivism a revival of the scholastic absurdities which Science had so triumphantly overcome. What can be, or has been, done to remedy this asymmetry, to make credible the assertion of the telic character of living things? That is the question we have still to ask.

V

In the Cartesian universe, in which, I have argued, the minds of scientists and philosophers still dwell, the knowing mind, wholly secure and self-aware in its wholly explicit and self-guaranteeing knowledge, is the fitting counterpart of the one-level, one-sort, spread out, physical world, which by its nature it is equipped to know. These two Cartesian realities have shrunk in our time to shadows of themselves, but such as they are–tautologies or sense data on the one hand, space-time co-ordinates on the other–they constitute, for many people, the total furniture of the universe.

Now the key to this strangely reduced conception of what there is lies still in the Cartesian clear and distinct idea: in the ideal of totally explicit knowledge; and the key to its denial therefore lies also, as I have all along been arguing, in the substitution for this ideal of a more adequate concept of the unit of knowledge. Cartesian extended nature was suited to geometrizing Cartesian mind. A new nature will become intelligible to us only when we have assimilated a new concept of our own activity in knowing. Such a concept we have found in Polanyi's theory of personal knowledge, with its unit of tacit knowing, and its distinction between focal and subsidiary awareness. Very close to the same theory is Merleau-Ponty's account of the phenomenology of perception with its distinction between 'positing' and 'non-positing' consciousness.[30] Throughout the preceding chapters I have been trying, from one vantage point or another, to guide the reader toward an acceptance of this new conception of the activity of knowing, and of the nature of the unit of knowledge. I need not repeat the lesson once more here.

In the present context, however, there are two further steps to be taken, both of which have also been in part anticipated but which do, I believe, need to be taken more expressly and emphatically before we rest our case.

First, it is obviously not enough, in itself, to accept the paradigm of tacit knowing, to admit that every act of knowledge entails the apprehension of a reality in terms of clues bearing on it, themselves not focally apprehended, but assimilated to ourselves as clues to the central object of our attention. For if the world *were* a Cartesian world, such a re-reading of the cognitive situation, far from curing us of our alienation from reality, would only aggravate it the more. Such a proceeding would seem, as indeed it does to the objectivist, a mere subjective crying in the dark. It would be a re-echoing of Kierkegaard's 'subjectivity is truth', cutting us off irrevocably from the outside, objective world of science and common sense. No, what we need is a pointer *from* the paradox of personal knowledge *to* the changed reality which our changed conception of knowledge shows us that we know. This step has been anticipated in the preceding chapter, in our outline of levels of organic existence: for the act of comprehension *by* which we recognize living things turned out there to be, at an advanced level of organization, an example of the very kind of comprehensive entity we had all along been recognizing. We may consolidate this insight here, however, by referring to Polanyi's formulation of the same analogy in a lecture on 'The Emergence of Man'. I have already spoken of the comparative reality of the problem and the paving stone, and of the generalization of this comparison to apply to the reality of human skills in general. For such a skilful performance as the playing of a game of chess, for example, it is plain that my understanding of the playing of the game parallels the structure of playing the game itself. Having come this far, Polanyi argues, we can then reasonably conclude that, for all cases of tacit knowing, 'the structure of comprehension reappears in the structure of that which it comprehends'. We can go even further 'and expect to find the structure of tacit knowing duplicated in the principles which account for the stability and effectiveness of all real comprehensive entities'.[31]

In what would such a parallel consist? In tacit knowing, Polanyi reminds us, first, we rely on our awareness of the parts of a whole in order to attend from the particulars to the whole. And secondly, as we have noticed, for example, in the knowledge of minds, if we attend focally to the particulars, we lose sight of the whole to which we had been attending.[32] Comprehensive entities if they mirror our tacit knowing of them should display an analogue of both these properties:

> (1) The principles controlling a comprehensive entity would be found to rely for their operations on laws governing their particulars in themselves.
> (2) At the same time the laws governing the particulars in themselves would never account for the organizing principles of a higher entity which they form.[33]

We have seen both in our survey of levels of organic form and in our description of telic phenomena, that living things do in fact display this double parallel with the activity of knowing. We rely on the particulars of a message in the interpretation of genetic events, for instance, to understand the message; the organism relies on the DNA code to grow into the type of organism it is. Moreover, the particulars themselves would not constitute a message except in the context of the organism whose growth they subserve, any more than the enumeration of a particular string of organic bases would constitute in and of themselves an understanding of genetics. The principle of ordinal complementarity, as I have called it, holds equally of the structure of our explanation and of the structure of the development so explained. This is as true of our world as of ourselves. Indeed it is true of ourselves because it is in relation to our world, as a concretion in and of the world, that we have our being.

What I am asking, in the last analysis, both in this and in the preceding chapter, is that as philosophers we take seriously the routine admission—granted in one breath by biological writers but rescinded in the next—that there *are* levels of organization of real entities which are at the same time levels of achievement. It must be noted, however, that this is *not* to reinstate either a Cartesian dualism or any other ontological pluralism of this kind. It is precisely the alternative between materialism and mind-body dualism which we are trying to overcome, and which the nature of the phenomena demands that we overcome. I have already referred to the way in which psychologists take the disjunction of a mindless reality or machine-ghost duality as the only possible choice before them. The same choice, if we believe Passmore's lecture on the two-world hypothesis, seems to confront philosophers as well.[34] Passmore is not only persuasive, but correct, I believe, in his insistence that Cartesian separate secret mind is indeed dead and deserves only burial. But his inference seems to be the Rylean one that, the ghost once laid, we can go on working, learning, philosophizing, in reliance on 'ordinary language', with no more metaphysical pangs at all. Here psychologists like Beloff are, though mistaken, at least more candid than the philosophers: for they recognize that there *is* a metaphysical problem which must be faced.[35] But neither psychologists nor Rylean philosophers have yet at their disposal the conceptual tools with which to work at the problem. The psychologists therefore give a wrong answer, whether in a materialist or a Cartesian sense: both answers belong to the past. And the philosophers pretend there is no problem at all.

In contrast to both these, what we need, again, is to articulate an analytical pluralism, a metaphysic which will allow us to acknowledge the existence of a rich variety of realities, not all of which need exist in identifiable, spatio-temporal separateness. Minds are not separate from bodies, yet persons capable of 'minding' are richer and more highly endowed than persons, or individuals, not so capable. And achievements of responsible persons, such as laws, works of art, or forms of worship, may again be richer in reality than those persons themselves. That does not mean that such performances, such products of human skill, somehow exist 'in themselves', separately from the existence of those who contrive, support, and also depend upon them. The alternative 'separate mind' or 'no mind', two reals or one real only, has been too long dominant over western thought. We need to recognize once more the richness of thought in comprehending what cannot be wholly reduced to so explicit a pair of formulae. And equally, we need to recognize the richness of reality, including the achievements of human persons and human traditions. For this transcends even the profoundest acts of comprehension, harbouring for future knowers consequences not yet imagined: harbouring them just because the nature of these realities is more complex, involves more strands and levels and ways of being, than we had thought. Not only in extension, but in intensity, in depth of being, the world has more to say to us, in a greater range of types of discourse, than our Cartesian imprisonment has allowed us to believe.

VI

But we have still said too little. One more step is needed, and that a hard one. It is all very well to pronounce that the structure of tacit knowing mirrors the structure of the entities known, that in personal knowledge our minds are once more at home in a world ontologically suited to contain them. But in asking philosophers and scientists to accept a many-levelled universe, a universe containing, really containing, a multiplicity of forms and ends, we are still asking the nearly impossible. And we have still to seek out the change in philosophical paradigm which could truly enable us to think in these new, or renewed, pluralistic terms.

It is in fact a change that has been repeatedly described, and prescribed, only to be repeatedly ignored. It is, in one form or another, the philosophical reform central to the thought of Bergson, Whitehead, Collingwood, Heidegger, Merleau-Ponty. That is the reform which would make *time* the fundamental category of metaphysics. This looks, at first sight, easy. Have not, as Collingwood said, the prominence of evolutionary concepts on the one hand and the growth of modern historical scholarship on the other, brought the categories of history, of process and development, squarely onto the centre of the intellectual stage? Perhaps–but as we have already seen, the orthodox interpretation of organic evolution is still essentially reductivist in import, and the philosophical analysis of history, as for example by Dilthey and Rickert, or more recently by W. B. Gallie,[36] has for the most part tended simply to set historical understanding over against the pure objectivity of science. Our problem will not be solved, however, until we treat history as our basic phenomenon and draw the world of science, as a limiting case, out of historical reality. Descartes's profoundest error, I have argued earlier on, was his disregard of time. Newton, to construct a satisfactory dynamics, had to abandon the Cartesian time-atom for 'true absolute mathematical time', but this was still time as non- and anti-historical. This was still the homogeneous time which, as Kant rightly demonstrated and as Bergson too insisted, *we* have constructed out of a living medium. Neither Kant's inner sense, however, nor Bergson's metaphysical time provides an adequate base from which to start. Kant is still hampered by his Newtonian optimism and Bergson is crying out, vehemently, but in essence negatively, against the Newtonian denial of life.

In the cosmology of Whitehead, on the other hand, there is a conceptual framework ready to hand, truly founded on the priority of process. It was this cosmology, as well as the cruder outline of Alexander's system, on which Collingwood in *The Idea of Nature* grounded his optimism about the 'modern' as against the 'renaissance' concept of the natural world. But, once more, it needs a frankly epistemological approach to metaphysics to set right the epistemological errors of Descartes with which modern (or in Collingwood's sense 'renaissance') philosophy began. It is Polanyi's theory of tacit knowing, therefore, I believe, which can start us on the right path, coalescing as it does with the existentialist-phenomenological approach of Merleau-Ponty, and it may be, in large part at least, something not unlike the philosophy of *Process and Reality* that will emerge. It is my belief, in particular, that with Polanyi's starting point we can come to a metaphysic of process convergent with Whitehead's, except that it will eliminate the strange doctrine of eternal objects. Starting from the human situation, we remain with the tension of a *claim* to universal validity, and do not need separate real universals to support our concept of form. But that is by the way. Meantime, we do need to take, as I have said, one more step beyond (1) the acknowledgment of tacit knowing, and (2) the recognition of the parallel structure of comprehensive entities, and see where these two steps can direct us in our search for an adequate concept of history and of time, concepts on which alone an adequate theory of knowers and of knowable entities can be built.

Let us think back once more to the structure of tacit knowing and the parallel with comprehensive entities. On the one hand we have the Cartesian myth of total explicitness and the Cartesian atomicity of time. On the other we have the tension of the act of tacit knowing in which we attend from the clues which we know only subsidiarily *to* the object of our focal attention. This directedness, from the *proximal* to the *distal* pole of tacit knowing, is a reaching out from ourselves to the world–and by the same token a reaching out from past to future, a reaching drawn by the focal point of attention, which *is* future. Knowing is essentially temporal activity, directed temporal activity, drawn by the future pull of what we seek to understand. Knowing, I have argued earlier, is essentially learning; and learning is a telic phenomenon, in which the end in sight, even only guessed at, draws us toward a solution. In the knowing at least of comprehensive entities, moreover, this pull from the future, reflected in our effort to understand, characterizes likewise the reality we are striving to know. For achievement, as we have seen, is a pervasive character of life; and achievement, that is, success or its contrary, failure, are temporal categories, categories constituted by the future, by their eventual result. For living things, therefore, past and present depend on the *future* as primary. That is my first thesis: time itself, as lived time, is telic in structure.

This principle is reminiscent of Heidegger. That, as one might say, the primary tense of existential time is future, is perhaps the central insight of *Sein und Zeit*; but the difference from my present thesis is significant. While Heidegger's future is the cessation of life, death only, Polanyi's unit of tacit knowing, or the parallel structure of comprehensive entities, comprises an open multiplicity of tensions— or, in Husserl's term, *protensions*, that is, ways in which the future pulls us towards it. In the yet unsolved problem, the developing embryo, the dance half-performed, the melody half-sung, the nesting behaviour in course of enactment: everywhere in the living world the same future-drawn structure is evident. What spreads out before us here in the variety of life's achievements is not so much Heidegger's 'being to death' as Tillich's 'openness to the future'. Each protension, each foreshadowed end, is indeed definite and limited, and its achievement or the failure to achieve it will be definite and limited as well. Yet the number and variety of *kinds* of *telos* is open and unlimited. This principle is closer also to Whitehead; it is indeed equivalent to Whitehead's 'prehension', or the lure of form as yet unrealized. It is the contrary equally of the Cartesian independent instant, and of the Newtonian absolute time which flows uniformly in one direction. Protensions are temporal arches, curved times reaching back from their goals to the steps that lead on to them.

Yet surely, it will be protested, the one-dimensional advance of time is undeniable. As Reichenbach has demonstrated, it is in fact the one absolute left untouched by relativity.[37] One-dimensional, yes, in the sense that it is irreversible. What has been cannot not be, or be again in the same way, for the first time. There *is* a rectilinearity in time, indeed, but that rectilinearity results only when the pull of the future and the sheer facticity of the past are seen together from outside as the smooth flow of an eternal quasi-present. As lived, time is both protensive: lure, future pull; and facticity: sheer given pastness, *before* it is the smooth flow that everyday timekeeping and physics make of it.

Notice, however, that I am speaking here, again, in an analytic sense, pluralistically. There are, as I have already pointed out, many and various definite pulls of the future, neither one only to death, nor one general push forward as in Bergson's *élan vital*. In every comprehensive entity, a skilful performance, a life history, the growth of an institution, or whatever it be, something not yet born is striving toward a being that pulls it forward to maturity. The existence of such entities often entails interdependence and even, as we shall see, overlapping or actual congruence, yet they are nevertheless distinguishable and different. The performance of *Swan Lake* tonight at Covent Garden does not exist, as a time span, 'separately' from the corresponding segments of the life-spans of the performers. Yet even this segment of his life has, for each participant, a somewhat different rhythm from that of the performance as a whole, and each whole life span has its own temporal pattern again. The differences, though analytical, have not simply conceptual, let alone linguistic, but *metaphysical* significance: they are differences in *being*. There is no single unique timing even of the temporal structures constituting the activities of a given organism. Whitehead's 'fallacy of simple location' must be applied to time as well as space.

A second principle is plainly entailed by our first thesis, and a principle equally revolutionary for the traditional concept of time. Time as a multiplicity of protensions is neither atomistic in the Cartesian way nor is it a smoothly flowing continuum like Newton's true mathematical time. Nor is time merely the relation between events otherwise defined, as Leibniz would have had it, for events *are* already temporal units. What then is the *unit* of temporality? It is a *duration*, a finite, structured *stretch* of time, the stretch defining one real aim, one real process or another. Not moments, but *durations* are time's units. Nor are these units strung along in a single chain. It is not a question of substituting cylinders of finite length for Cartesian instants or for the Newtonian one-dimensional continuity. Time is not one dimension, but a host of them. It is the whole class of durations which together constitute the totality of process. These overlap in an undetermined and, for any single knower, non-determinable number of ways. Take for example a sheep jumping a gap in a hedge. The duration of this piece of organized behaviour is one temporal unit; it can be localized as part of the temporal unit that is this sheep's life-span, or the unit that will be the life span of the species in the history of mammals, or of vertebrates or of life as a whole. But it also overlaps with the temporal span of the hedge's existence, the poachers after rabbits who knocked the gap in the hedge last winter, their life histories, the span of a rural culture, now dying, which included such activities, and so on. In fact, there are already involved in the mention of a sheep or a hedge or a man thousands of intricately interlacing temporal rhythms: those maintaining the sheep's body temperature, for example, its equilibrium, its gait. Or there is its watchfulness for a place to get across into the sweeter pasture over the fence, a plainly future-directed pattern, as stubbornly resistant to time-atomistic analysis as the pattern of the leap itself. As every living being is structured through a multiplicity of forms, physico-chemical, metabolic, and, in the case of animals, neurological and psychic as well, so the same series of levels and multiplicity of form-matter relations constitutes, looked at historically, rhythmically, a complex interlocking of time-spans.

The conceptual apparatus through which we may learn to think in these new terms is yet to be created: only when it has been thought of and articulated, and, more than that, when we have come to dwell in it, as we have dwelt so long in the one-level nature of the Cartesian tradition, only then will we truly have acknowledged, fundamentally, ontologically, the primacy of time. At the explicit, conceptual level at which, in philosophy, we have to begin, the most interesting suggestion for such new basic concepts that I have seen is that of Professor David Bohm for a new topochronology for quantum mechanics. Starting from a critique of the Copenhagen school, Bohm argues that quantum mechanics leads to its well-known paradoxical consequences, not out of logical necessity as such, but out of a more limited logical necessity created by the limited premises from which the physicists' reasoning starts. It is still assumed by physicists, as Kant had assumed, that the concepts of classical physics are simply a refinement of our everyday concepts, which are *the* concepts of common sense, or of human nature. And contrariwise, all rational thought on any subject is held to entail the use of the concepts of classical physics. Bohm easily shows that this is not in fact the case. 'Let us concentrate', he suggests,

> on an essential feature of the concepts of space and time as they are used in classical physics, namely, the description of the location of an object or an event in terms of a set of *continuous Cartesian co-ordinates*. Is it really true that we have no other way to think of space and time except in terms of such a concept? We may ask, for example, whether in everyday experience we would describe the pencil as being on a certain desk, which is in a certain room, which is in a certain house, on a certain street, etc. In other words, we locate the pencil with the aid of a series of *topological relations*, in which one entity is *within* or *upon* another.[38]

The same is true, he argues further, of all laboratory experience:

> For in no one experiment does one ever give an exact co-ordinate of anything (i.e. to an infinite number of decimals). Rather, in a typical measurement, one places a point *between* certain marks on a scale, thus once again locating it by means of a topological relationship. Indeed, in every experiment that can possibly be done, the notion of a precisely

defined co-ordinate is seen to be just an abstraction, which is carried out when a topologically described experimental result is translated into the language of continuous co-ordinates.[39]

There is, Bohm concludes, a more fundamental topological framework underlying the use of classical or approximately classical concepts. A topology, or better, a topochronology constructed on the basis of this more truly common-sense frame of reference would start, as Whitehead's metaphysic does, with the fundamental concept of an *event*. All events, moreover, are to be considered, axiomatically, as 'constituting regions, having some spatial extension and temporal duration'.[40] Objects, Bohm points out, 'will then consist of repetitive, persistent, and organized patterns of events'.[41] Further, such events enter into a relation of 'containment' to one another: so 'for example a flash of light can be in the space between a certain pair of marks on a ruler and occur while a given clock pointer is between a certain pair of marks on its dial'.[42] Next, Bohm introduces the concept of an *elementary process*, defined as 'a relationship between two different events, in which one becomes the other'.[43] Such a process, though potentially divisible, is in itself essentially indivisible: if divided it becomes something else, not itself. Then Bohm introduces the total cosmic process, 'in which all events that have been, are, and will be, are in principle taken into account' in their proper topological order.[44] To each event in this total process one can associate a characteristic wave function. This gives us a Leibnizian universe in modern dress:

> In effect, every such event is regarded as furnishing a unique and individual perspective on the cosmic process (in the sense that in a certain way it 'perceives' its past, in the form of a trace or a set of marks left by this past in this particular event).[45]

Mathematically, the perspective of a given event, Bohm explains, is 'represented by the wave function associated with that event'. And further, this wave function 'determines potentialities for the development of the cosmos subsequent to the event in question'.[46] Again, like Whitehead's cosmology, this is a picture analogous to the Leibnizian monadology, but such that the actual world *develops*, rather than simply changing in accord with an eternal formula.

Professor Bohm's theory, which he has presented elsewhere in more mathematical detail, may well provide a more adequate basis for a metaphysic of time than philosophers have yet put forward. For our present argument, however, it also poses a serious problem.

I have put forward the principles listed above in response to the needs of epistemology on the one hand and biology on the other, and I have not ventured to decide how inorganic nature as such is to be included in the ontology I am sketching. Bohm, on the other hand, has been driven to his innovation by the difficulties neither of philosophy nor of biological science but of physics. In this, of course, he is at one with Whitehead, for whom the categories of event, conceptual aim, prehension and so on are pervasive for all the realities of our cosmic epoch. This gives us a comprehensive metaphysic, satisfying, so far, to the aesthetic sense: but producing, as I have suggested earlier, serious epistemological difficulties. I have preferred, therefore, to start from Polanyi's epistemological inquiry, and so to reunite mind and living nature. In this case, however, the inorganic world seems, so far, to remain a foreign body outside this reconciliation. Yet at the same time every comprehensive entity, no matter how complex, how rich in reality, depends, Polanyi would insist – and rightly insist – on lower level realities for its existence. *All* reality, so far as our situation shows us, is body-bound. A metaphysic recognizing this general truth must assimilate *in*organic reality to its world view. However 'analytic' our pluralism, we must not take matter, as Aristotle does, *simply* as the last level of analysis. 'Matter' *is* both the last resistance to, and the necessary support of, form. Polanyi's treatment of universals may give us a clue for such an undertaking: the laws and theories through which exact scientists understand non-living nature have as their objects 'thinner' realities than the comprehensive entities studied by biologists. But they are, in a reduced sense, also comprehensive entities, though not of the kind which can achieve individuality. I should not like to embark here and now, however, on the solution of such a knotty problem. I only want to suggest that Bohm's analysis of the unit of physical occurrences seems to harmonize well with the need for a unit of *duration* arising from the demands of my own argument.[47]

It should also be added that just as Bohm's new topology involves a rethinking of our concepts both of time and space, so a radical ontology of process must also entail the reorganization of our concept of spatial location. The basic concept of orientation in the world entails a break with Cartesian-Newtonian extension as well as with Cartesian-Newtonian time.

We want to think, then, in terms of stretches of time pulled from the future. But is this not, after all, despite my earlier disclaimer, simply a revival of that most hoary of philosophical antiquities, Aristotelian final cause? This question I have already admitted we should have to ask, and the answer, partly indicated already in Chapter Two as well as at the beginning of this chapter, is instructive. It is indeed the issue of the process which draws the steps to their fitting conclusion: that is to say, however, that the *potential* elicits existence from the *merely actual*, and that is the very contradictory of Aristotelian nature. For Aristotle the actual always precedes the potential; for us, the opposite is the truth. Granted that the actual, viewed as eternal, is all that is of intrinsic value, whether as beautiful, true or good; it is form considered as it *is*. Yet in the rhythm of becoming, what is actual is always already dying: it has its life, as living, from what it may yet become. For Polanyi, as we have seen, the paradigm case of mind at work is found in heuristics, in the original mind *en route* to discovery. Even at a more ordinary level, we have admitted, knowing is essentially learning, whereas for Aristotle learning is a queer case to be dealt with in the refutation of the *Meno*, not made central, in itself, to the method of science. Straus mentions Aristotle's illuminating if brief statement at the beginning of the *Metaphysics*: all animals by nature desire to know, and wonders why Aristotle never carried further his insight here.[48] Straus is right also in finding an answer to his own question in the nature of Aristotelian logic, or better Aristotelian methodology. To deny the primacy of learning is central to the Aristotelian concept of the sciences as finished, eternal edifices in a finished, eternal world, where actuality keeps potency firmly within bounds. Man rooted in the eternal and the simply necessary: that is the Aristotelian theme. In direct contrast is Polanyi's description of the 'society of explorers' whose existence he is concerned to justify: 'man rooted in potential thought'.[49] The power of what is not yet draws us on, whether to achievement or to failure, to knowledge or to error. From that ultimate dubiety there is no escape, just because it is in the last analysis process, not eternity, contingency, not necessity, in which we have our roots. But if there is no end to our peril, neither is there any end, so long as life lasts, to our hope. Aristotelian finitude is perfect in itself but stifling; our finitude as we understand it is infinite in its dangers, but infinite also in its aspirations, never complete in its present. Our 'teleology' is like Aristotle's in affirming the telic character of living nature, without affirming Paleyan planning in the universe. But it is radically unlike Aristotle's in placing potency, ontologically, before actuality, not after it. Actuality in the sense of the factual does indeed limit potency, yet it is itself in every case the product of history, the particular concretion of past potentialities, the realization of one, the failure of others.

Potency before actuality: this principle entails contingency, and the contingency of time looked at in focus becomes negativity: the nothingness so loudly vaunted by existentialist philosophers. It is not, however, or not necessarily, the negativity of despair or of the absurd: it is the negation that lies first at the heart of time as such, and secondly at the heart of consciousness as the 'upsurge of time', self-consciousness as the expression of reflective, critical history.

Time everywhere entails negativity. The protensive pull of the future is the lure of what is not yet, what may be or may not. The past has been exactly itself and nothing but itself—definite and ineluctable —yet it is no more. The factual, absurd, irrational *that* is, but is over. The horizon of possibilities, with its scope, its guessed at unknown fulfilments or failures, gives us breathing space for our projects, but is a dream only. It is not yet and we cannot know what, when it is, it will be, or will have been. For only when it has been is it, unequivocally, what it was. Straus puts this in terms of the contrast between particular and general: every moment, he says, is particular as past though general with respect to the future.[50]

It is this ambiguity of past and future, perhaps, that drove science, seeking total objectivity, total exactitude, to ignore time and try to escape into the present. And yet as every philosopher of time since Augustine has insisted, the present is the most evanescent tense of the three. If time is essentially a class of durations, indeed, how *could* there be a present? For how could we grasp it? Thrown into the world by the force of facticity, making ourselves and making our world through our thrust forward into the future, where shall we find a present? For Heidegger the 'normal' present is forfeiture, betrayal of our true transcendence, forgetful of our essential task in the scattering demands of convention and the crowd. For Whitehead there is a true present, but it is wholly subjective and wholly fleeting: the enjoyment of the experienced moment, the aesthetic aspect of experience caught, instantaneously, on the surface of flux. Both these again have their moment of negativity. Heidegger's everyday present is itself denial; and, as against this, the authentic present, the present of the Heideggerian man of resolution, is even more thoroughly denial: it is the awareness of destiny as being-to-death. This, I have tried to say, is an overstressing of *one* temporal rhythm; but we could say that the true present, or at least *one* true present, is realized in the awareness of destiny, the awareness that this moment is part of a temporal pattern. This is a positive present, though negative in that it is caught in the arch from future through past to future. And on the other hand, Whitehead's present, 'enjoyment', is positive, even absolute in its quickly perishing immediacy; yet it is also a negation of time as such, in that, as absolute, as enjoyed, it is wholly out of the stream of process. It is the *kairos*, the moment *par excellence*, the aspect of eternity which, though it fulfils, yet gives the lie to process as a whole. Thus reality as process issues in what Nicholas Cusanus called the coincidence of opposites. That is, again, why science and the rationalist tradition have feared to face it. The metaphysics of time is perilous.

Yet the metaphysics of time can give us tools for solving philosophical riddles which all the efforts of rationalism are unable to disentangle, and I may point in conclusion to one of these: a central problem for the point of view I have been supporting in this book. If knowing is one of the kinds of activity perfected by living persons, then we need a metaphysic which provides an adequate conception of activity. We must have a tenable theory of action as responsible and as free. A theory of wholly explicit knowledge is a determinist theory: this is brought out, for example, in the argument of Dr Beloff referred to above. A blind hope of free agency is left over against the rigid determinism that 'science' would decree. But if we start from the structure of temporality, the situation is different. Existentialists have told us over and over: we are bound by facticity, we are what history makes us, yet we are free, even totally free, wholly responsible for, wholly creative of, each action of our own. How can this be? The answer is paradoxical if you will, as time is, and as, therefore, reality is, but simple. It parallels the argument of Straus already quoted. What is past is determinate just because it is past; we can study, as sociologists or psychologists, only what is past. Therefore all human behaviour as the object of study is determined, but what is future is still, in Straus's terms, general, that is, indeterminate.[51] Within the bounds left by the past I must make what my new past is going to have been. The scope and richness of such generality varies immensely from species to species, from person to person, from circumstance to circumstance. There are, as everyone in this century knows or ought to know, circumstances of confinement, deprivation, torture, so suffocating that only the strongest and greatest human beings can find, within them, a core of freedom. And it is primarily because they strangle freedom that they are so terrible. That is, in general, why pain is terrible: it robs us of potentiality, makes life wholly present and therefore wholly meaningless, it deprives us of the protensive pull of our transcendence that is the core of conscious life. Where we are spared such levelling pressures, freedom lives in the openness to the future that is the meaning of the past. In every act of every responsible person the totality of the past is brought to bear, is focussed on the discovery of a meaning still to be known. The structure of tacit knowing is mirrored in the structure of comprehensive entities because they both mirror the metaphysical structure of time.

Appendix

Statistics and Selection:
An Analysis of Fisher's Genetical Theory

I

SIR RONALD FISHER'S argument in the *Genetical Theory of Natural Selection*, has played a decisive role in the rise of the present orthodox theory of evolution. Not all theories of evolution, not even all neo-Darwinian theories, share this structure; but Fisher's argument has been so very widely influential that it seems worthwhile to examine it in some detail.[1] I shall take the mathematical core of the theory for granted, but want to examine the concepts carried by the mathematical formalism. As Fisher writes, 'the rigour of the demonstration requires that the terms employed should be used strictly as defined'.[2]

II

It is the principal thesis of all Darwinian and neo-Darwinian theories that evolution is the result of the joint action of random variation (or mutation) and environmental pressure (or natural selection). How is this basic thesis supported by Fisher's argument in the *Genetical Theory*? I am not asking whether evolution is in fact a function of random variation times natural selection, but whether or to what extent Fisher has proved it to be so. The crucial text we have to consider is Chapter Two, on the Fundamental Theorem, although much that is said in the chapters on the evolution of dominance and on mutation and selection is also relevant.

What is to be demonstrated in Chapter Two, Fisher tells us at the start, is that 'the rate of improvement of any species of organism in relation to its environment is determined by its present condition'.[3] 'Improvement in relation to environment' seems to mean 'increased adaptation'; but the term 'adaptation' is formally introduced only later, where it is defined in terms which appear to presuppose the concept of 'improvement':

> An organism is regarded as adapted to a particular situation, or to the totality of situations which constitute its environment, only in so far as we can imagine an assemblage of slightly different situations, or environments, to which the animal would on the whole be less well adapted; and equally only in so far as we can imagine an assemblage of slightly different organic forms, which would be less well adapted to that environment.[4]

In other words, an organism is regarded as adapted, if one can imagine its condition as an improvement over another possible condition that would be slightly less favourable.

Thus the concept of improvement is central to the argument, and we must find out what it means. And there is also the question, in what sense the present condition of an organism 'determines' its 'improvement in relation to its environment'. Does 'determine' here mean 'cause'; if so, how, or if not, what does it mean?

III

Fisher's procedure is to establish a table of reproduction, analogous to a life table, and to specify a parameter of population increase m, expressing the 'relative rate of increase or decrease of a population when in the steady state appropriate to any such system'[5]—i.e. when the distribution of age groups in the population is constant. Fisher calls this the 'Malthusian parameter of population increase', and it is said to 'measure *fitness* by the objective fact of representation in future generations'.[6] Now suppose we are measuring a particular character, such as tallness, in a population. And suppose we assume, as in the light of modern genetics we do, that all persistent changes in organisms are produced by changes in their genetic make-up.[7] Then we may calculate the average effect on the character in question of a given gene substitution, and also the effect of this one gene substitution on m, that is on the chance of leaving posterity. We then calculate a summation of these gene changes *and* their effects on m for all the genes in the population, and we get what Fisher calls the 'genetic variance'—in this case for example, the genetic variance of tallness. Now suppose further that what we are measuring is not tallness but fitness itself. We then find, by further calculation, that '*The rate of increase in fitness of any organism at any time is equal to its genetic variance of fitness at that time*'.[8] This statement Fisher describes as 'the fundamental theorem of Natural Selection'.

'm', or the 'rate of progress of a species in fitness to survive', is, as Fisher says, 'a well-defined statistical attribute of a population'.[9] It is the increase (or decrease) in the chance this population has of leaving posterity at some future date. 'Fitness' in this sense would seem to be the same for all organisms: it is simply a statistical measurement, which has, so far, nothing to do with the particular structures or functions of particular organisms as suited to particular environments. In fact, it has, so far, nothing to do with environment at all, nor with 'improvement' in any sense other than the very restricted quantitative one: that a gene or an individual or a population may be said to be 'improved' when its chance of having descendants at some future date has risen. This is 'improvement' in the sense in which a patient has improved when he is more likely to survive.

IV

If this were the whole story, there would be no problem. It would be possible, as indeed happened far and wide in the wake of the publication of Fisher's book, to make valuable calculations, resembling actuarial tables, by which to record the gradual increase or decrease of certain genetic factors in Mendelian interbreeding populations. Some of the great array of experimental work in which Fisher's techniques were in fact applied is referred to in the later edition.

It seems odd, however, to speak in this connection of 'improvement in relation to environment' or of 'Natural Selection'. 'Improvement in relation to environment' suggests a correlation which has so far not been considered; and similarly, 'Natural Selection' seems to describe not a purely numerical relationship, but something qualitative as well; i.e. the elimination of characters less well adapted to a particular environment in favour of those slightly better adapted to that environment.

In what sense, then, is the Fundamental Theorem a theorem of 'Natural Selection' (concerned, *a fortiori*, with 'improvement in relation to environment')? In introducing the notion of 'reproductive value', the probability that a given individual of a given age will have descendants at some future date, Fisher remarks that this value is of interest, since '*the action of Natural Selection must be proportional to it*'.[10] This is indeed true. If, as Fisher points out, the reproductive value of the inhabitants of Great Britain decreased between 1911 and 1921 as a result of the First World War, then whatever selective effects might take place, must take place only upon that declining group; and therefore the action of Natural Selection would be proportional to the decline. And conversely, where there is Natural Selection taking place, its operation can be investigated and measured by the use of Fisher's techniques. The fact of industrial melanism, for example, has been known for many years; but Kettlewell has recently studied it with great care and precision in terms of modern population genetics.[11] Thus if normal peppered moths are taken by predators in industrial areas in greater numbers than the darker carbonaria mutants, then the increase of carbonaria and the decrease of light coloured individuals can be recorded as a decrease in reproductive value of the normal form (which is more likely to be eaten before reproducing–and its offspring also and so on) or an increase in the reproductive value of the carbonaria, i.e. an increase in the probability that there will be carbonaria in future. In other words, once we know that selection has in fact taken place in a particular situation, we can record and elaborate this knowledge in the statistical terms of Fisher's theory.

This statement about reproductive value, moreover, holds equally for the fundamental theorem itself, which generalizes the notion of increase in reproductive value for an active interbreeding population, and equates it with the increase in probability of survival of the particular genes forming the genetic constitution of the population in question. Thus *either* (as in the decline of the British population) the fundamental theorem expresses the limits within which Natural Selection can operate; *or* (as in the case of industrial melanism) the occurrence of Natural Selection (as known from other sources) entails the truth of the fundamental theorem.

V

But it is not at all clear that the fundamental theorem entails Natural Selection. In fact, in the example of reproductive value cited by Fisher, the effect of war, the change in reproductive value is notoriously one in which the better adapted are eliminated in favour of the less well-adapted: the very opposite of a natural selection effect. For natural selection expresses the tendency to *increased*, not to *decreased* adaptation.[12] More generally, we should recall also that, as Darwin himself admitted, natural selection is applicable only to such characters or functions of living things as are both heritable and adaptive (whether for good or ill)–i.e. relevant to viability or the reverse in a given environment. But we might record the increase or decrease of all sorts of characters in populations without regard to their 'adaptive' value one way or another. Supposing for example that red hair is increasing, and hence the probability of larger numbers of future redheads is also increasing; this does not in itself tell us anything about the usefulness of red hair, unless we know from some other source that all characters that are increasing in the population must be of use to it. Darwin was well aware of this restriction on his theory, but was confident on the whole that most characters of organic beings were adaptive. And what Darwin demonstrated in the first four chapters of the *Origin* was that given the largely adaptive nature of organisms, and variation, and inheritance, and Malthusian population increase, natural selection necessarily follows.[13] But Fisher's statistical proof does not appear to be rich enough in its premises to permit this conclusion. In terms of the 'strictly defined' concepts it uses, the fundamental theorem is not a theorem of natural selection, but a statistical device for recording population changes. Nor is the situation altered by calling such changes 'genetical selection'. We must still distinguish between 'genetical selection', which is purely statistical, and Darwinian selection, which is environment-based and causal. They remain two distinct concepts with a common name.

VI

It is important to keep this distinction in mind when interpreting the use made by Fisher himself and by others—notably, e.g. Huxley, Haldane, Simpson—in applying his formula. The fundamental theorem has been stated, Fisher says, for idealized populations 'in which fortuitous fluctuations in the genetic composition have been excluded'.[14] He then calculates the error due to such 'fortuitous fluctuations'. The standard error turns out to be $\frac{1}{T}\sqrt{\frac{\overline{W}}{2n}}$, where T is the time of a generation, n is the number of the population, and W the rate of increase in fitness of a population measured in terms of the summation of the effect in particular genes on m. In terms of this formula, it turns out that the rate of increase in fitness becomes irregular only when it is so slight as to be of the value $1/n$. Only then, in other words, do the random fluctuations produced in a single generation by mutation (given random mating) affect the exactness of the statistical measurement, or, as Fisher puts it, 'the regularity of the rate of progress'. And more than this: if a long enough time is allowed, even this irregularity will recede to vanishing point. For even if the value of m for different genotypes were so delicately balanced in a given generation as to show only a $1/n$ distinction, and hence a fluctuation in m and the summation of the effects of genes on m, still over a span of 10,000 generations, the deviations from regularity would be just a hundredfold less.

Now this argument is taken to show that 'very low rates of selective intensity' are effective in nature. But if we have interpreted the fundamental theorem correctly, what it shows in fact is that very slight trends in the frequency of characters in populations may be recorded if they persist over a long period of time. Whether such trends are the result of a process that can reasonably be called 'natural selection' is another question altogether.[15]

How does Fisher deal with this question? What he argued in his 1932 paper in *Science Progress*[16] was that such trends are not, in large populations, the result of mutation, since mutations are too infrequent and advantageous mutations still more infrequent, and therefore it must be natural selection that directs the trends which his statistics describe. This follows, however, only if mutation and natural selection are the only two possible causes of evolutionary change: and that is what the theory is supposed to prove, not to presuppose.

Nor is the argument of our present text more satisfactory, for it moves in an even narrower circle.[17] Since only mutation rates around the 1/n value are 'selectively neutral', Fisher says, random variation, i.e. mutation, will very seldom indeed be an effective factor in evolution. But what does 'selectively neutral' mean? It means precisely: with a mutation rate, i.e. a rate of gene substitution, around the 1/n value or less. Similarly, '1 per cent selective advantage' *means* 1 per cent increase in numbers of a particular gene substitution. Any mutation rate more substantial than 1/n therefore automatically becomes 'selective advantage' and so the product of selection, not mutation; and any lesser mutation rate remains 'selectively neutral', that is, counts as mutation, not selection. All this will be a more than verbal argument only if we know from other evidence that selection, in the environment-related, Darwinian sense, is always the cause of such statistical advances. In short, genetical selection is entailed by and measures but does not entail Darwinian selection.

VII

Let us return for a moment to Fisher's opening statement (at the beginning of Chapter Two) and put it alongside the fundamental theorem. 'The improvement of any organism in relation to its environment is determined by its present condition.' 'The increase in fitness of any organism at any time is equal to its genetic variance in fitness at that time.' In the context of Fisher's argument, 'improvement' etc. clearly refers to increased probability of leaving descendants, for whatever reason. And 'present condition' means present genetic variance in fitness, i.e. in the probability of leaving descendants. In other words, it means the summation of such probabilities itemized in the gene pool of the relevant population. What does it mean, finally, to say that the second of these 'determines' the first? The fundamental theorem asserts that the rate of increase in fitness of any organism at any time is exactly equal to the genetic variance in fitness at that time. But Fisher has just said that the rate of increase in fitness here means rate of increase in fitness *due to all changes in gene ratio*.[18] Now the genetic variance in any measurement in population means according to Fisher's earlier definition[19] the summation, for all genes, of the effects on m of the excess of any one gene over its alleles. But this *is* precisely the summation of the effect on m of all changes in gene ratio. To say that the rate of increase in fitness is due to changes in gene ratio is to assert a fundamental belief of modern genetic theory. To identify the increase so caused with the 'genetic variance in fitness' is to assert an identity. How can such a statement be said to 'determine' anything? We have present increase in fitness = improvement; genetic variance in fitness = present condition. Either the second determines the first in the sense that we are simply stating an identity; and this tells us nothing about organic phenomena except as formalizing what we already know–that, as Professor 'Espinasse has put it,[20] wherever there are characters there are some genes that cause them. Or else the fundamental theorem is meant to direct our attention to the tables of reproduction which can be used to chart the trends in populations both at the level of individuals and at the genetic level and to correlate trends in other measurements with trends in m. We could say, for example, that the overall increase in tallness of a population is equal to its genetic variance in tallness; because we believe that whatever trend a population is showing in respect to a given measurement has some genetic basis. To say that its overall trend in fitness is equal to its genetic variance in fitness is not to express any further 'determination' over and above this. Again, the only determination expressed here is the determination we know of from genetics, and the statistical measurements of m add nothing to this. There may of course be other causal connections in nature, in predator-prey situations and so on, and our statistical measurements may guide us in our analysis of, and perhaps even our search for, these. But in themselves statistics cannot specify such connections. In other words, the fundamental theorem is a guide to statistical technique which is overlaid on the causal relation of heredity and can be used as underpinning for the causal study of Darwinian selection; but in itself it asserts neither.

VIII

But how can the imposing edifice of modern neo-Darwinian theory rest on so narrow a base? In fact, it does not. It rests on the broader foundation of Darwinian thinking which is drawn into the circle of Fisher's statistical theory in virtue of the ambiguity of its central concepts. We have only to look at Fisher's comments on the fundamental theorem to see how this works. He likens this principle to the second law of thermodynamics, as a statistical law that reigns supreme over a vast area of nature. But fitness, he says, though measured by a uniform method, 'is qualitatively different for every different organism'.[21] Now this is not fitness in the sense of the mathematical chance of leaving descendants, which is a quantity, and cannot be 'qualitatively different' for each organism. On the contrary, Fisher is here referring to fitness in the sense which he goes on to amplify later in the same chapter, in section added in the second edition but implicit in the usage of the first edition also: that is, he is talking about fitness in the qualitative sense of an 'advantage' (of a particular kind) to the individual organism.[22] 'Fitness measured by m' will again become extremely important in the theory of the evolution of dominance (Chapter Three), where the biologist's concern is with the probability, for certain genetic factors, of leaving a remote posterity, even though these factors may lie deeply hidden in the present population, phenotypically considered. But here (in the latter part of Chapter Two) the statistical concept of fitness has been translated into old-fashioned Darwinian fitness: in terms of our previous example, the benefit to a Manchester moth of being black and the harm to his cousin of being speckled. Of course if mostly peppered moths are eaten and black ones spared, the population will come to include more black and fewer speckled individuals. But the statistical result to the population in the future and the immediate benefit to this sooty moth in this grimy tree trunk today are not the same thing. Yet through the identity of the word 'fitness', the insistence that selection has to do with present advantage, not 'trends' (which would be orthogenetic, finalistic and wicked) is here attached to Fisher's original, stricter concept of 'fitness', which thus becomes Darwinian as well as genetical and immediate as well as long-run. So we have genetical selection for later and Darwinian selection for now fused under a single word 'fitness'.

And 'progress' is equally elastic. We have 'progress' in fitness-measured-by-m: e.g. progress in the height of the population if tall individuals are on the increase (never mind why); and at the same time we have progress in an advantageous character in the sense of increased adaptation, if, say, tallness (as in the proverbial giraffe) actually, for some reason, causes its possessor to get more to eat than his shorter brothers and therefore causes, rather than simply measuring, survival.

IX

There is more to it than this, however. The advantage to the individual organism on which Fisher insists is not just the traditional one of an advantage in facing predators or the like, that is, as against our contemporaries, a lesser chance of death. It is also (and must be, in an evolutionary context) the chance of reproduction. 'It will be observed', Fisher writes,

> that the principle of Natural Selection, in the form in which it has been stated in this chapter (i.e. the fundamental theorem) refers only to the variation among individuals (or co-operative communities), and to the progressive modification of structure or function only in so far as varia-

tions are *of advantage to the individual in respect to his chance of death or reproduction.* It thus affords a rational explanation of structures, reactions and instincts which can be recognized as profitable to their individual possessors. *It affords no corresponding explanation for any properties of animals or plants which, without being individually advantageous, are supposed to be of service to the species to which they belong.*[23]

Now if we omit the qualification 'or reproduction', this is a fair statement of the situation described by Darwin. It is the chance of death that selection controls. True, we may also infer that, since the chance of reproduction is obviously tied to the chance of death, the future numbers of organisms possessing immediately advantageous characters, given certain environmental conditions, will increase in numbers also, if and when those conditions persist. Moths that are eaten cannot reproduce thereafter. But the *'immediate advantage'* to the moth in this case is not reproduction, but the omission of being eaten. Reproduction would be an advantage to the moth's descendants, and indirectly to the moth insofar as it is advantageous to it to satisfy its instincts; but in the situation of Darwinian selection—as in this case of the black moth on the black tree trunk—it is the character that keeps one alive that counts. Reproduction as the continuation of the species is a matter that is indirect and inferred; it is staying alive that is the immediate benefit.

Yet the 'or reproduction' alternative is essential to Fisher's *genetical* selection—and again, to the future-directed character, in particular, of the evolution of dominance: where in present-day recessives—which may some day become dominant—we are dealing, as he says himself, with the 'chance of leaving a remote posterity' by storing up characters that will some day be useful in some distant future environment. Such a chance is surely meaningless in terms of 'advantage to the individual' unless in some Biblical sense that a man feels he is cut off from immortality if he is cut off from having living descendants. In short, we have tied together in the concept of fitness three kinds of 'selection': genetical selection, which is future-directed but only in a Pickwickian sense selection at all; Darwinian selection for now, directed to immediate advantage; and Darwinian selection for later, in reference to future advantage. The first specifies progress in the purely statistical sense of increased chance of survival of some genes rather than others; the second in the sense of short-run increase in adaptation; the third, long-run increase in adaptation.

Finally, added to these, we must notice another of Fisher's comparisons between his theorem and the Second Law. While physical systems run downhill, he says, evolution tends on the whole to produce 'progressively higher organization of the organic world'.[24] This is progress in a new sense, and one which escapes all Darwinian considerations, though again its existence, once admitted on other grounds, might be recorded with the help of statistical methods.

Thus the larger conceptual structure of the theory is both richer and less exact than the proof of the fundamental theorem would lead us to expect. It consists of a network of concepts, in which statistical and deterministic, genetical and Darwinian meanings, short-run and long-run assessments, reinforce one another in a self-confirming circle.

X

This self-enclosing ambiguity will become clearer if we pinpoint the sense in which the concept of 'improvement' occurs in the argument and consider their evolutionary import.

First, there is the strict statistical meaning of the Malthusian parameter: the increase in the probability that organisms possessing certain characters will leave offspring. Such an increase, though calculated for an infinitesimal period, has meaning only over time. What it asserts about organisms in time may be taken in two ways: either as a tautological statement: what has survived has survived, what is on its way to surviving is on its way to surviving; or as the retrospective appraisal of an achievement: what has survived is not what has failed to survive, but what has succeeded. But this says nothing of *why* that might have happened, either in terms of adaptive relations to environment or anything else. Tables of reproductive value record the multiplication of some characters and the disappearance of others; that is all one can say in these terms. And in terms of these tables, one may assert the probable increase of some genes rather than others.

In this sense of 'improvement' Fisher is right in saying that organisms must show 'improvement' up to the moment of extinction. In terms of the increase of some genes as against their alleles, they doubtless do. For since the sum of any gene and its alleles in any population always $= 1$, we can always take the increasing rather than the decreasing gene (or genes, where there are multiple alleles) and so get a picture of 'improvement'. This is really why, in the fundamental theorem, the calculated value is always positive. Not only is the time interval, dt, necessarily positive, but the changing gene ratios also can always be taken in this sense.

XI

Alongside this statistical formulation, however, consider what Fisher says about the universality of 'improvement' in his comment on the fundamental theorem. His first comparison with thermody-namics is to this effect:

> The systems considered in thermodynamics are permanent; species on the contrary are liable to extinction, although biological improvement must be expected to occur up to the end of their existence.[25]

The phrase 'biological improvement' brings us back to the 'improve-ment in relation to environment' from which we started; it is what Fisher describes elsewhere as 'progress determined by Natural Selection', the full Darwinian improvement so emphatically under-lined in the second edition. According to this conception, organisms are in fact constantly becoming better adapted to their niches in nature, as natural selection weeds out the imperfectly adapted; and therefore it follows, further, as Fisher in fact argues in some detail, that the explication of all cases of extinction must be referred to deterioration of the environment. Thus when the dinosaurs died out, e.g., something must have gone wrong in their environment to bring this about. That this is actually so in nature, however, cannot be inferred from the fundamental theorem by taking 'improvement' in its strict and statistical sense.

We are dealing here, in other words, with a second concept of improvement. We are asserting that there is improvement in the sense of the appearance of adaptive relations with immediate effectiveness here and now, characters or functions which are genuinely advan-tageous in relation to their bearer's actual environment, and which may therefore, as compared with their absence, be called 'improve-ments'. These are the improvements effected by Darwinian selection, and the concepts presupposed in the assertion of such improvement are not by any means the same as those supporting the statistical concept. While statistical 'improvement' entails the conception of the organism as an aggregate of gene effects, Darwinian improvement entails in addition the conception of the organism as a machine with parts adapted to the performance of their special functions. The improvement that is effected here is that of increasing adaptation in the sense of specialization, of fitting in better and better to a special niche in nature. The evolutionary import of such improvement is *katagenetic*, to use a term introduced by the German evolutionist Rensch. That is, it is evolution downhill, in the sense that species break up into varieties and subspecies as specialized demands are made on them. Darwin's finches are a classic example.

As against genetical 'improvement', which is meaningful only as an assessment of a trend over a lapse of time, this kind of improve-ment is short-run. On the other hand, it is not intelligible, as the statistical concept purports to be, in terms of gene ratios alone. Its assessment depends on the recognition of phenotypes, as wholes, not as aggregates of genes, and on the recognition of the relation of such wholes to their environment, to predators, to climate, and so on and so forth. It is neither future moths, nor gene pools, to whom it is advantageous not to be taken by a bird, but this black moth on this tree trunk today. And the evolutionary trend which establishes and maintains a phenomenon like melanism expresses the accumulation of millions of such individual escapes and individual disasters, not to genes or gene pools, but to moths, whether today or yesterday or (from some cause other than the industrial revolution) a million years ago.

XII

So much for my first pair of 'improvements'. However, as critics of natural selection theory have long been saying, there seem to be other adaptive relations which develop only slowly, and which do not appear to benefit their possessors at the beginning of their development. Such long-run adaptation appears to entail a third meaning of 'improvement'. It refers to characters or functions which will be 'better' for future phenotypes in future environments. Such improvement we may call *quasi-anagenetic*; it still concerns particular adaptive relationships and specialization, but specializations which accompany the emergence of new forms (rather than new sub-styles of old forms) and which develop slowly over a very long period of time. Now this seems to be the kind of situation which Fisher explicitly excludes, exiling the 'benefit of the species' approach as teleological and irrational. In terms of what he says there, one would conclude that all ultimately useful characters must have been in some direct way useful even in their minute beginnings. And it is true that this has been shown to be possible or even likely in a number of cases, for instance, primitive photoreceptors, electric organs, feathers and so on. One can, if one likes, extrapolate such instances to all cases of clearly adaptive characters. Yet the forward reference, as distinct from immediate utility, seems essential to Fisher's own extremely important case of the evolution of dominance. Here we have recessives, either useless or even harmful, hidden away in a population over a long period of time—up to the moment of a new environmental situation which makes them advantageous and so calls forth modifiers that turn them into dominants. Only the reference to 'remote posterity' makes sense of this story. True, there is the case of sickle-cell anaemia : where we have a gene which is lethal in the homozygote, but in the heterozygote actually gives protection against malaria, and is kept going in the population by this beneficial effect. Supposing a situation in which sickling were no longer harmful, we could imagine that a character now maintained, but in a recessive state, because of the advantageous nature of the heterozygote, might become dominant and pervade the population much more completely. And we might then extrapolate this kind of process to all cases of the retention of recessives apparently for the sake of their future usefulness, but really for the sake of some other present benefit. Yet even then, the modifiers which will eventually make the now-recessives dominant must be lurking in the population ready to leap into action when the environment demands, and thus the future-directedness of the whole procedure is simply transferred to them. It seems strange to say, as Darlington does, that the genes are 'gifted with automatic foresight',[26] yet the reference to 'remote posterity' which necessarily dominates Fisher's argument on dominance does indeed suggest some such idea.

But how can Fisher and other evolutionists who follow him remain so happily unaware of this third and uncomfortably long-term 'improvement'? What happens, I think, is something like this. Improvement 1, statistical selection, is the measure of improvement 3, long-run adaptation. But long-run adaptation is *adaptation*, and where there is adaptation there must, in the light of the Darwinian theory of natural selection, be improvement 2, Darwinian selection— for Darwin has proved that that is how adaptation is produced. So improvement 3, which is in fact unintelligible in terms of the dictum of improvement 2 (since in its terms all adaptation bears on immediate, not remote benefit) is nevertheless subsumed under it through the measurement of both of them by the techniques of improvement 1. Moreover, improvement 1 is expressed by a differential, which can be interpreted as a summation of gene changes *now*— short-run trends–or over as long an interval as you like–long-term trends; but at the same time, since it is one statement (the fundamental theorem) it must express one relationship, and since in Darwinian terms improvement 3 would be nonsense, this one relationship must be the situation covered by improvement 2.

The way in which 1, 2 and 3 are assimilated to one another is most evident if we place the argument about the fraction $1/n$ and the efficacy of very slight 'selective intensities' alongside the argument about immediate advantage. As Fisher himself argues, irregular variation in the rate of increase in fitness as measured by m is more apparent in a single generation than over a longer period, and therefore very small 'selective values' are sufficiently strong to establish themselves *over a long enough time*. This statistical observation is often used against those who object to natural selection theory because of the difficulty of accounting for the first beginnings of what will ultimately be useful traits. Selection can do so much 'because it has so long'.[27] Yet if one speaks of trends in evolution, of orthogenesis or the like, one is told that this is nonsense because evolutionary modification always consists in the selection of the immediately useful at each step, in each generation.[28] So improvement 3, long-run adaptation, with its statistical measure in improvement 1, is used to answer one objection, while improvement 2, which can also be expressed by the same statistics, applied to short-run situations, is invoked to answer another.

We must mention, finally, a fourth meaning of improvement, which is truly an advance to higher forms of life. Such improvement is explicitly mentioned only in Fisher's remark about his fundamental theorem and the tendency to 'higher organization' (as contrasted with the Second Law and entropy). This is the kind of improvement which represents true *anagenesis* in the sense of emergence, or the appearance of genuine novelty at a higher level of richness or complexity. But this is also a kind of improvement which neither statistical genetics nor selectionist biology can handle, since it is neither quantitative nor adaptive. It is best for selectionists to ignore it, as Darwin warned himself to do when he wrote in his copy of the *Vestiges* 'Never speak of higher or lower in evolution.' Yet the great outlines of the fossil record are there, and demand to be spoken of, especially since the fact that we can speak of them is one of the surprising results of the process they record. But evolution as macro-evolution, as the emergence of life and of higher forms of life, outruns both the concepts of gene-substitution, and of improvement in relation to environment. It makes sense only as an achievement—an achievement for which statistical methods can measure the necessary, but not the sufficient conditions.

Notes

Chapter 1

1 Michael Polanyi, 'Commitment to Science', Lecture delivered at Duke University, February 24, 1964, p. 2 (microfilmed and copyrighted as *Duke Lectures*, Pacific School of Religion, 1964.)

2 Michael Polanyi, *ibid.*, p. 12; Sir Karl Popper, 'On the Sources of Knowledge and of Ignorance', *Proceedings of the British Academy*, XLVI (1960), 39–70, pp. 47–48. The same point is made by P. Lachièze-Rey in a passage quoted by Merleau-Ponty; see note 11 below.

3 *Meno* 70A. Passages from the *Meno* and *Protagoras* are from the Loeb translation.

4 *Phaedrus* 249B.

5 *Meno* 79D.

6 *Protagoras* 314A–B.

7 *Symposium* 212A.

8 *Meno* 80D.

9 *Loc. cit.*

10 *Loc. cit.*

11 P. Lachièze-Rey. *L'Idéalisme Kantien*, pp. 17–18, quoted in Maurice Merleau-Ponty, *Phenomenology of Perception*, translated by Colin Smith (London: Routledge and Kegan Paul, 1962), p. 371.

12 Merleau-Ponty, *loc. cit.*

13 Michael Polanyi, *Personal Knowledge* (London: Routledge and Kegan Paul, 1958; Chicago: University of Chicago Press, 1958; 2nd. ed., 1962), pp. 55–65 and *passim*.

14 On Plato's relation to eristic, see Rosamund Kent Sprague, *Plato's Use of Fallacy* (London: Routledge and Kegan Paul, 1962).

15 *Meno* 81A.

16 *Seventh Letter* 341D.

17 *Meno* 86C.

18 *Seventh Letter* 344B.

19 See R. S. Bluck, *Plato's Meno* (Cambridge: Cambridge University Press, 1961), Introduction.

20 *Meno* 86B.

21 *Ibid.*, 86B–C.

22 *Ibid.*, 100A (*Odyssey* X 494).

23 *Meno* 98B.

Chapter 2

1 *Posterior Analytics*, Book I, Chapter 1, 71a 1–11. Quotations from the *Posterior* and the *Prior Analytics* are from the Loeb translation.

2 *Ibid.*, 71a 29–30.

3 Book II, Chapter 21.

4 *Prior Analytics*, Book II, Chapter 21, 67a 8–21.

5 *Ibid.*, 67a 22–26.

6 *Posterior Analytics*, Book I, Chapter 1, 71a 19–28.

7 See Chapter One, note 11.

8 *Categories*, Chapter 5, 2b 5–6.

9 D. W. Hamlyn, *Sensation and Perception* (London: Routledge and Kegan Paul, 1961; New York: Humanities Press, 1961).

10 C. I. Lewis, *Mind and the World Order* (New York: Scribner, 1929).

11 *De Anima*, Book II, Chapter 12, 424a 17 ff. Quotations from the *De Anima* are from the Hicks translation.

12 *Ibid.*, 424a 24 ff.

13 *Ibid.*, 424a 33 ff.

14 *Ibid.*, Book III, Chapter 3, 428b 24 f.

15 In speaking of sensory 'discrimination', Aristotle is not, as is sometimes said, confusing sensation with judgment. It is perception as discriminating that he is talking about. The 'discriminating' power of judgment is distinct from this.

16 Merleau-Ponty, *op. cit.*, p. 212.

17 Wilhelm Szilasi, *Wissenschaft als Philosophie* (Zürich and New York: Europa Verlag, 1945).

18 Richard B. Braithwaite, *Scientific Explanation* (Cambridge: Cambridge University Press, 1953; New York: Harper, 1960), p. 210.

19 Aristotle's concept of each thing's 'being-what-it-is' I have treated at some length in my *Portrait of Aristotle* (London: Faber, 1963; Chicago: University of Chicago Press, 1963). Polanyi's view as developed since the publication of *Personal Knowledge* is stated in the lectures delivered at Duke University in 1964 (see Chapter I, note 1).

20 Such is the approach not only of Merleau-Ponty (*op. cit.*), but, for example, of Erwin W. Straus in *The Primary World of Senses* (New York: Free Press of Glencoe, 1962) or John Wild in *Existence and the World of Freedom* (Englewood Cliffs, N.J.: Prentice Hall, 1963).

21 Michael Polanyi, 'Tacit Knowing: Its Bearing on Some Problems of Philosophy', *Reviews of Modern Physics*, XXXIV (1962), 601–16.

22 *Ibid.*, p. 608.

23 *Loc. cit.*

24 *Ibid.*, p. 609.

25 *Loc. cit.*

26 *Loc. cit.*

27 *Ibid.*, p. 609.

28 Except that Polanyi's starting point is epistemological, while Plato's universals are primarily moral.

29 In the *Republic* (523D) Socrates insists that *qualities* are better starting points than *things* for learning about the Forms.

30 Polanyi, 'Tacit Knowing', p. 610.

31 *Loc. cit.*

32 *Loc. cit.*

33 *Ibid.*, p. 609.

Chapter 3

1 First Meditation. *Philosophical Works of Descartes*, translated and edited by E. S. Haldane and G. R. T. Ross (Cambridge: Cambridge University Press, 1931; New York: Dover Publications, 1955), vol. I, p. 145. All quotations from Descartes are from the Haldane and Ross translation.

2 *Rules for the Direction of the Mind*, Rule III, H. and R., vol. I, p. 7.

3 *Ibid.*, Rule VIII, H. and R., vol. I, p. 28.

4 *Ibid.*, Rule II, H. and R., vol. I, p. 3.

5 *Loc. cit.*

6 *Ibid.*, Rule II, H. and R., vol. I, p. 4.

7 *Ibid.*, Rule II, H. and R., vol. I, p. 5.

8 *Loc. cit.*

9 *Ibid.*, Rule III, H. and R., vol. I, p. 5.

10 *Ethics*, Part II, Prop. XLIII.

11 Supplement to *Replies to Objections II*, H. and R., vol. II, pp. 52–59.

12 See for example *Posterior Analytics*, 71b 35 ff.

13 Personal communication.

14 This is Heidegger's term for our condition of being 'thrown into the world'. It corresponds roughly to Sartre's 'facticité.'

15 Carl Hempel, 'On the Nature of Mathematical Truth', in H. Feigl and W. Sellars, *Readings in Philosophical Analysis* (New York: Appleton-Century-Crofts, 1949, pp. 222–49), p. 235.

16 For a very simple statement see R. Blanché, *Axiomatics* (London: Routledge and Kegan Paul, 1962; New York: Free Press of Glencoe, 1962), pp. 56–58. For a more detailed but still non-technical account, see Ernest Nagel and James Roy Newman, *Gödel's Proof* (New York: New York University Press, 1958).

17 Imre Lakatos, 'Proofs and Refutations', *British Journal for the Philosophy of Science*, XIV (1963–64), 1–25, 120–39, 229–45, 296–342, p. 7.

18 For our purposes, α may be taken as equivalent to V.

19 *Loc. cit.*, n.

20 Rule I, H. and R., vol. I, p. 1.

21 *Loc. cit.* My italics.

22 *Loc. cit.*

23 *Loc. cit.*

24 *Loc. cit.*

25 *Loc. cit.*

25a *Loc. cit.*

26 See Polanyi, *Personal Knowledge, passim.*

27 H. H. Price, *Thinking and Experience* (London: Hutchinson, 1953; Cambridge, Mass.: Harvard University Press, 1953), p. 345.

28 *Ibid.*, pp. 86–87.

29 Merleau-Ponty, *op. cit.*, p. 197.

30 H. Plessner, *Die Stufen des Organischen und der Mensch* (Berlin and Leipzig: De Gruyter, 1928).

31 This emphasis goes back to the work of von Uexküll early in this century, although contemporary writers have modified his position through distinguishing the human world (Welt) from the animal environment (Umwelt) of which he wrote. See J. J. von Uexküll, *Theoretical Biology* (London: Kegan Paul, 1926); and compare for example A. Portmann, *Zoologie und das neue Bild des Menschen* (München: Rowohlts deutsche Enzyklopädie, 1956), p. 135. See also Chapter VI below.

32 W. H. Thorpe, *Learning and Instinct in Animals*, 2nd ed. (London: Methuen, 1963), p. 173.

33 A similar point was made by G. H. Mead in terms of the contrast between the 'me', the product of organised social relations, and the 'I', which is formed only in response to the social self. See for example *Mind, Self, and Society* (Chicago: University of Chicago Press, 1934), pp. 184 ff.

34 Samuel Alexander, *Space Time and Deity* (London: Macmillan, 1920), 2 vols.

35 Merleau-Ponty, *op. cit.*, pp. 415–16. ['unalloyed' = 'en personne', 'absolute self-evidence' = 'une évidence dernière.']

36 *Ibid.*, p. 416.

37 *Loc. cit.*

38 *Loc. cit.*

39 *Loc. cit.*

40 *Ibid.*, p. 428.

41 *Loc. cit.*

Chapter 4

1 Alfred North Whitehead, in *Modes of Thought* (New York: Macmillan, 1938), pp. 173–232.

2 *Ibid.*, p. 180.

3 *Ibid.*, pp. 180–1.

4 *Ibid.*, p. 181.

5 *Loc. cit.* Whitehead is still speaking of 'perception' as conceived in empiricist terms; in a theory like Merleau-Ponty's, Whitehead's 'causal efficacy' as well as 'presentational immediacy', would be included in perception in the full meaning of that term.

6 *Ibid.*, pp. 183–4.

7 *Ibid.*, p. 184.

8 *Ibid.*, pp. 185–6.

9 John Maynard Keynes, 'My Early Beliefs', in *Two Memoirs* (London: Rupert Hart-Davis, 1949; New York: A. M. Kelley, 1949), p. 102.

10 Hume, *Treatise of Human Nature*, Book I, Part IV, Section VII. Selby-Bigge edition (Oxford: Clarendon Press, 1955), p. 272.

11 *Ibid.*, Book I, Part I, Section I. S.–B., p. 4.

12 *Ibid.*, Book I, Part I, Section III. S.–B., p. 10.

13 *Ibid.*, Book I, Part I, Section IV. S.–B., pp. 10–11.

14 Hume distinguishes further between 'impressions of sensation', including bodily feelings of pleasure and pain, and 'impressions of reflexion', arising from the former, that is, the emotions (*Treatise*, Book II, Part I, Section I). This distinction, however, need not concern us for the moment.

15 See the argument of the Third Meditation.

16 W. V. Quine, *Word and Object* (New York and London: John Wiley and Sons; Boston: Technology Press of M.I.T., 1960).

17 *Treatise*, Book I, Part IV, Section I. S.–B., p. 183.

18 *Ibid.*, Book I, Part III, Section XVI. S.–B., p. 176.

19 *Ibid.*, Appendix. S.–B., p. 636.

20 *Ibid.*, Book I, Part IV, Section II. S.–B., p. 209.

21 *Dialogues Concerning Natural Religion*, Part One. Hafner Library of Classics edition (New York: Hafner, 1948), pp. 9–10.

22 *Treatise*, Book III, Part III, Section I. S.–B., p. 583.

23 *Ibid.*, Book III, Part III, Section III. S.–B., p. 606.

24 *Ibid.*, Book III, Part III, Section III. S.–B., p. 603.

25 *Ibid.*, Book III, Part III, Section III. S.–B., p. 604.

26 Hume's *History of England*, vol. VI, Chapter LV.

27 *Treatise*, Book II, Part II, Section III. S.–B., p. 418.

28 See *History of England*, vol. VII, Chapters XVIII and XIX.

29 'Whether the British Government inclines more to Absolute Monarchy, or to a Republic', in *Essays Moral, Political, and Literary*, vol. I (ed. Green and Grose, London: Longmans, Green and Co., 1912), p. 126.

30 *Loc. cit.*

31 *Loc. cit.*

32 *Dialogues*, Part VIII. Hafner ed., p. 54.

33 *Treatise*, Appendix. S.-B., pp. 634–5.

34 Boswell's *Private Papers*, ed. Scott and Pottle, vol. XII (New York, 1931), pp. 227–32; quoted in Norman Kemp Smith's edition of Hume's *Dialogues* (2nd. ed.; New York and Edinburgh: Nelson, 1947), p. 77.

35 Letter from Adam Smith to William Strahan, November 9, 1776, published with *My Own Life* (London: Strahan and Cadell, 1777); reprinted in Kemp Smith's edition of the *Dialogues*, pp. 247–8.

36 Bertrand Russell, *An Inquiry into Meaning and Truth* (London: George Allen and Unwin, 1940), p. 7.

37 R. B. Braithwaite, *Scientific Explanation* (Cambridge: Cambridge University Press, 1953; New York: Harper, 1960), p. 10.

38 G. H. Von Wright, *The Logical Problem of Induction* (2nd. ed., Oxford: Blackwell, 1957).

39 Russell, *Human Knowledge: Its Scope and Limits* (London: George Allen and Unwin, 1948; New York: Simon and Schuster, 1948).

40 See note 37 above.

41 *Human Knowledge*, Allen and Unwin ed., pp. 265 ff.; Simon and Schuster ed., pp. 257 ff.

42 *Ibid.*, Allen and Unwin ed., pp. 166–170; Simon and Schuster ed., pp. 148–154.

43 *Ibid.*, Allen and Unwin ed., p. 189; Simon and Schuster ed., p. 174.

44 *Loc. cit.*

45 *Ibid.*, Allen and Unwin ed., p. 325; Simon and Schuster ed., pp. 307–8.

46 *Ibid.*, Allen and Unwin ed., p. 182; Simon and Schuster ed., pp. 167–8.

47 *Ibid.*, Allen and Unwin ed., p. 201; Simon and Schuster ed., p. 185.

48 *Ibid.*, Allen and Unwin ed., p. 448; Simon and Schuster ed., p. 432.

49 See for example H. Feigl, 'Induction and Probability', in Feigl and Sellars, *op. cit.*, or William Kneale, *Probability and Induction* (Oxford: Oxford University Press, 1949).

50 See Rudolph Carnap, *Logical Foundations of Probability* (Chicago: University of Chicago Press, 1952).

51 *Human Knowledge*, Allen and Unwin ed., p. 189; Simon and Schuster ed., pp. 174–5.

52 Russell lists five such principles.

53 W. V. Quine, 'Two Dogmas of Empiricism', in *From a Logical Point of View* (Cambridge: Harvard University Press, 1953), pp. 20–46.

54 *Human Knowledge*, Allen and Unwin ed., p. 526; Simon and Schuster ed., p. 507.

55 See Polanyi, *Personal Knowledge*, pp. 305–6.

56 Braithwaite, *op. cit.*, pp. 131, 151 ff.

57 Sir Ronald Fisher, *The Design of Experiments* (7th ed., Edinburgh: Oliver and Boyd, 1960; New York: Hafner, 1960).

58 Braithwaite, *op. cit.*, pp. 153 ff.

59 *Ibid.*, pp. 212–13.

60 *Ibid.*, p. 213.

61 *Ibid.*, p. 174.

62 *Treatise*, Appendix. S.-B., p. 636.

Chapter 5

1 *Critique of Pure Reason*, B IX. All references are to the second edition (B) unless the first edition (A) is specified.
2 *Loc. cit.*
3 *Loc. cit.*
4 *Loc. cit.*
5 B IX–X.
6 *Loc. cit.*
7 B X.
8 *Loc. cit.*
9 Descartes, Rule III, H. and R., I, p. 7.
10 B X–XI.
11 B XI–XII.
12 B XII.
13 *Loc. cit.*
14 B XII–XIII.
15 B XIII.
16 B 197.
17 These are treated as follows: Objective deduction stated: A 92–93: B 124–7. O.D. expanded: B 129–43 (A 95–98 perhaps parallel to this?). Subjective deduction: A 98–110, 115–125; B 144–159. O.D. reinforced by S.D.: A 110–115, 126–130; B 159–169. For further details, see H. J. Paton, *Kant's Metaphysic of Experience* (London: Allen and Unwin, 1936), vol. II.
18 The expression 'homogeneous time' is Paton's (*op. cit.*). Paton has failed, however, to see the importance of time (as against space) in Kant's theory of the imagination. See my *Heidegger* (London: Bowes and Bowes and New York: Hillary House, 1957), Chapter IV.
19 Martin Heidegger, *Kant und das Problem der Metaphysik* (Bonn: F. Cohen, 1929); *Kant and the Problem of Metaphysics*, translated J. S. Churchill (Bloomington: Indiana University Press, 1962).
20 R. G. Collingwood, *The Idea of History* (Oxford: Clarendon Press, 1946), p. 77.
21 B XII–XIII.
22 J. B. Conant and Leonard K. Nash, eds., *Harvard Case Histories in Experimental Science* (Cambridge, Mass.: Harvard University Press, 1957), vol. I, p. 71.
23 Thomas S. Kuhn, *The Structure of Scientific Revolutions*, International Encyclopedia of Unified Science, vol. II, no. 2 (Chicago: University of Chicago Press, 1962).
24 Michael Polanyi, *Personal Knowledge*, p. 404.
25 Kant, *Critique of Judgment*, Part II, Division II, paragraph 75 (2nd. and 3rd. editions, p. 338).
26 A. D. Lindsay, *Kant* (London: E. Benn Ltd., 1934), Chapter V, section 4.
27 William James, *Principles of Psychology* (New York: Henry Holt and Co., 1890; Dover, 1950), vol. I, pp. 288–9.
28 Wolfgang Köhler, *The Mentality of Apes*, 2nd. ed. (London: Routledge and Kegan Paul, 1927), p. 191.

Chapter 6

1 C. K. Ogden and I. A. Richards, *The Meaning of Meaning*, 8th ed. (New York: Harcourt Brace and Co., 1956).

2 See for example Mrs Philippa Foot, 'Moral Beliefs', *Proceedings of the Aristotelian Society*, N.S. LIX (1958–59), 83–104; or P. T. Geach, 'Good and Evil', *Analysis* XVII (1956–57), 33–42.

3 This general thesis is implicit in Polanyi's epistemology; it could, I think, be developed more formally than I have stated it here.

4 Bertrand Russell, *Inquiry into Meaning and Truth* (London: Allen and Unwin, 1940).

5 *Ibid.*, p. 139. Russell's example is 'That is red', but since 'this' and 'that' are treated by him as logical equivalents, we may safely ignore the difference here.

6 *Ibid.*, p. 95.

7 *Ibid.*, p. 97.

8 *Ibid.*, p. 112.

9 *Ibid.*, p. 113. Russell claims to eliminate 'I' also, as parasitic upon 'this'. His argument seems dubious, but it is in any case irrelevant to my argument at this juncture. In terms of the position adumbrated in this book, of course, it is absurd to pretend to eliminate 'I' from cognitive discourse.

10 See Chapter III, note 32 above.

11 Wolfgang Köhler, *Gestalt Psychology* (New York: Liveright, 1929), pp. 167–8, 233–4.

12 Hume, *Treatise*, Book I, Part I, Section 1, S.–B., pp. 5–6.

13 G. E. M. Anscombe, *An Introduction to Wittgenstein's Tractatus* (London: Hutchinson, 1959), pp. 25–30. See also James Griffin, *Wittgenstein's Logical Atomism* (Oxford: Clarendon Press, 1964). It does seem likely that Carnap and Neurath at least saw the difficulty of taking protocol sentences as observation statements; see Russell's exposition of their view as in effect a 'coherence theory' (*Inquiry*, Chapter X).

14 Such an undertaking is suggested, for instance, by Peter Winch's *Idea of a Social Science* (London: Routledge and New York: Humanities Press, 1958).

15 In an exchange of letters in the press.

16 Russell, *Inquiry*, p. 151.

17 Elizabeth B. Gasking, 'Why was Mendel's Work Ignored?', *Journal of the History of Ideas*, XX (1959), 60–84.

18 *Ibid.*, pp. 75–76.

19 *Ibid.*, p. 77.

20 Polanyi, *Personal Knowledge*, Chapter VII.

21 Admittedly, I have, in previous chapters, accepted as true, and as fundamental to my argument, Polanyi's theory of tacit knowing. According to this view, there is no knowledge which is wholly explicit, carried wholly by the surface of the spoken or written word. But neither, in the human world, is there any knowledge capable of systematization or communication which is wholly tacit, which is not mediated by speech. I have therefore in effect been arguing that all human knowledge entails evaluation.

22 F. J. J. Buytendijk, *Mensch und Tier* (Hamburg: Rowohlt, 1958). cf. W. N. and L. A. Kellogg, *The Ape and the Child* (New York: McGraw-Hill, 1933); Cathy Hayes, *The Ape in Our House* (New York: Harper, 1951).

23 Buytendijk, *op. cit.*, p. 95.

24 *Loc. cit.*

25 *Ibid.*, p. 112.

26 *Ibid.*, p. 73.

27 *Ibid.*, p. 87. See Erwin W. Straus, 'Der Mensch als ein fragendes Wesen', *Jahrbuch für Psychologie und Psychotherapie* I (1953), 139–54; reprinted in E. W. Straus, *Psychologie der menschlichen Welt* (Berlin: Springer, 1960), pp. 316–35.

28 *Loc. cit.*

29 E. W. Straus, 'The Upright Posture', *The Psychiatric Quarterly*, XXVI (1952), 529–61, p. 7 ff.; see also 'Zum Sehen Geboren, Zum Schauen Bestellt', in *Werden und Handeln* (v. Gebsattel Festschrift, Stuttgart: Hippokrates-Verlag, 1963), 44–73. Also 'Die aufrechte Haltung. Eine anthropologische Studie', in *Psychologie der menschlichen Welt*, pp. 224–35.

30 *Wahrnehmen* and *bemerken*.

31 Buytendijk, *op. cit.*, p. 41.

32 'Gabe und Aufgabe'.

33 *Loc. cit.*

34 *Ibid.*, pp. 76–77.

35 Buytendijk here stresses the absence of formal patterns of behaviour in the higher apes; this belief has been discredited by recent ethological research. See for example the bibliography in A. Portmann: 'Die Stellung des Menschen in der Natur', *Handbuch der Biologie*, vol. 9 (Konstanz: Akademische Verlagsgesellschaft Athenaion, 1964), pp. 437–60. The fundamental contrast of 'nature' and 'culture' in the social life of apes and men still holds, however, as Portmann's essay emphasizes.

36 *Loc. cit.*

37 *Ibid.*, p. 78.

38 *Loc. cit.*

39 *Loc. cit.*

40 Primo Levi, *If this is a Man* (New York: Orion Press, 1959).

41 See for example Ivo Kohler, 'Die Methode des Brillenversuchs in der Wahrnehmungspsychologie mit Bemerkungen zur Lehre von der Adaptation', *Zeitschrift für experimentelle und angewandte Psychologie*, III (1956), 381–417. The philosophical importance of these experiments is emphasized in Polanyi's *Duke Lectures*.

42 Buytendijk, *op. cit.*, pp. 66–67.

43 R. J. Pumphrey, *The Evolution of Language* (Liverpool: University Press, 1951).

Chapter 7

1 *The Autobiography of Charles Darwin*, edited by Nora Barlow (London: Collins, 1958; New York: Harcourt Brace, 1959), p. 87.

2 Sir Julian Huxley, *Evolution in Action* (London: Chatto and Windus. 1953), p. 146.

3 David Lack, *Evolutionary Theory and Christian Belief* (London: Methuen, 1957).

4 Quoted in Francis Darwin, ed., *Life and Letters of Charles Darwin* (New York: Basic Books, 1959; 2 vols.), vol. II, p. 77.

5 Sir Gavin De Beer, *Embryos and Ancestors*, 3rd. ed. (Oxford: Clarendon Press, 1958), p. 174. My italics.

6 Sir Gavin De Beer, 'The Darwin-Wallace Centenary', *Endeavour*, XVII (1958), 61–76, p. 76. Also *Evolution*, British Museum Handbook (London, 1958), p. 32.

7 Sir Ronald Fisher, *The Genetical Theory of Natural Selection* (Oxford: Clarendon Press, 1930; 2nd. ed., New York: Dover, 1959). See Appendix.

8 See Chapter VI above and Gasking, *op. cit.*

9 Fisher, 'Measurement of selective intensity', *Proc. Roy. Soc. B.*, CXXI (1936), 58–62.

10 De Beer, 'Darwin-Wallace Centenary', p. 63, and *Evolution*, p. 19.

11 *Loc. cit.* (and in *Evolution*, p. 20).

12 Sir James Gray, 'The Case for Natural Selection', *Nature*, CLXXIII (1954), 227.

13 *Autobiography*, p. 119.

14 Gertrude Himmelfarb, *Darwin and the Darwinian Revolution* (London: Chatto and Windus, 1959), pp. 83-89.

15 *Ibid.*, p. 85.

16 *Ibid.*, p. 87.

17 H. B. D. Kettlewell, *Nature*, CLXXV (1955), 943; *Heredity*, IX (1955), 323 and X (1956), 287; *Proc. Roy. Soc. B.*, CXLV (1956), 297. (See also Appendix.)

18 C. H. Waddington, 'The genetic assimilation of an acquired character', *Evolution*, VII (1953), 118-26; cf. also 'The genetic assimilation of the bithorax phenotype', *Evolution*, X (1956), 1-13.

19 P. M. Sheppard, *Natural Selection and Heredity* (London: Hutchinson, 1958; New York: Philosophical Library, 1959), p. 113.

20 John Maynard Smith, *The Theory of Evolution* (Harmondsworth, Middlesex: Penguin Books, 1958).

21 See for example A. M. Dalcq, 'Le problème de l'évolution est-il près d'être resolu?', *Annales de la societé zoologique Belgique*, LXXXII (1951), 117; O. Schindewolf, *Grundfragen der Paläontologie* (Stuttgart: Schweizerbart, 1950); A. Vandel, *L'Homme et L'Evolution*, 2nd. ed. (Paris: Gallimard, 1958).

22 Waddington, *The Strategy of the Genes* (London: George Allen and Unwin, 1957; New York: Macmillan, 1957), p. 64.

23 George Gaylord Simpson, *Major Features of Evolution* (New York: Columbia University Press, 1953), p. 351.

24 T. S. Westoll, 'Some aspects of growth studies in fossils', *Proc. Roy. Soc. B.*, CXXXVII (1950), 409-509. See also Simpson, *op. cit.*, pp. 283-4 and Maynard Smith, *op. cit.*, pp. 253-4.

25 See De Beer, *Embryos and Ancestors.*

26 A. M. Dalcq, 'Sur la notion de vie', in *Colloque Orient-Occident* (Brussels 1958), pp. 81-89.

27 *Autobiography*, p. 93.

28 Lack, *op. cit.*, p. 104.

29 See Waddington, *Strategy of the Genes*, pp. 1-10 and 188-190.

Chapter 8

1 Berlin: Springer, 2nd. ed., 1956. I am quoting from the English translation, *The Primary World of Senses* (New York: Free Press of Glencoe, 1963).

2 *Ibid.*, pp. 298-9.

3 C. F. A. Pantin, 'The Recognition of Species', *Science Progress*, XLII (1954), 587-598.

4 This is a paradigm, not necessarily a piece of history. That Kekulé's reliance on structural concepts was by no means unambiguous is suggested by a paper by W. V. and K. R. Farrar, 'Faith and Doubt: The Theory of Structure in Organic Chemistry', *Proceedings of the Chemical Society*, 1959, pp. 285-90.

5 Max Born, *Theory and Experiment in Physics* (Cambridge: Cambridge University Press, 1943; Dover reprint, 1956), pp. 12-13. Norman Campbell in *What is Science?* (Dover edition, New York, 1952, p. 156) uses the same example. Cf. Polanyi, *Personal Knowledge*, pp. 145-9.

6 Paul Dirac, 'Quantum Mechanics and the Aether', *Scientific Monthly*, LVIII (1954), p. 142.

7 Sir Harold Jeffreys, *Scientific Inference*, 2nd. ed. (Cambridge: Cambridge University Press, 1957).

8 *Ibid.*, p. 77.

9 R. B. Braithwaite, *op. cit.*, pp. 163 ff. See also Chapter IV above.

10 G. S. Fraenkel and D. L. Gunn, *The Orientation of Animals* (Oxford: Clarendon Press, 1940).

11 Polanyi, *Personal Knowledge*, pp. 348–54.

12 Professor D. Lewis, address on 'The New Molecular Genetics', Joint Biology Conference, London, 24 October, 1959.

13 London, 27 September, 1661. Translated in A. Wolf, *The Correspondence of Spinoza* (London: George Allen and Unwin, 1928), p. 80.

14 R. B. Goldschmidt, *Theoretical Genetics* (Berkeley: University of California Press, 1955), p. 250. My italics.

15 See for example Campbell, *op. cit.*, pp. 53–55 or Russell, 'On the Notion of Cause' in *Mysticism and Logic* (Pelican edition, 1953), pp. 171–96.

16 The point I am making here is related to the argument of *Personal Knowledge*, Chapter XI, especially pp. 331–32; but the role of 'causal' concepts in explanation needs further analysis along the lines suggested there.

17 Walter M. Elsasser, *The Physical Foundations of Biology* (New York: Pergamon Press, 1958); 'Quanta and the concept of organismic law', *Journal of Theoretical Biology* I (1961), 27–58; 'Physical aspects of non-mechanistic biological theory', *Jl. Theor. Biol.* III (1962), 164–91. Cf. Barry Commoner, 'In Defense of Biology', *Science*, CXXXIII (1961), 1745–1748.

18 G. W. Leibniz, *Mathematische Schriften* (ed. Gerhardt, Berlin and Halle, 1849–1855), vol. VI, pp. 129–35. English translation in Leibniz, *Philosophical Papers and Letters* ed. L. E. Loemker (Chicago: University of Chicago Press, 1956), vol. I, pp. 538–43.

19 H. S. Jennings, *The Behavior of the Lower Organisms* (New York: Columbia University Press, 1906; 4th reprinting, 1931), p. 336.

20 Polanyi, *Personal Knowledge*, pp. 361–63.

21 Dr. W. H. Thorpe, who has kindly read part of this chapter, points out that this impression is invalidated by modern cinemaphotography of the process of growth. Yet there does seem to be a line to be drawn somewhere!

22 Quoted by Fraenkel and Gunn, *op. cit.*, p. 4, from G. J. Romanes's *Mental Evolution in Animals* (London: Kegan Paul, 1885), p. 279. It is interesting to note that Romanes's argument is introduced in support of his enthusiastically Darwinian position: an instinct so often lethal must have some explanation in terms of adaptive relationships.

23 See J. A. Bierens de Haan, 'Animal Psychology and the Science of Animal Behaviour', *Behaviour*, I (1948), 71–80.

24 N. Tinbergen, *The Herring Gull's World* (London: Collins, 1953; New York: Basic Books, 1960).

25 *Ibid.*, p. 141.

26 *Ibid.*, p. 154.

27 *Ibid.*, p. 54. Tinbergen adds: 'The ceremony is understood by other gulls.'

28 *Ibid.*, p. 60.

29 *Ibid.*, p. 137.

30 Cf. also Tinbergen's account of van Dobben's method of gull control: 'A limited area in a colony is selected as the future site of the reduced colony. In this area all eggs are shaken, and outside the area all eggs are taken. Part of the outside gulls will start a new clutch in the same area, but part change over to the central area, where there is, *from the limited point of view of the gulls*, no egg-robbing.' *Ibid.*, p. 173. My italics.

31 *Ibid.*, p. 51. My italics.

32 *Ibid.*, p. 79.
33 *Ibid.*, p. 81.
34 *Ibid.*, p. 167. See also the reference to 'tradition' in the account of chick-stealing, p. 174.
35 *Ibid.*, pp. 84–85.
36 *Ibid.*, pp. 72–73.
37 Campbell, *op. cit.*, p. 156.
38 Polanyi, *Personal Knowledge*, Chapter VI, p. 174.
39 *Loc. cit.*
40 *Loc. cit.*
41 *Ibid.*, p. 379.
42 R. O. Kapp, *Science vs. Materialism* (London: Methuen, 1940); *Mind Life and Body* (London: Constable, 1951).
43 Also in the Duke Lectures already quoted.
44 Fourth *Duke Lecture*, pp. 4–5.
45 Plato, *Laws* X, 892A–B.
46 Personal communication.
47 Jean Paul Sartre, 'Merleau-Ponty vivant', *Les Temps Modernes*, XVII (1961–62), 304–76, p. 363: 'La nature est en haillons'.
48 See the treatment of form and matter in Edward Pols' *The Recognition of Reason* (Carbondale, Ill.: Southern Illinois University Press, 1963). Pols has taken this problem much farther than I have been able to do; I should have written this and the preceding chapter differently, had I had the good fortune to read his book before completing mine. I have not the courage to start afresh, but hope that the convergence of our arguments, as it seems to me, will strengthen them both.

Chapter 9

1 R. G. Collingwood, *The Idea of Nature* (Oxford: Clarendon Press, 1945), p. 13.
2 Aristotle, *Physics* II, Chapter VIII, 199b 15–16.
3 *Ibid.*, 199b 18–19.
4 R. B. Goldschmidt, *The Material Basis of Evolution* (New Haven: Yale University Press, 1940).
5 Collingwood, *op. cit.*, p. 83.
6 *Ibid.*, p. 136.
7 These lectures were incorporated in *Modes of Thought*. See Chapter IV above.
8 Collingwood, *op. cit.*, p. 136.
9 P. F. Strawson, *Individuals: An Essay in Descriptive Metaphysics* (London: Methuen, 1959), p. 57.
10 Charles Darwin, *The Origin of Species*, Chapter XIV, section on 'Morphology'.
11 C. F. A. Pantin, *Science and Education* (Cardiff: University of Wales Press, 1963), pp. 19–26.
12 See Chapter VII note 18.
13 Aristotle, *Physics* II, 193b 14–15.
14 See J. S. Nicholas, 'Regeneration of Vertebrates', in Benjamin H. Willier, Paul A. Weiss, and Viktor Hamburger, *Analysis of Development* (Philadelphia: Saunders, 1955), pp. 674 ff.

15 T. Dobzhansky, *The Biological Basis of Human Freedom* (New York: Columbia and London: Oxford, 1956), p. 17.

16 Paul G. 'Espinasse, 'The Concept of the Gene', paper read to the British Society for the Philosophy of Science, 20 February, 1959.

17 A. F. Baker, 'Purpose and Natural Selection: A Defense of Teleology', *Scientific Journal of the Royal College of Science*, IV (1934), 106–19, pp. 107–8.

18 *Ibid.*, p. 108.

19 *Ibid.*, p. 109.

20 *Loc. cit.*

21 *Ibid.*, p. 110.

22 Paul Weiss, in *The Chemical Basis of Development*, ed. William D. McElroy and Bentley Glass (Baltimore: John Hopkins Press, 1958), p. 846.

23 See for example R. R. Sokal, *Journal of Theoretical Biology*, III (1962), 230–67; also G. G. Simpson, *Principles of Animal Taxonomy* (New York: Columbia, 1961).

24 Jane Oppenheimer in Willier Weiss and Hamburger, p. 36.

25 *Loc. cit.*

26 C. P. Raven, 'The Formalisation of Finality', *Folia Biotheoretica* B, vol. V (1961), 1–27.

27 *Ibid.*, p. 22.

28 R. C. Lewontin, 'Evolution and The Theory of Games', *Journal of Theoretical Biology*, I (1961), 382–403.

29 W. T. Williams and D. A. Barber, 'The Functional Significance of Aerenchyma in Plants', in *Mechanisms in Biological Competition, Symposia of the Society for Experimental Biology*, no. XV (1961), 132–144.

30 Merleau-Ponty, *op. cit.*, e.g. pp. 258, 397 f.

31 Fourth *Duke Lecture*, p. 5.

32 Chapter III above.

33 Fourth *Duke Lecture*, p. 6.

34 J. A. Passmore, *Philosophical Reasoning* (New York: Scribner, 1961).

35 See his *Existence of Mind* (London: McGibbon and Kee, 1962).

36 W. B. Gallie, *Philosophy and the Historical Understanding* (London: Chatto and Windus, 1964).

37 Hans Reichenbach, *The Philosophy of Space and Time* (New York: Dover, 1958).

38 David Bohm, 'Classical and Non-Classical Concepts in the Quantum Theory', *British Journal for the Philosophy of Science*, XII (1962), 265–80, p. 273.

39 *Ibid.*, pp. 273–4.

40 *Ibid.*, p. 276.

41 *Ibid.*, p. 277.

42 *Loc. cit.*

43 *Loc. cit.*

44 *Loc. cit.*

45 *Ibid.*, p. 278.

46 *Loc. cit.*

47 See also D. Bohm, 'A Proposed Topological Formulation of the Quantum Theory', in I. J. Good, ed., *The Scientist Speculates* (London: Heinemann, 1962) pp. 302–14 and Professor Bohm's inaugural lecture at Birkbeck College, London: *Problems in the Basic Concepts of Physics* (London: J. W. Ruddock & Sons, 1963). Broader philosophical implications of Professor Bohm's approach are suggested in his article 'On the Relationship between Methodology in Scientific Research and the Content of Scientific Knowledge', *British Journal for the Philosophy of Science*, XII (1961), 103–16.

48 E. Straus, 'Der Mensch als ein fragendes Wesen', p. 140. (See Chapter VI, note 27).

49 See the *Duke Lectures*.

50 Straus, *Primary World of Senses*, p. 95.

51 This argument is suggested in the *Duke Lectures*.

Appendix

1 It is often said that Fisher has 'proved mathematically' the truth of neo-Darwinism. The confidence with which the 'synthetic' theory has been asserted on the basis of Fisher's argument is reflected, for example, in the contributions by Huxley, Mayr and Fisher in Huxley, Hardy, Ford, *Evolution as a Process* (London: Allen and Unwin, 1954), or in the conclusion of the third edition of de Beer's *Embryos and Ancestors* (Oxford, Clarendon Press, 1958), or in P. M. Sheppard's *Natural Selection and Heredity* (London, Hutchinson, 1958)–to mention but a few examples among many. (And see Chapter VII above.)

2 Sir Ronald Fisher, *The Genetical Theory of Natural Selection* (Oxford, 1930; New York: Dover, 1959), p. 38. I am following the Dover edition, which is in part revised, but not, with one exception, to be noted later, in ways that are philosophically relevant.

3 *Ibid.*, p. 22.

4 *Ibid.*, p. 41.

5 *Ibid.*, p. 26.

6 *Ibid.*, p. 37

7 I am speaking here (as Fisher is doing) of genic inheritance. The question of cytoplasmic inheritance introduces another dimension altogether into the evolutionary problem.

8 *Loc. cit.* (My italics.)

9 *Ibid.*, p. 40.

10 *Ibid.*, p. 27.

11 See Chapter VII above, and references in note 17.

12 Or if, alternatively, we say that in war it is the 'normally' mal-adapted who are *better* adapted, and vice versa, then we are using 'better adapted' to mean 'surviving' and are saying only: 'those who survive, survive'.

13 The demonstrative character of Darwin's argument was pointed out by C. F. A. Pantin (in *History of Science*, London: Cohen and West, 1953); cf. the discussion by A. G. N. Flew, in *New Biology*, no. 28, 1959, pp. 25 ff.

14 Fisher, *op. cit.*, p. 38.

15 If one has set up a selection experiment, of course they are so.

16 R. Fisher, 'The Bearing of Genetics on Theories of Evolution', *Science Progress*, 27 (1932), pp. 273–87.

17 *Op. cit.*, pp. 131–2.

18 *Ibid.*, p. 37.

19 *Ibid.*, pp. 30–32.

20 In an address to the British Society for the Philosophy of Science in February, 1959.

21 Fisher, *op. cit.*, p. 39.

22 This section is added in the second edition, but what Fisher says here is implicit in the usage of the first edition also.

23 *Ibid.*, p. 49. (My italics.)

24 *Ibid.*, p. 40.

25 *Loc. cit.* For an excellent discussion of the logical place of biological

improvement in Darwinian and neo-Darwinian theory, see the article by Flew mentioned in note 13 above.

26 C. D. Darlington, *Evolution of Genetic Systems*, 2nd. ed. (Edinburgh: Oliver and Boyd, 1958), p. 239.

27 See, for example, the contributions of Huxley and Fisher to the Huxley, Hardy, Ford volume, referred to in note 2 above, or Huxley's *Evolution in Action* (New York: Harper, 1953).

28 *Loc. cit.*

Index